# Drama
# and
# Resistance

# MEDIEVAL CULTURES

**SERIES EDITORS**
Rita Copeland
Barbara A. Hanawalt
David Wallace

*Sponsored by the Center for Medieval Studies
at the University of Minnesota*

Volumes in the series study the diversity of medieval cultural histories and practices including such interrelated issues as gender, class, and social hierarchies; race and ethnicity; geographical relations; definitions of political space; discourses of authority and dissent; educational institutions; canonical and noncanonical literatures; and technologies of textual and visual literacies.

*For other books in the series, see p. 211*

# Drama and Resistance

BODIES, GOODS, AND THEATRICALITY
IN LATE MEDIEVAL ENGLAND

Claire Sponsler

Medieval Cultures
Volume 10

University of Minnesota Press
Minneapolis
London

Published by the University of Minnesota Press
111 Third Avenue South, Suite 290, Minneapolis, MN 55401-2520
Printed in the United States of America on acid-free paper

**Library of Congress Cataloging-in Publication Data**

Sponsler, Claire.
  Drama and resistance : bodies, goods, and theatricality in late medieval England / Claire Sponsler.
     p.  cm. — (Medieval cultures ; v. 10)
  Includes bibliographical references and index.
  ISBN 0-8166-2926-9 (alk. paper). — ISBN 0-8166-2927-7 (pbk. : alk. paper)
  1. English drama—Middle English, 1100–1500—History and criticism.  2. Mysteries and miracle-plays, English—History and criticism.  3. Christian drama, English (Middle)—History and criticism.  4. Theater—England—History—Medieval, 500–1500.  5. Moralities, English—History and criticism.  6. Literature and society—England—History.  7. Civilization, Medieval, in literature.  8. Social history—Medieval, 500–1500.  9. Social problems in literature.  10. Body, Human, in literature.  I. Title. II. Series.
PR641.S66   1997
822′.051609—dc21                        96-40235

For Jeff

# Contents

✢

# Preface

✝

*Drama and Resistance* is a study of subjectivity, theatricality, and commodification in late medieval England. It examines key discourses through which late medieval subjects were "disciplined" and matches those disciplining discourses with theatrical performances that can be said to have "undone" them, at least in part. This study continues and develops my interest in how cultural productions are received, used, and modified by specific audiences of readers, viewers, or listeners. Its methodology thus draws on cultural studies—particularly the work of cultural historians and ethnographers—and reception studies, which encourages us to pay attention to the consumers of texts and performances.

In writing this book I have incurred many debts, beginning with the teachers whose considerable talents have shaped this study at the most fundamental level. I am particularly grateful to Larry Clopper, Al David, Barbara Hanawalt, Paul Meyvaert, Sheila Lindenbaum, and Paul Strohm for encouraging my interest in the historical period of medieval culture and for providing exemplary scholarly models, and to Clifford Flanigan, whose unflagging enthusiasm, prodigious intellect, and inestimable generosity is sorely missed. I am also indebted to my students at George Washington University, the Bread Loaf School of English, and the University of Iowa, who willingly allowed me to try out many of these ideas on them and whose perceptive and often refreshingly resistant reactions and observations were much appreciated. I have also profited from the astute suggestions of Theresa Coletti and Michal Kobialka, whose perceptive critiques provided extremely valuable help on revisions. Friends and colleagues—particularly Kathy Ashley, Bob Clark, Huston Diehl, Barbara Eckstein, Connie Kibler, Jim Maddox, Teresa Mangum, Kim Marra, Gail Paster, Judith Pascoe, Pam Sheingorn, Margaret Soltan, Etsuko Taketani, Jon Wilcox, and Tara Ghosal Wallace—have provided crucial support and encouragement at the various stages of this project. To my parents Jean and Clair Sponsler and parents-in-law Pat and Herb Porter: thanks for everything.

The staffs of the Folger Shakespeare Library, the Newberry Library, the Library of Congress, and the Walters Art Gallery deserve special mention for their helpfulness in tracking down the material that made its way into this book. I also wish to thank Rita Copeland and Barbara Hanawalt for their interest in the project, as well as Lisa Freeman and Gretchen Asmussen of the University of Minnesota Press for their help in preparing the manuscript and Anne Running for her skillful copyediting. Thanks also to George Washington University and the University of Iowa for supporting the research and writing of this book with grants and research assistance. Portions of chapter 1 appeared as "Narrating the Social Order: Medieval Clothing Laws," *CLIO* 21 (1992): 265–83; I am grateful to the editors of *CLIO* for permission to incorporate that material here.

Finally, special thanks to Jeff Porter for seeing me through this project to the very end.

# Introduction

✣

## Bodily Transactions: Performance, Identity, and Commodification

*Where there is power, there is resistance.*
—Michel Foucault, *History of Sexuality*

This book takes up the question of discipline as it applies to medieval subjects by investigating how commodity culture, discourses of bodily control, and theatricality converged in late medieval England as part of the "disciplining" of individuals. In particular, I consider both the technologies of power that structured the individual and the tactics of consumption that made possible a refiguring of and resistance to power. Although the cultural practices and representations I examine all predate the modern period, both my interest in this topic and my means of exploring it are indebted to the present—to often contentious contemporary debates over identity politics, subjectivity, and processes of commodification. The late-twentieth-century industrialized world has been forced to confront new and often unsettling patterns of embodied subjectivity and its cultural meanings within a consumer society. From the denatured body of the cyborg to the mesmerizing simulacra of shopping-mall culture, we have been bombarded by objects and events that profoundly question established notions of identity. In the process, we have come to see ourselves less as self-directing, unified persons than as, in Terry Eagleton's words, "decentered network[s] of libidinal attachments, emptied of ethical substance and psychical interiority, the ephemeral function of this or that consumption, media experience, sexual relationship, trend, or fashion."[1] No longer the autonomous agents we once might have imagined ourselves to be, no longer the confident knowers privileged by the economy of signs, we recognize ourselves instead as subjects who are constituted at the whim of unstable cultural forces abuzz all around us. As a consequence, we view the socially constructed body as a site of both cultural crisis and a subjectivity that is always-already disappearing.[2]

Medieval subjectivity, however, has often been construed in terms that are entirely alien to postmodern understandings of the self and the social. When framed within a society that is seen—as it often is—as monolithic, orderly, hierarchical, and God-centered, medieval subjectivity looks as un-interesting as it appears uncomplicated.[3] But recent work in medieval history has eroded the notion of a harmonious Middle Ages within which individual identities were unproblematic. Instead, the communities that took shape from 1200 to 1500 are now increasingly imagined by historians to have been distinctly disharmonious and the subjects inhabiting them to have been anything but secure, stable, and unaware of themselves as subjects. Under the impetus of such late medieval cultural forces as monastic reform movements, the development of parliaments and national dynasties, and the growth of professional elites and trade associations, individual identities and the self's location within the social were challenged in unprecedented ways. As a consequence, subjectivity was opened to active exploration as individuals sought to place and understand themselves in reaction to new boundaries, dogmas, alliances, and laws.[4] Any investigation of medieval subjectivity has to begin with a recognition of these diverse and often conflicting traditions, discourses, and practices that informed the cultures of medieval Europe. All of these forces suggest that medieval subjects were constructed not within a consensus of social harmony but out of heterology.

## Embodied Subjects

Like other cultural historians I argue that the self is embodied, inhabiting a corporeal form that is in turn invaded and shaped by relations of power, especially, as Foucault asserts, by "disciplinary power," the prescriptive demands of institutional authority.[5] Central to my thinking is the idea that both self and body are imprinted by material and discursive forces that give them their being and their meaning. The body acts as the screen on which the self reads external events and situations; it is the place where the self acquires a sense of its boundaries and of its connections with outside forces. The individual self gains its awareness of identity first from the body, and it is also through the body that the self is constituted as a social being. It is therefore perhaps not surprising that all cultures seek control of the body.

The centrality of the body to both self and the social was an accepted tenet of medieval thought.[6] By the late medieval period, a systematic theory of physiognomy had been developed, drawing on such Aristotelian and pseudo-Aristotelian texts as *De physiognomia*, which categorized human character according to physical features, especially the features of the head. The assumption behind these texts was that physiognomy represented a way of calculating the invisible through the visible, of seeing the inner through the outer and hence of identifying the true self through the external signs of the body. As John Metham put it in his fifteenth-century physiognomic essay, "Be thyse tokynnys off the face . . . ye may knowe the trwth."[7]

Certain official views of society likewise drew on the image of the body as an organizing unity, conjuring up a notion of membership that played on the unified assemblage of body parts. Modeled on the *corpus Christi* as described by Paul in Corinthians, the urban community in particular was often envisioned as an organic entity within which each of the community's members, like each part of the human body, had a specific and hierarchically determined function leading to the survival of the whole. The head ruled the hands and feet, which worked in turn to sustain the head, and the whole organism was ruled by God. Within this scheme, individuals were assumed to exist primarily to further the survival of the whole.[8]

Although these understandings of embodiment should by no means be taken as describing the entirety of the lived experiences of real individuals, they nonetheless formed a powerful ideological field within which subjects were positioned and against which they could stage their resistance. Pierre Bourdieu's notion of the *habitus* within which social agents internalize dominant social values through the medium of the body is obviously useful in theorizing this ideological field. Bourdieu defines the *habitus* as the totality of general dispositions or unarticulated and internalized norms and values that govern human behavior. The *habitus* is what makes possible the internalization of dominant social values, a process that occurs as an ordinary, largely unnoticed part of social life. For Bourdieu, an important aspect of the education of the individual into the *habitus* is the inscription of social power relations onto the body. As "embodied history," the *habitus* is produced and expressed through bodily gestures, movements, postures, and behaviors. In Bourdieu's formulation, the socially produced body is thus the political body, which becomes in turn a reminder of power relations whose traces can be read on it.[9]

## Commodified Subjects

Although Bourdieu is primarily interested in the impact of discourse on the body, social theorists argue that changes in the nature and uses of the body are often tied to changes in commodity production and consumption.[10] Following their lead, I stress the role of material culture on the construction of late medieval subjectivities. Few studies have taken up the question of commodification's effects on premodern subjects.[11] In part this is because the preindustrial period is often seen as an age of such small-scale production that a dearth of commodities meant freedom from the insidious forces of consumption. But although the range of commodities might have been more limited, late medieval consumers nonetheless were confronted with an array of goods that many could afford to purchase.[12] Constructions of subjectivity in the late Middle Ages took place within a context of new patterns of production and consumption. As Christopher Dyer has observed, the English economy between 1350 and 1750 was characterized by important changes in the workforce and in the kinds of labor performed, by an increase in manufacture and trade that made urban areas more important, by rising standards of living, by shifts in social attitudes toward labor and consumption, and by an increase in rules governing work and the use of consumer goods.[13] The late Middle Ages were, as Dyer and others suggest, marked by new models of consumption that responded to the filling up of the private world with goods. As a consequence, attempts to control consumption became a consistent part of the disciplining of subjects. In addition, both the disciplinary discourses and the theatrical performances I discuss were caught up in a culture of commodification, themselves produced and consumed as material goods—as texts and performances—a fact that has important repercussions for their ideological impact.

Not only were medieval men and women avid consumers of goods, texts, and theatrical performances, but they were consumers Michel de Certeau would surely have recognized, consumers who became producers. Ordinarily understood, consumption is characterized by passivity and inertia, waste and absence. In de Certeau's view, however, consumption is a creative activity, a way of transforming the commodities that the dominant culture assumes will be passively ingested. De Certeau defines consumption not as passive ingestion but as the realm of the use of an object by those who are not its makers.[14] For de Certeau, these moments of the use of an object are acts of antidiscipline in which subjects can, through various strategies and tactics, appropriate and reshape the subject positions handed to them by the producers of power. Through this formulation, de Certeau turns consumption into a mode of resistance rather than a passive absorption of mass culture's projects. Everyday life, according to de Certeau, invents itself by "*poaching* in countless ways on the property of others," deflecting the intended flow of goods and altering their meanings. In this way consumers become active participants in the processes of both production and consumption, constantly adapting the material conditions of the dominant culture to their own ends.[15] In late medieval England, poaching on the property of others provided, as I hope to show, a powerful way of resisting disciplining forces.

## Discourses of Control and the Theater of Resistance

Against this backdrop of embodied and commodified subjects, *Drama and Resistance* tells two entangled stories. The first story is about dominance, control, and the "disciplining" of bodies and commodities. Chapters 1, 3, and 5 discuss three separate authoritative discourses—clothing regulations, conduct literature, and books of hours—that tried to dictate the proper use of goods and bodies by disseminating authorized codes of dress, behavior, and devotional practices. Here, I argue, we can see the dominant culture at work writing what might be called official scripts for living that focus on regulating both bodies and items of consumption. Such official scripts represented the social order as elites, particularly urban elites, wished to see it, settling the less privileged—especially women—precisely where those in power wanted them, in subordinated positions. To be effective, however, these official scripts had to appeal to the very subjects they sought to control. A controlling discourse might have achieved its intended effects through brute coercion, but by enlisting the aid of an appealing rhetoric that asked the subject willingly to join in with the cultural project of subordination, its task was made easier, its reach broader, and its effects more pernicious. In these three chapters I therefore also examine the persuasive strategies employed in making certain subject positions *desirable*. At the same time, I analyze the contradictions and inconsistencies in these official discourses that opened up a breach for the production of the dissident stances found in the theater. The disciplinary discourses I discuss were part of cultural processes of iterability that attempted through the repetition of norms to regulate and constrain behavior. As such, they were cultural fictions that served as mechanisms for controlling the human body and its insertion into systems of production and consumption. Although they often attempted to present a univocal and unconflicted understanding of the self, they were also open to disruption. As Judith Butler has said, "If the regulatory fictions of sex and gender are themselves multiply contested sites of meaning, then the very multiplicity of their construction holds out the possibility of a disruption of their univocal posturing."[16]

While the body is central to the reproduction of often repressive social relations, as Bourdieu notes, it can also function as a source of subversion, since it can never be entirely invaded by power. Discourses that seek to control can also be resisted. The second story my book tells is thus about liberatory practices that defy regulatory regimes. In chapters 2, 4, and 6, I look at transgressive acts staged in Robin Hood performances, morality plays, and Corpus Christi pageants, instances that indicate how, within the licensed space of the theater, official scripts for living could be rewritten—no matter how fleetingly or contingently—to explore alternate possibilities of action and being. In these performances, I argue, bodies and commodities were reassembled in deviant ways that countered authoritative models of subjectivity, reappearing engaged in such forbidden acts as cross-dressing, social and sexual misbehavior, and violence against the body to challenge the codes promulgated by official discourse. Disciplines were in turn thus disciplined in the late medieval theater when, in a dramatic reversal, authoritative norms were subverted in performances that not only suggested different models of subjectivity but also imagined ways of reinventing prescriptions for the "proper" use of goods and bodies.

Theatrical performances in late medieval England, which have been linked to a growing self-consciousness at national, civic, and personal levels,[17] played a significant role in late medieval life because they were social events to which a wide range of people had access and within which various contested cultural issues could be acted out. In my analysis of medieval theater, I do not, however, make hard-and-fast distinctions between the performativity of everyday life and the specific theatricality of the stage. Instead, I have found it instructive to view identity—whether onstage or off—as the performance of the self through the medium of the socially interpreted body. As Erving Goffman has shown, even though individual subjectivity is socially determined—largely through the roles made available to participants within a culture—that condition does not rule out the possibility of individuals exerting some degree of control over both the choice and performance of social roles.[18] It would therefore be inaccurate to take the theater as the only place where identities can be creatively reimagined.

Despite the inseparability of theatricality in everyday life and on the stage, dramatic performances played a privileged role within late medieval culture. Like the pub or the tavern, the theater was a social site where resistance could be practiced, articulated, enacted, and tried out, protected by the codes of theatricality from the full scrutiny of authority, even when authority sponsored the performance. In the late Middle Ages, the theater represented at least in part what James Scott has called the "hidden transcript," that set of speeches, gestures, and practices through which subordinated groups rebel against the official version of social reality promulgated by elites.[19] It allowed for covert opportunities whereby subordinated groups could act out contrapuntal, nonhegemonic, and dissident alternatives to hegemony. However, since late medieval theater had a complicated and ambiguous relationship with dominant cultural groups—at times sponsored by them, at times repressed—performances cannot be seen as the pure expression of marginalized groups using subversive discourse to evade or redefine official ideologies.

Just as official discourses are seldom unilaterally coercive, so too dramas of resistance are rarely entirely transgressive. Complicitous as they often were with dominant forces, the theatrical performances I discuss could often only gesture toward alternate behaviors and practices existing beyond the reach of authoritative discourse.[20] Late medieval theater was involved in the practice of staging identities, but that was a complex ideological business in which the consumption of its product was indeterminate and open to conflicting understandings, and its effects on individuals as well as groups were more plural than singular. In some instances medieval performances led to real rebellion, as in the case of certain insurrections inspired by Robin Hood performances; on other occasions the dissident potential remained largely untapped and was quietly reabsorbed, whatever its individual psychosocial effect might have been.

In the chapters that follow I describe tactics of control used by authoritative discourses, delineating some of the specific representational forms and historical subjects for whom those representations did their cultural and ideological work, while also pointing to the traces of a lingering obstinacy on the part of medieval subjects toward being disciplined. In the process, I heed Bourdieu's injunction against objectivist discourse's tendency to treat "its constructions—'culture,' 'structures,' 'social classes,' or 'modes of production'—as realities endowed with a social efficacy," trying instead to recognize the constructedness of the terms and categories I employ while also seeking to remain aware of the ambivalence of my position writing in the present about past events and texts that are the product of a long history of textual transmission and historiographic work.[21] My readings of these dominant and transgressive texts and cultural practices will, I hope, be taken as they were undertaken—as attempts to write about the elusive struggle of competing forces fighting on and over the bodies of medieval subjects.

CHAPTER 1

✛

# Fashioned Subjectivity and the Regulation of Difference

*God suffreth weel ther be a difference*
*Touchyng array, as men been of degre.*
— Lydgate, *Fall of Princes*

In August 1976, the Mashpee Wampanoag Tribal Council, Inc., sued in federal court to reclaim possession of some sixteen thousand acres of tribal land constituting three-quarters of the town of Mashpee, Massachusetts. What was in dispute was not whether the Mashpees had a legal claim to the land, but whether they did indeed constitute a distinct and separate "Indian tribe" and so would be eligible to argue for their rights to land ownership. For several months in 1976, James Clifford, a historian who has made a career of studying and critiquing the discipline of anthropology, attended the Mashpee trial, subsequently writing an account of his observations. In Clifford's view, the Mashpee trial was "less a search for the facts of Mashpee Indian culture and history than it was an experiment in translation, part of a long historical conflict and negotiation of 'Indian' and 'American' identities."[1] The difficulty faced by the Mashpees was that they did not obviously form a "tribe," at least not in the eyes of the white, middle-class Americans who made up the jury: they spoke English; they were chiefly Baptists; they had intermarried with blacks and whites; they were "businessmen, schoolteachers, fishermen, domestic workers, small contractors."[2] To all appearances, the Mashpees were indistinguishable from their neighbors. Looking nothing like the sepia-tinted photographs taken by Edward Curtis—prints that for over a hundred years had powerfully shaped American perceptions of "Indianness"—the Mashpees failed miserably at fitting into the imaginative space allotted to Native Americans in the minds of the dominant white culture.

In Clifford's account, appearance and ways of looking became the trial's central issues. Looked at one way, the Mashpees formed a distinctive social group; looked at another way, they did not. In a crucial exchange that starkly condensed the complexities of the trial into one iconic image, a teenager known as Chiefy took the stand, wearing a bandanna

*1*

wrapped around his head. Apparently glad to be presented at last with what he could take as a sign of genuine Indian identity, the judge asked Chiefy about the bandanna's significance. Chiefy replied simply that he wore it to keep his hair out of his eyes. When the judge pursued the matter, asking how he had come by the bandanna (perhaps hoping Chiefy would dramatically reveal that it had been handed down to him by his forebears), Chiefy once again refused to use his bandanna as a marker of "Indian" identity as the judge seemed to want him to, stating flatly that he had bought it at the local dimestore. At the end of this inconclusive exchange, with which Clifford tellingly winds up his essay, we are left with provocative questions not only about the Mashpees' claim to tribal status, but also, and more important for my present purposes, about clothing's role in processes of constructing and displaying subjectivities. Could Chiefy's bandanna be seen as a token of "Indianness" even though it was a common item of consumption that might be purchased and worn by anyone? Could the bandanna mark Chiefy as a Mashpee even though he used it—again as anyone might use it—for functional, not ceremonial, purposes? Could something as insignificant and ordinary as a bandanna bear the symbolic weight necessary to inscribe its wearer into determinate social groupings? And, finally, who decides what clothing means—wearers or onlookers?

As Chiefy's bandanna suggests, clothing is a complex sign, one that is open to multiple and conflicting interpretations, interpretations often arrived at under the oversight of powerful and vested interests.[3] Although clothing might seem to promise instant recognition of others, their social condition, and their relation to the viewer's self, it often leads to confusion, deception, and misrecognition as well. Moreover, as a commodity clothing is entangled with mechanisms of production and consumption that complicate its social meanings. If clothing's signifying gestures are in many cases hard to restrict, so too are its paths of acquisition. A T-shirt imprinted with the logo of a college in the United States can find its way to a rice farmer in Indonesia, while huaraches handmade in Central America wind up on the feet of a banker in London. Easy to acquire and readily traded from one person to another, clothing has social uses and cultural values that are flexible and shifting. What clothing means is thus nearly endlessly open to revision as it shifts from owner to owner and context to context.

The issues of commodification and signification raised by Chiefy's bandanna might appear to be unique to the late twentieth century, but they are not.[4] In the Middle Ages, although items of dress might have traveled shorter distances and have leapt fewer cultural barriers, conflicts over dress were nonetheless widespread and the stakes high. In late medieval England, what fashion historians have identified as a virtual revolution in dress had the result of making clothing a focal point of tensions over consumption and subjectivity. The salient features of this revolution are as follows. Before 1340, according to fashion historians, clothes were longer, looser, more flowing, and relatively unmarked for gender or status. During the 1340s, however—as the result of such forces as the development of mercantile capitalism, the growth of cities and courts as centers of cultural dissemination, technological innovations in textile manufacturing, and greater social, economic, and geographic mobility—a tighter, fitted style using buttons and lacing to accentuate the body became popular. Men's tunics were now cut short and tight; women's dresses, although still worn long, were close-fitting and often low in the bodice. Sleeves were shaped close to the arm, ending in voluminous pieces of cloth that trailed to the ground. Elaborate belts, embroidery, fur trimming, and expensive imported cloth were frequent adornments. Edges of garments were "dagged," or cut into points, scallops, or other complicated patterns. Men's shoes developed long curved tips, called "pikes"; women's hats became almost monstrously fanciful.[5] Although precise information about who had the wealth or connections to acquire fashionable clothes is hard to come by, evidence suggests that rising standards of living put the new styles within reach of a fairly wide range of consumers, widening the scope of the fashions' potential impact and linking them with deeper concerns about social and economic changes.[6]

From our point of view in a culture of novelty and hyperconsumption, such developments might seem unremarkable, but for many elites in late medieval England these changes were profoundly disturbing and were registered as a sign of rupture of the normative social order. New styles were frequently denounced by male political and ecclesiastical authorities in an overblown rhetoric that equated the wearing of fashionable clothes with the demise of tradition and virtue and the rise of social and economic unrest. Typical is a passage from *The Brut* that rails against how the English "ordeyned and chaungyd ham euery ȝere diuers schappis of disgyngeȝ of cloþing," having abandoned "al old honeste and good vsage."[7] What is revealed in this and other similar denunciations is not just a revulsion against novelty or a nostalgic longing for a golden age now lost, but also a profound fear of the enhanced expressive possibilities of these newly and widely available fashions—especially a fear of the diversity their "diuers schappis" opened up. In response to this fear, discourses of sartorial control sought to restrict access to these commodities. In so doing, they treated dress as a proxy for the socially constructed bodies beneath, seeking to regulate subjects by prescribing what might be worn. Through what could be described as an early form of commodity fetishism, dress effectively displaced individual subjects as the target of authoritative surveillance, a move that quite deliberately mistook commodities for living bodies.[8] As Marjorie Garber has said, quoting from a newspaper wedding announcement that lavishly describes the bride's wedding gown while treating the woman who wears the gown as no more than an inert mannequin, "What gets married *is* a dress."[9] The bride's identity becomes established in her dress, and it is the dress as much as the person within it that participates in the wedding ceremony. In a similar way late medieval subjects were located within a materialist terrain, and their social relations were mapped out by explicit reference to consumer goods. Not only were the individual's desires understood to be channeled toward consumption, but the individual was also assumed to be to a large extent the product of the satisfaction of those desires. It is thus important to recognize that the subjectivity articulated by medieval fashion regulations is intractably materialist, shaped in relation to the market and to the world of goods produced by it.

If diversity in the form of "diuers schappis" of clothing had become a cause for alarm, it was in large part because such diversity seemed to threaten the stable social positioning of individual subjects by producing an abundance of signs of difference that could be displayed on the body. What was particularly troubling about these signs of difference, from the perspective of authorities, was that they made it difficult to match individuals up with fixed and identifiable subject positions. As a result, attempts to regulate dress in late medieval England have to be seen as allied with a larger cultural apparatus for producing and controlling gender, status, and, less often, racial differences. Because dress was taken as a proxy for the bodies of individuals, control of dress seemed to promise the chance to control those bodies as well, especially through the policing of the signs of difference visible in clothing. Questions of *difference* were thus at the heart of late medieval conflicts over dress.

But dominant attitudes toward difference were riddled by contradictions—contradictions that, as I shall suggest later, undermined efforts aimed at controlling clothed bodies. On the one hand, fashion's ability to produce difference was valued by authorities, as Lydgate's remarks (quoted in the epigraph to this chapter) favoring a divinely ordained "difference touchyng array" indicate, since it seemed to promise that differences in status or gender could be made visible and could thereby be stabilized, stabilized in ways that favored particular vested interests, that is. On the other hand, difference was feared because it challenged the idea of a limited and ordered social system. Although officialdom required the production of differences precisely to maintain its privileges by defining itself as *other than* subordinated groups, limiting the degree and kinds of difference displayed on the clothed body proved difficult, given both the variety of fashion choices and their accessibility. While clothing regulation can be seen as an attempt to control unruly bodies by regulating the seemingly more manageable category of consumer goods, those goods turned out to be just as resistant to control as the bodies that wore them.

This chapter examines the strategies used in late medieval England by various regulatory discourses, particularly sumptuary laws, sermons, and social advice literature, in their attempts to control clothing—and through clothing, embodied subjects. My chief interest lies in the descriptive or rhetorical methods adopted by these discourses to structure the conceptual and ideological space for controlling dress, thereby reaffirming or fixing specific patterns of social relations. In a fascinating move whose implications I will explore, regulatory discourses endeavored to naturalize certain subject positions—in the sense of making those subject positions seem innate, customary, and unquestionable. They did so primarily by constructing a fiction of the essential, originary subject untainted by signs of fashion excess and intrinsically obedient to the demands of authority. In this fiction, the phrases "unnatural," "counterfeit," "excessive," and "inordinate" crop up again and again, constructing a silent standard—the natural, the real, the moderate, and the orderly—against which fashion (and its wearers) could be measured. Much of the persuasive power of these regulatory discourses derives from their ability to define fashion consumption as an act against nature, against order, and against propriety.

What these regulatory discourses also reveal is how hegemonic power works to make itself plausible and even attractive. Relying not primarily on brute force, but rather on the power of language and representation to shape reality and motivate behavior, regulatory discourses assembled an array of rhetorical appeals and ideological constructs to make their agenda seem both reasonable and desirable, even for the subjects whose bodies and goods were being controlled. In this way, regulatory discourses enlisted language and representation to aid their cause, crafting an imaginative social order in which properly dressed individuals willingly took up their allotted roles.

I wish to make clear that in my analysis I view these disciplining discourses as complex interventions within a complicated and shifting social field that is itself a series of interrelated but also inconsistent processes. This social field can be described as, in Victor Turner's words, "a set of loosely integrated processes, with some patterned aspects, some persistences of form, but controlled by discrepant principles of action expressed in rules of custom that are often situationally incompatible with one another."[10] Within this social field, regulatory discourses should be seen not as inert sources of documentary evidence about cultural attitudes, but rather in terms of the dynamic practices that they created, modified, and disseminated.[11] This means that regulatory discourses ought to be understood not just as registering complaints about excess consumption and unruly subjects but also as contributing to the production of those subjects and to the commodification of clothing. I read these regulatory discourses, then, as themselves social practices whose inscription and transmission are part of broader and continually shifting social alliances and economic concerns.

Moreover, as Bourdieu has suggested, laws are both structuring and structured, both gendering and gendered.[12] Which is to say that regulatory discourses are produced by as well as produce social forces, and are themselves constructed, not passively recorded. Hence laws are never and cannot be simple or unilateral expressions of power, but take their place within an always changing social field. Although it is beyond the scope of the present study to give a detailed account of the forces that called forth agents of fashion regulation, I shall try to suggest something about the specific interests that were brought to bear on clothing control, sketching out who was concerned with fashion excess and why. Fashion regulation was part of the cultural representation of social life in late medieval England and therefore part of the social construction of reality. As this suggests, discourses of sartorial discipline were caught up in contests over what social reality was and how bodies and goods should behave within it. The rhetorical tactics adopted by fashion critics had, then, a bearing on how subjects understood themselves and their social positions.

I also wish to stress that like all attempts to constrain signification and limit differentiation, fashion control was open to resistance, recalling Foucault's rule of "the tactical polyvalence of discourses," whereby discourse acts not only as an instrument of power, but also as "a hindrance, a stumbling-block, a point of resistance and a starting point for an opposing strategy."[13] Despite their concerted efforts to do just the opposite, regulatory discourses ended up promoting the very thing they tried to inhibit—the consumption of clothing along with its transgressive social consequences—so that what was forbidden emerged from the regulatory machine looking even more desirable. The story of this chapter thus has to do with both the discursive techniques of fashion control and the ultimate deconstruction from within of the regulatory project. Power, at least as seen through the lens of late medieval conflicts over dress, comes to seem less an abstract expression of monolithic hegemonic attitudes than a relationship that is always changing. And if power is an ever-shifting relationship, then even at its most pervasive and imperious moments opportunities are constantly being created for resisting it, opportunities such as those I shall consider in the following chapter.

## Unnatural and Counterfeit

One powerful way of containing difference is to style its production as outside the boundaries of the permissible and beyond the limits of socially acceptable activities. In the case of the control of gender and status differences produced by clothing after 1340, this containment involved a double move of first defining the body as a natural and transparent sign of identity and then describing clothing, in contrast, as unnatural and deceptive. Late medieval discourses of sartorial control typically begin by creating just such a dichotomy between the natural, divinely created body and the body tainted by human intervention. Robert Mannyng's *Handlyng Synne*, for example, has this to say about women who, through the use of face powder, try to make themselves more beautiful:

Of þese [wymmen] þat are so foule & fade
Þat make hem feyrer þan god hem made,
Wyþ oblaunchre or wyþ ouþer flour
To make hem whytter of kolour,
Gret pryde hyt ys & vyle outrage,
Þat she ys nat payd of goddys ymage.[14]

These lines manage to invest the innocuous act of powdering the face with sinister force, turning the use of cosmetics into an unnatural intervention against nature and a rebellion against divine will. In this construction, adornments worn on the female body are understood to be deceptive, while men are cast as the victims of the deceit, unwittingly taken in by the feminine masquerade. What seems to be at issue for Mannyng is not so much the dangerous sexual allure of the powdered female body, although that is certainly a subtext of his complaint, but rather the concealing of "true" identity and "real" value in a process that transforms what is ugly into something fraudulently beautiful. Obscuring nature with artifice, face powder attracts the unsuspecting masculine gaze, maneuvering the observing male into a bad bargain by offering up false goods rather than the genuine product.

The counterfeit coin of the self put into circulation by cosmetics stands in contrast to the ideal image of the naked body that transparently reveals innate human identity. A sermon by Thomas Wimbledon explains how nakedness manifests the real self, since it is the state into which humans are born: "For we beþ / nouȝt gete wiþ riche cloþis, neiþer bore wiþ gold ne wiþ / siluer. Ynakid he bryngeþ vs in to þe world, nedy of mete, / cloþynge and drynke."[15] Although Wimbledon is explicitly criticizing fashion excess with his reference to "riche cloþis," he is also implying that all clothes, not just fashionable ones, are unnatural. But since no one was advocating the complete abandonment of clothing, distinctions had to be made between appropriate and inappropriate kinds and uses of dress. In a sermon on Mary Magdalene, Bishop Rypon tries to mark out some of these distinctions. Before sin, he argues, the body was naked,

but after sin clothing was made from animal skins to cover human nakedness. Later, as pride grew, men used wool and then linen and silk, worn
for vanity rather than necessity.[16] The point for Rypon is that simple
clothes worn out of need and to cover the shamefully naked body are permissible, but anything worn beyond necessity is not. Rypon's remarks,
like Wimbledon's, express a deep mistrust of fashionable clothing, which
is set up in conventional terms as postlapsarian, hence problematic. In
opposition to the pure, originary body—naked and hence natural—the
fashionably clothed body was by definition debased, the result of sin and
a sign of it.[17]

The link between dress and sin becomes especially apparent in attacks
on the eroticizing powers of dress, which might have been behind such
sumptuary legislation as the 1463 prohibition against men's wearing of
short jackets.[18] *Handlyng Synne* goes so far as to define lechery expressly
as the use of clothing to incite desire: "Lechery ys also gret ȝernyng / To
be desyred þurgh feyre cloþyng."[19] Although Mannyng's formulation is
gender neutral, the desire to be desired was usually attributed to women,
not to men. As *Jacob's Well* puts it, men are led into lechery by women
who dress themselves so as to capture the male gaze:

Men may synnen ofte in syȝt of wommen; as nyce wommen þat
dyȝten hem qweyntly to make men to mys-vsyn here syȝt on hem,
and ȝit þei wenyn þei synnen nouȝt, for þei consentyn noȝt to hem.
but þei synne grevously, for þei are cause þat þe soulys of manye
men are lost. ȝif þe womman in here entent doth so in here aray, þat
men þat beholdyn here hadde desyre to don foly wyth here, þanne
sche is cause of here synne.[20]

This passage is particularly striking for the way it emphasizes the power
of appearance to inflame desire, causing men to "misuse" their sight and
stray into sin. Notice here that it is not the woman's naked and natural
body, as we might anticipate, which is condemned for having the power
to lead men astray; instead it is the *clothed* and therefore unnatural female body that is the object of censure.

In a surprising rewriting of the story of Judith and Holofernes, retold
in a Middle English sermon, this theme of the dangers of female dress is
given full narrative treatment. In this sermon, Judith is described as
deliberately making herself "as freshe as she cowȝth be in aray" in order
to attract Holofernes, thus gaining the opportunity to cut off his head.
Judith, not Holofernes, is here cast in the role of evil seducer, and the
man, not the woman, becomes the victim. Rather than praising Judith's
resourcefulness and heroism while a captive victim of Holofernes' lust—
the theme of the biblical version—the sermon goes on to lament how a

prince "was distrowed by þe nyce aray and atyre of a womman." In a dramatic reversal, the biblical story is given a new moral with the warning that "muche pepull is stered oft, ʒe! and assenteþ to lechery by þe nyse aray of wommen."[21]

Attempts to rein in the dangerous sexual allure of the clothed female body could be almost comically encyclopedic, as in this passage from a sermon that catalogs a whole wardrobe of items of female costume:

> Wommen with here hedes y-horned, schort clokes unnethe to the hupes, with bendels, chapellettes and frontelles y-set above the heued y-lyche to a wylde beste that hath none resoun. Sche hath also fylettes, skleyres, crymyles, kyrcheves, y-colored garlondys of perreye to have upon the top—though that the heved be al calwe on the cronne, they chargeth it nouʒt—and chapellettes y-poudryd wyth perry, and of many nyce dysgysynges of atyre: so that y nouʒt wryte ne discryve suche dyvers thynges as men and wommen use now a day.

> [Women with their horned headdresses, short cloaks reaching scarcely to the hips, with bands, caps, and frontelles set above their heads like a wild, irrational beast. They also wear fillettes, veils, plaits, kerchiefs, colored garlands of jewelry on top—even though their heads are all bald on top, they do not care—and little caps sprinkled with jewels, and many "nyce dysgysynges" of dress: so that I cannot write or describe such diverse things as men and women use nowadays.][22]

This enticing list of items of dress points up the diversity of clothing choices available to the consumer, a diversity that is seen as at once uncontrollable and beyond the scope of language, prompting the writer's complaint that he cannot "wryte ne discryve" the variety of things men and women now wear. Again, this diversity is positioned as unnatural (through artifice women transform themselves into wild beasts) and counterfeit (they disguise themselves with their clothes, deliberately ignoring the messages sent by the body beneath, in this case a bald head that clashes with the fancy head coverings). In a creative use of an old topos, the very indescribability of the fashion items becomes evidence of their alarming proliferation; even linguistic invention cannot keep pace with clothing's rampant spread, this passage suggests.

The reference in this passage to clothing choices as "dysgysynges of atyre" is particularly loaded. The term "disguise" could imply new, elaborate, showy, and ostentatious clothing or strange, unfamiliar, and extraordinary dress—meanings that share a fear of the out-of-the-ordinary.[23]

More significant, the term "disguise" was also associated with various kinds of dramatic performances and entertainment, such as the "disguysings" held by the Tudor court in 1501 to celebrate the marriage of Katherine of Aragon and Henry VII's eldest son, Prince Arthur,[24] and so suggested the act of dressing up in elaborate or fanciful costume. In this usage disguise is linked with festivity and entertainment, but also, and more troublingly, with the masking of "real" identity.[25] Part of the anxiety that lurks behind the notion of fashion as disguise has to do with the counterfeiting of identity, that is, with the fear that clothing offers people the chance to alter their appearance with the intention to deceive, not just during a courtly entertainment, but also in everyday life, where the consequences might be more alarming.[26]

Perhaps the most dangerous form of disguise through attire was cross-dressing. Certain strains of thought tolerated cross-dressing by women on the grounds that it made sense for women to wish to "better" themselves by becoming more male, even if only in appearance.[27] Aquinas, for instance, had argued that women should be allowed to dress like men when necessary, especially in order to escape from enemies;[28] in most instances, however, women were strongly discouraged from impersonating men. Henry Knighton's *Chronicon*, for example, berates women who come to tournaments dressed in masculine attire.[29] Men were also warned against dressing in ways that seemed to conceal or undo their sexual identities. The author of the chronicle *Eulogium historiarum sive temporis*, for instance, in his commentary on the year 1362 criticizes men for dressing like women and for looking more like minstrels and actors than knights, suggesting that masculinity hinges on its display and construction through dress.[30] Likewise, when Beggar in Hoccleve's *Regement of Princes* complains that the new fashion of tippets (long, trailing sleeves) makes it difficult for men to come to their lords' defense since such wide sleeves are heavy and cumbersome, he seems to be explicitly identifying appropriate male dress with appropriate male behavior, suggesting that the new fashions make men effeminate and incapacitate them for their masculine duties. Beggar underscores his concerns by urging lords to acquaint their men with Mars, who "loueth non array / That hurtyth manhode at preef or assay."[31] Since dress was supposed to match up with the body underneath, which was assumed to possess an innate identity, wearing the wrong clothing could "hurt manhood." What is particularly intriguing about Hoccleve's position is that by recognizing the power of clothes to produce gendered identities—to fashion the male and female subjects who wear them—he is also acknowledging that clothing has considerable signifying power, which can be "misused" to construct subjects who are gendered in ways other than those desired by such spokesmen for the normative order as himself. So Hoccleve is forced to try to suppress the deviantly expressive possibilities of clothes. His bind, I might add, is shared by other discourses of fashion regulation, with similarly conflicted results.

Clothing's power to construct and display not only gender but also status was similarly a concern. The naked, natural, originary body might be unmarked for status, but once the body is clothed, the possibility of deception based on the erasure of class markers arises. Medieval critics of fashion often posit an imaginary past in which the visible signs of identity coincided with innate identity, a time when the symbolic and the real were one and the same. In this imaginary past, which they seek to extend into the present, the clothed body reflects innate status distinctions and makes social standing immediately apparent. At the beginning of the *Regement of Princes*, for instance, Beggar complains about the poor man who dresses like a lord, "counterfete / In his array."[32] Once it was possible, Beggar continues, to tell people apart by their clothing, but now "a man schal stody and musen a long throwe / Whiche is whiche."[33] Hoccleve's words describe a fantasy past of clear social distinctions when it was simple to tell "which is which"; the present, in contrast, is characterized as a time of deceptive social identities that result from clothing's ability to counterfeit "real" social standing. Serving as visual proof for Hoccleve's complaints, manuscript illuminations, such as those in the Bodleian Romance of Alexander (ca. 1344), show the extent to which the costumes of different ranks and professions were often indistinguishable.[34]

English sumptuary laws offer perhaps the most concerted response to the perceived problem of counterfeit status.[35] In a series of statutes enacted over the course of two and a half centuries, parliament took on the task of regulating the dress of citizens of the entire country. Since pressure for these laws originated chiefly in the House of Commons, the interests they most directly reflect are those of the representatives to that legislative body, a group of men drawn not from the aristocracy but from the prosperous middle social groups. Because the focus of the fourteenth- and fifteenth-century sumptuary laws, unlike later laws that emanate from the monarchy, is on these middle groups rather than on the aristocracy or the peasantry, the gaze of the laws' promulgators has a curiously self-directed quality to it. Sumptuary laws aimed at restricting clothing choices to a range of options identifiable with a particular rank or income level so that at a glance an individual's "genuine" social position would be apparent. The laws typically set out a gradient of styles of dress, as well as specific fabrics and accessories permitted to different social groupings, with the least choice allowed to those in the lowest social and economic groups—such as the carters, ploughmen, and other agricultural laborers who in the 1363 statute are permitted to wear only cheap russet wool costing twelve pence ("blanket & russet, laune de xii d").[36]

Although they sometimes couch themselves as protectionist in intent and hence aimed at limiting the import of foreign goods, suppression of status counterfeiting is a key goal of these laws. The 1463 statute, for example, prohibits esquires and gentlemen or anyone below the degree of knight from wearing counterfeit silk ("contrefet drap le soie resemblant a le mesme") or any cloth made to look like velvet or satin or ermine ("resemblantz a velewet ou a satain fugeree, ou ascun pellur dermyne").[37] Although the focus here is on the deceptiveness of the cloth itself, the concern is clearly with the issue of counterfeiting. Wearing counterfeit goods, this statute suggests, would allow someone to assume an identity not necessarily ratified by wealth or rank, making possible social posturing at various levels.

Haunting these attacks on disguise and counterfeiting was the desire to establish an innate, essential identity beyond the reach of fashion's signifying power, an identity that could be employed in the service of a social order in which status difference was immediately visible. This desire was difficult to realize, however, since exactly how to determine "real" status was a vexed issue. In the absence of a clear-cut consensus that birth alone assigned social standing, sumptuary laws were forced to grapple with the problem of what defines "real" status by trying to correlate various factors such as wealth, occupation, and rank in determining what dress would be allowed to an individual.[38] The statute of 1363, for instance, allows merchants, citizens, burgesses, artificers, and handicraftsmen with incomes up to five hundred pounds per annum to dress in the manner of esquires and gentlemen with incomes of one hundred pounds. But those same groups, if they have higher incomes of one thousand pounds a year, may dress like esquires or gentlemen with two hundred pounds a year.[39] Money in this statute is used to justify a more privileged style of dress than might otherwise be one's due. In this way not just dress but status itself is treated as a marketable item that can be purchased like any other commodity. This statute makes a strong statement about commodification and subjectivity, suggesting that the self is to some degree for sale.

The frank acknowledgment of the marketability of status in the 1363 statute was not, however, repeated in later statutes. In the 1463 statute (3 Edward IV) it is in fact no longer possible to use money to buy higher status. Income in this statute is mentioned for only a few social groups who apparently had justifiable reasons for displaying the trappings of social prestige or who could influence the legislative process, for example, mayors and aldermen, who are permitted to dress like esquires and gentlemen having incomes of forty pounds per year.[40] For everyone else, income no longer permits the purchase of the visible signs of a higher social standing.

The apprehension found in sumptuary laws that clothing could actively *produce* status, not just passively reflect it, is echoed in other discourses of fashion regulation, especially sermons. In a typical passage, one homilist warns about the social consequences of the free flow of items of fashion: "For we may se now al day that, be it never so pouer a man, and a have on a gay gowne of selk or ell[s] a pair o curel bedes hongyng abowte his nekk, eny man is fain to make him cher and also for to be mek and lowliche to him."[41] If a man, no matter how poor he might be, can command immediate respect by wearing a necklace of coral beads, then the language of fashion is certainly something to reckon with. Dress codes are here configured as an explicit line of defense against what is perceived as an immanent social upheaval that, it is feared, could be readily enabled by clothing—and hence averted by regulating clothing choice.

The task of regulatory discourses aimed at limiting the counterfeiting tendencies of clothing was made easier by the widespread cultural acceptance of using dress to mark affiliation with a specific group. Livery provides a particularly striking instance of people obligingly wearing dress that is strongly socially coded. The wearing of livery by members of guilds and households—whether in the form of a badge, hood, or full costume— had the effect of making immediately apparent an individual's association with a particular group while also indicating rank within that group.[42] Ordinances prohibiting the selling of livery (not until two years after a man's death) and regulating when livery could be worn (not to work, which might soil it) suggest some of the ways in which livery was understood to be an important signal of guild membership.[43] Honorary membership in a guild could be created by bestowing a suit of livery on outsiders, as the Tailors did in 1399 when they gave livery to the king, the prince, and the mayor of London. Alternately, it became fashionable for some members of the more powerful guilds to take the livery of the mayor and sheriffs, stressing their alliance with urban governments.

Willing conformity in dress also played an important role in certain ceremonial events, when the projection of apparent unity was desired. On the occasion of Prince Edward's visit to Coventry in 1474, for instance, the mayor and his associates, along with "the diuers of Cominalte of the seide Citie," all uniformly clothed in green and blue, met Edward on his entrance into the city.[44] Similarly, for the welcome of Henry VII to York in 1486, a castle was ordered to be set up in the Common Hall wherein "Citisyns" "shall appeir in clothing of white and greyne, shewing þer trueth and herty affection vnto the kinge."[45] In a display of class solidarity that transcended gender differences, Richard II's team at the Smithfield Tournament of 1390—men as well as women—all wore the king's livery with his emblem of a white hart, offering spectators the image of a fellowship of equals.[46] These moments of compliant self-regulation of costume

*13*

provided a common ideological ground from which attacks on the counterfeiting possibilities of clothing could be launched. In these instances of conforming dress, the dream of discourses of sartorial control was realized as individuating differences were subordinated to the overarching goal of a visible, orderly, harmonious, and fixed social system. In contrast, counterfeiting dress that seemed to allow the wearer to create new identities releasing the individual subject from existing social configurations could be styled deviant and unnatural, hence deserving of suppression.

## Excessive and Inordinate

One reason why the counterfeiting tendencies of dress proved so hard to contain was because control of the differentiating powers of clothing was closely tied to clothing's accessibility. As commodities available through a variety of official and unofficial exchange mechanisms—including purchase, inheritance, gift, and theft—items of apparel must have been difficult to keep out of circulation, even though we now have only glimpses of how clothes were acquired and by whom. A particularly vivid example comes from Caxton's *Vocabulary in French and English*, a language handbook designed to aid the English traveler to France. One of Caxton's sample dialogues presents a lively negotiation over the purchase of cloth for clothes, a dialogue that was apparently included in the *Vocabulary* because it was an activity the traveler would frequently engage in and need linguistic help with.[47] Although Caxton's traveler is male, records from the borough of Halesowen in 1290 suggest women's involvement in the trade in clothes, describing a woman named Isabel of Bracton, a dealer in clothes who sells a range of commodities, including hoods, gowns, tapestries, and linen sheets.[48]

Wills are another place where we can see clothes in circulation from wearer to wearer. A will of 1433, for example, leaves "myne aray for my body, armure, gownes, hodes, girdels . . . to Johne my sonne." Another will of 1444 bequeaths "to my doghter Issabell, my coufer with all my array."[49] Indirect evidence for increased access to clothing comes from economic trends, which point to a wider availability of commodities and greater purchasing power in the late Middle Ages. R. H. Britnell claims that between 1330 and 1500, despite a general decline in commerce, altered patterns of trade within England supplied a declining population with more comforts. Of particular interest in terms of fashion and its regulation, rising standards of living shifted consumer demand from cheap, locally produced goods to better-quality commodities made in recognized centers of cloth making and marketed by merchants to a broad range of the population, including laborers and servants.[50]

Trade in commodities such as clothing might also have taken place in informal ways, through theft, cast-offs, hand-me-downs, and the second-hand clothes market. A complaint from the reign of Henry VIII makes reference to one such informal exchange route. Attacking the careless-ness of the upper classes that enables the lower social groups to acquire fashionable clothes, the writer describes how noblemen's clothing is often "given away or it be half worne, to a symple man, the whiche causeth hym to weare the same," inciting his fellows, in turn, to want similarly fancy outfits.[51] Expensive clothing, out of the reach of poorer consumers if purchased new, might also have been acquired as secondhand goods. Although most references to the secondhand clothes trade date to the eighteenth century, the trade itself might have existed for much longer before being extensively commented upon in written records.[52] A few early references have in fact survived—such as a list of fines for second-hand clothes dealers in Norwich in the Conesford ward—suggesting that such a trade did indeed exist in late medieval England.[53] Court records also indicate that theft of clothing was a frequent crime, as in the exam-ple of John Banyard, who in 1315 was accused of robbing Robert of Dirby, parson of Hethersett, of a brightly colored robe, three hoods with fur of miniver, and two miniver furs.[54]

The fact that it must have been difficult to limit access to items of dress did little to discourage, and in fact probably incited, repeated legislative attempts to control these commodities. In what can be taken as implicit recognition of the proliferation of items of clothing in the marketplace, a persistent concern of sumptuary laws is with what they call "excess" in dress, which lawmakers typically claim is impoverishing the country, destroying morals, and generally leading to, in the words of the 1483 statute, "great misery and poverty" ("graund miserie & poverte").[55] Cloth-ing was seen as excessive and inordinate in at least three senses: in the economic sense that it was a sign of conspicuous consumption, in the moral sense that it represented the sin of pride, and in the social sense that it often seemed to cross the bounds of moderation and seemliness. But in all three instances, a common cause for alarm was clothing's super-fluity of signification, its tendency to escape the bounds of not only mar-ket controls but also the discursive limits to which it was continually asked to submit.

At its simplest, excess in array could be understood as too many clothes or too much cloth used to make an outfit, the latter a frequent complaint, given the voluminous cuts of many of the new fashions. This is what Hoccleve has in mind when he condemns the new styles as "A foul wast of cloth and an excessyf."[56] In Caxton's translation of *The Book of the Knight of La Tour-Landry*, excess in sheer numbers of items of dress is cause for parental concern. In a section aimed at deterring his daughters from extravagance, the Knight of La Tour-Landry recounts for their benefit the story of a knight who loses his wife. When the knight consults a hermit to try to locate her, he finds out that his wife has been taken to hell for crimes that included owning ten different gowns and coats—a number apparently indicative of extreme profligacy in dress. The Knight concludes that "a good woman shulde arraie her after her husbondes pusaunce," which presumably would mean in a nonexcessive way.[57]

Excess in clothing could also refer to the excessive cost of items of apparel. The supposedly extreme amounts of money being spent on clothing were often described in inflated terms as contributing to national economic collapse. The statute of 1463 is typical in its claim that the use of "excessive and inordinate array" has led to the "impoverishing of this Realm [of England], and to the enriching of [other] strange Realms and Countries, and to the final Destruction of the Husbandry of this said realm" ("enpoverissement de cest dit Roialme, & enricher de Roialmes & pais estraunges, a finallement destruccion del hosbondrie de cest dit Roialme").[58] This insistence on the deleterious effect of clothing excess on the country's economy, although often interpreted by historians as evidence of the essentially protectionist impulse behind English sumptuary laws, should also be seen as a rhetorical move that appropriated the powerful language of economic necessity in order to intensify the attack on clothing, raising the stakes for violation of dress codes.[59]

If the vision of impending national economic crisis were not deterrent enough, personal impoverishment was also often cited as the direct consequence of excess in dress. Revealing the masculinist and elitist bias behind clothing control, the people construed as being harmed by these expenditures were apt to be either husbands, reputedly brought to poverty's door by their extravagant wives, or masters whose apprentices were said to improvidently squander all their wages on fancy clothes. Fears of personal impoverishment were in these instances cleverly used to appeal to the interests of husbands and masters, a group that would be particularly perturbed by the new fashions' ability to destabilize existing sexual and status hierarchies.

The fact that regulatory discourses focused to such an extent on the excessive amounts of money spent on clothing by women and young men indicates just how much obedience and submission were key issues in fashion control. Among the many meanings of the word "inordinate," which was frequently used to describe the new fashions, were the connotations of "undisciplined," "unruly," and "rebellious," connotations that seem to describe not the clothes but rather the embodied subjects who wore them.[60] Many fashion critics assumed that it was the responsibility of the husband and master as overseer of wife and apprentices or servants to control his subordinates' fashion excess. The *Regement of Princes*, for instance, argues that if servants dress excessively, it is the fault of lords for letting their men "Vsurpe swiche a lordly apparaille."[61] Playing on this theme, a Tudor sumptuary law made masters legally responsible for servants who transgressed the law by wearing inappropriate dress.[62] Sumptuary laws expressed a similar paternalism, regulating women's dress as a subset of the dress allowed to her husband or father and thus assuming that the status of the male head of the household should determine the subordinated woman's permissible clothing. Sumptuary laws further attempted to reinscribe obedience and submission onto the bodies of potentially unruly subjects by arguing that the commons have always been prone to excess in dress and, like wives and apprentices, need to be reined in. By reiterating that the commons always require control, the promulgators of the laws made their own role seem a matter of benevolent necessity—a self-serving position, needless to say.

"Inordinate" clothing that called attention to the wearer was likewise proscribed for its flaunting of individual subjectivity in ways that violated obeisance to authority. The Knight of La Tour-Landry, for example, advises his daughters not to be the first to wear new fashions and not to call attention to themselves through their clothing, actions that he presumably sees as representing both feminine immodesty and social pushiness. Instead, he recommends that they "holde the mene astate of the good women and of the commune astate of the rewme," and so position themselves unobtrusively in the social mainstream.[63] The self-display made possible by new fashions also comes under scrutiny in *Handlyng Synne*, which tells the story of a knight "þat louede nouelrye" and who had made for himself "A kote perced queyntly wyþ pryde." Riding home one day he is killed by his enemies. His friends bury his body at the church and give away his goods to the poor, but no one wants the "coat of pride" except a clerk, who when he puts on the coat is struck by a fire that burns him to the ground. The moral of this story is that "þere shewede god weyl þe þat cas / þat þe kote acursed was."[64] In both cases, the newness of the fashions, not their cost—although the newest styles would presumably have been expensive—is what causes concern, chiefly because novelty is taken as a sign of a socially disruptive and rebellious ostentation.

Ostentatious display was often attacked in moralistic terms as a manifestation of the sin of pride, a rhetorical move that had the effect of keeping the individual in line through the heavy, but effective, hand of moral coercion.[65] John Bromyard, for instance, describes the "Devil's Castle" in which stands the tower of Vanity and Pride, whose inhabitants can be quickly recognized by their long, fashionable beards and dagged garments.[66] Wimbledon similarly complains:

The devyl hath maryid Pride to wommen; for wommen settyn all here stodye in pride of aray of here hed and of here body, to lokyn in

myrrourys, in kemyng here heed, in here hornys, in peerlys, in
other ryche aray abowte the heed, in ryngys, in brochys, in hedys,
in longe trayles.[67]

*Jacob's Well* picks up the theme of Wimbledon's sermon with a story of a
countess damned for her pride. The countess, although "chast of body, &
gret in doing almes-dedys, devowt in prayerus," nonetheless was sent to
hell after her death. She then appeared to a Frenchwoman, "fowl as a
feend," and advised her to take heed of her example. Although the countess had been good in every other way, because she delighted in pride and
vainglory of dress—"in prowde aray of myn heuyd & of my body, in longe
traynes, & in brode hornys"—she was damned in spite of her other
virtues. The homilist ends with the comment that since even a countess
was condemned because of lavish dress, all poor folk, who are proud and
borrow money to purchase fancy goods, should be especially on guard.[68]
In a revisionist reading of Noah's flood, the *Book of the Knight of La
Tour-Landry* goes so far as to attribute the flood to "the pride and the dis-
guysinge that was amonge women."[69] Enlisting Christian ideology to aid
their cause, these homilists suggest that ostentatious dress is a quick
route to sin and damnation, hence something the sane and morally up-
right person desirous of salvation will avoid.[70]
  Reading through these attacks, it is hard not to admire their creative
use of commodity fetishism, but also hard not to be troubled by their in-
tents. In an ingenious move, these fashion regulators managed to trans-
late anxieties over the restlessness of actual individuals into the more
governable domain of clothing, where objects could stand in for subjects.
In the following example clothes explicitly become surrogates for the unruliness of individuals:

Nouȝ also the comyn peple is hie stied into the synne of pride.
For now a wrecchid cnave, that goth to the plouȝ and to carte . . .
there-as sumtyme a white curtel and a russet gowne wolde have
served suchon ful wel, now he muste have a fresch doublet of fyve
schillynges or more the price; and above, a costli gowne with
bagges hangynge to his kne, and iridelid [= perforated] undir his
girdil as a newe ryven roket [= surplice], and an hood on his heved,
with a thousande ragges on his tipet; and gaili hosid an schood as
thouȝ it were a squyer of cuntre; a dagger harneisid with selver bi
his gurdel, or ellis it were not worth a pese. This pride schulle ther
maistirs a-buye, whanne that thei schul paie hir wages. For, there-
as thei weren wont to serve for x or xii schillingis in a ȝer, now thei
musten have xx oor thritti and his lyverei also therto; not for he
wol do more werk, but for to meynten with that pride.[71]

No longer, we are told, are the lower classes content with their lot (as represented by a "white curtel and a russet gowne"); instead, they now demand ever more privileges (in the form of a "fresch doublet" and other items of apparel). Expensive clothing is here taken as an index of social discontent, representing both lower class unrest and threats to the established social order. Although the homilist is patently unable to disarm real master-worker antagonisms or to regulate the divisive social relations generated by the wage economy he describes, he does his best by focusing on clothing. The agenda of fashion regulation is here exposed for what it was: an attempt to police social bodies by using objects as simulacra for subjects.

Sumptuary laws use the same tactic of making the object-world of clothing stand for embodied subjects. In their elaborate schemes for correlating dress with social standing, these laws reveal their desire for a social system in which the signs of status difference are carefully controlled. Not surprisingly, sumptuary laws are heavily invested in the idea of containment. So deep is the emphasis on containment that it is actually embedded in the very structure of the laws. Each sumptuary law consists of three main parts: a formulaic preamble lamenting the detrimental effects of clothing excess, followed by a list of specific items of dress and groups of people being regulated, and ending with a closing exhortation that sets out penalties for violating the law. One effect of this fairly rigid and unvarying structure is to provide a restrictive cage for the objects and subjects in question that promises to hold them safely within bounds no matter how often they threaten to break out of the schematized frame.

Containment also features in the way the laws severely truncate or generalize the social groupings whose dress they regulate. The 1363 law (37 Edward III), for example, inventories a range of social groups at or below the rank of knight, ignoring the royal family and the aristocracy. Its social groups are neatly separated from each other under generic categories such as "knight," "yeoman," "merchant," or "esquire," assuming that all merchants, for example, fit into the same category no matter what their individual differences of wealth, power, or social standing might be.[72] The 1483 statute (22 Edward IV) is even more successful at controlling difference, largely because it relies more heavily on omission of potentially complex social groupings. The statute begins with the king and the royal family, then moves in descending order down through dukes, lords, knights, yeomen of the crown, esquires and gentlemen, ending up with agricultural workers and common laborers. But it completely omits the middle social strata, especially prosperous urban groups. The statute presents a social order made up of the highest and lowest groups alone, suggesting that only through calculated suppression can orderly hierarchy be achieved. The 1463 law (3 Edward IV), in contrast, reveals how social groupings can evade discursive control. This statute, unwisely from the perspective of containment, attempts to sift through and make explicit the various factors regulating social position. Unable to contain the proliferation of signs of difference, however, this statute ends up describing a remarkably disorderly social system of jumbled social groupings lacking clear hierarchy or order. What comes across forcefully in sumptuary legislation, however, even in such rhetorical failures as the 1463 law, is an attempt to use discourse to constrain fashion choice and through it social difference.

For legislators and fashion critics alike, the chief function of clothing was to assign an individual to a fixed social position and to make that position knowable at a glance. As a sign of a disordered social system, "excessive" and "inordinate" clothing menaced this goal, since it invented opportunities for social differentiation. What was attacked as excess in dress can be seen as a superabundance of fashion signifiers that presented new possibilities for individuation, possibilities that threatened the conservatively favored social order weighted in favor of husbands and masters. When new patterns of differentiation implicit in clothing shook the old hierarchies by making visible a multiplicity of uncontainable differences, those with vested interests in the status quo not surprisingly reacted by attempting to hold the line at already established patterns of status and gender organization.

As a complex semiotic system, dress in late medieval England became a key site where struggles over the mutability of the social order could be undertaken. For the male writers of sumptuary laws and fashion diatribes, who invested clothing with enormous powers of identity formation and social ordering, transgression of dress codes did not just signal social disruption but actually constituted it. For this reason, regulation of dress became a necessary part of the regulation of social bodies whereby limiting clothing choices was understood to be a way of directly intervening into the social structuring of embodied subjects. Through fashion regimes, it was thought, gender difference and status hierarchies could be produced and secured and subjects could be interpellated into their social positions—whether by coercion or, in the manner preferred by most regulatory discourses, by ideological persuasion.

These discourses of fashion control, I have been suggesting, made themselves persuasive through a variety of techniques, such as the use of scare tactics that raised the specter of domestic, social, and economic disaster; the appeal to other authorizing discourses, such as the languages of morality and economic necessity; or the recourse to existing cultural models that valorized willingly conformist dress. Through such techniques, these regulatory discourses sought to make themselves more than merely coercive, striving instead to construct an imaginative social universe in which acquiescence to fashion regimes offered the assurance of benefits for the individual. The socially conservative task of fashion regulators was made easier by the fact that, as cultural anthropologists have amply demonstrated, dress by its nature lends itself to the maintenance of normative cultural systems; by drawing upon other important cultural fields, including ritual, dress censors can cause individuals to *want to* follow fashion regulations.[73]

But the persuasive power of discourses of fashion regulation must have begun to diminish considerably outside the parameters of an audience predisposed to embrace its message of preservation of the social status quo. For the lower social groups, apprentices, and women who had the chance to put on the potentially transgressive and rebellious signifiers of fashionable clothing, these regulatory discourses would likely have held little appeal. Only if these wearers could be persuaded to see their own best interests represented in the regulatory regime—which is what a writer like the Knight of La Tour-Landry asks his daughters to do—would discourses of fashion control have found much acceptance among these groups. Thus the *persuasive* project of controlling social differentiation by regulating dress was limited by its inability to speak convincingly to those audiences it sought to regulate. Even in its most overtly punitive form in sumptuary laws, where the whole legal apparatus could be made to bear down on the transgressing dresser, the regulatory regime fell seriously short of its desired ends; it was unable to halt the proliferation of fashion, its availability to consumers, or the uses to which it was put. To a large extent, this failure was self-induced, deriving from the regime's own internal contradictions, which ended up making what was proscribed all the more desirable.

## The Allure of the Forbidden

The intended goal of regulatory fashion discourses was to discipline the bodies within the clothing, forcing them into their assigned social positions, a disciplining that was accomplished at least in part through the discursive strategies I have been discussing. By styling freedom of fashion choice as deviant—counterfeit, unnatural, excessive, and inordinate—these discourses seized the rhetorical and ideological high ground, marking violators of the norms they espoused as social monsters and underminers of the common good.

But no matter how repressive they might be, discourses by their very utterance open up the possibility of resistance. In the case of late medieval fashion, resistance can be glimpsed in a number of places. Resistance shows up in the apparent ineffectualness of and noncompliance with sumptuary laws, at least up until Elizabeth's reign, when surveillance became more thorough and punishment of transgression more certain.[74] The laws themselves testify to their inability to effect real control, repeatedly deploring the fact that in spite of past legislation people still continue to abuse dress. More important, resistance can be sensed in breaches unwittingly made by the regulatory discourses themselves, for instance in the enticing lists of desirable clothing items that typically accompany attempts to repress fashion display, lists that look like menus beckoning the consumer, or in the mechanisms for enforcement of sumptuary laws that strangely permitted others to confiscate the offending item of apparel and keep it for their own use.[75] As a way of getting forbidden items of dress out of circulation, this method of punishment would seem to be a failure, allowing the clothing to pass on to yet another, perhaps equally unauthorized, wearer. At the very least, the thought of a nation of subjects licensed to seize their neighbors' clothing conjures up the image of less, not more, fashion control and more, not less, social competitiveness.

An even more crucial mode of resistance unsuspectingly presented by would-be regulators has to do with the nature of surveillance itself. It seems particularly significant that both the vigilance prescribed against inordinate array and the punishment for it took the form of *looking*. As sumptuary regulations made clear, the only way to identify and thus apprehend violators was to observe them, to look at what they were wearing. In 1560 in London, for example, a precept was issued by the mayor to the aldermen urging them to "give a diligent eye" to what people in their wards were wearing.[76] But as *Handlyng Synne* and *Jacob's Well* recognize, looking at a fashionably dressed man or woman was what inflamed passion in the first place and hence led to sin. Regulatory surveillance could hardly have been immune to this dynamic wherein the gaze increased desire. Consider, too, the following punishment for fashion abuse. At the court of aldermen held in London on 24 January 1565, Richard Walweyn, a servant who had been arrested that day for wearing "a very monsterous and outraygous greate payre of hose," was ordered to be detained by the sheriff's officer until he had provided himself with more suitable hose. His "monsterous" hose were then impounded and put on display where they could be seen as "an example of extreme folye."[77] This act of holding up for public scrutiny offending items of dress, obviously intended by the authorities to deter future transgressions, highlights the difficulty of using surveillance to monitor visible signs of social difference. As punishment becomes advertisement, the line between deterrence and inducement is largely erased.

Finally, as this last example suggests, regulatory fashion discourses were by their very nature ultimately forced to betray their own intentions.

In the act of representing that which was forbidden, the regulatory theme was displaced by the allure of the representation itself. As they ranted against fashion excess, clothing critics described—and by describing made enticing—the very items of dress they wished to outlaw. Similarly, legislators crafting sumptuary laws called attention to social disarray through their very attempts at discursive containment of it. Wrenching social bodies into a coherent structure, the laws exposed the signs of social difference that they could not hope to master. At the same time, both diatribes and laws acted unwittingly as shopping lists for would-be consumers, laying out all the wares available for (forbidden) consumption. In the end, the more concerted the discursive attacks against dress, the more they were doomed to failure, undermined by the subversive power of representation itself. To paraphrase Garber, discipline is itself an erotics, and hence its effects are often more diffuse than the discipliners might wish and lead in directions they might not approve.[78]

In this way, regulatory discourses that sought to control fashion, and through fashion, signs of difference, inadvertently made a space for the more overtly transgressive play with dress that took place in the theater. They did this as discourse always does, by disseminating what it tries to suppress, by returning to the center what it seeks to exclude, by flaunting what it aims to hide.[79] As Sally Moore has said, writing about the legal system: "Established rules, customs, and symbolic frameworks exist, but they operate in the presence of areas of indeterminacy, or ambiguity, of uncertainty and manipulability. Order never fully takes over, nor could it. The cultural, contractual, and technical imperatives always leave gaps, require adjustments and interpretations to be applicable to particular situations, and are themselves full of ambiguities, inconsistencies, and often contradictions."[80] The always-already-there contradictions inherent in regulatory discourses and in the logic of signification and representation might sometimes or even often go unexploited, but under certain conditions their existence can open up antidisciplinary ways of constructing social reality. In the Robin Hood performances that are the topic of my next chapter, similar contradictions do not go unexploited as play with forbidden forms of dress opens the door to a range of unauthorized behaviors and activities.

# CHAPTER 2

# Counterfeit in Their Array:
## Cross-Dressing in Robin Hood Performances

*I'll be master of misrule: I'll be Robin Hood.*
—George Peele, *Chronicle of Edward I*

Robin Hood is now usually packaged for popular consumption as the quintessentially romantic hero. Living free in the forest with his loyal band of followers, he is construed as a valiant and charming character whose outlaw justice is nobly used to aid the poor and weak while fighting the rich and powerful. Whether bantering playfully with his men, gallantly wooing Maid Marian, or engaging in dashing feats of physical prowess, the modern Robin Hood, made familiar through such venues as Hollywood films and children's storybooks, is the very picture of charm, selflessness, nobility, and courage. The end product of centuries of sanitizing and sentimentalizing, this figure, however, bears surprisingly little resemblance to the Robin Hood of late medieval legend, a figure that, despite its alterity, can still be glimpsed in early ballads and performances. To encounter this earlier Robin Hood is to confront an outlaw given over to disruptive and transgressive acts unimaginable for his modern descendant.

Consider the following ballad.

Walking through the forest Robin Hood sees a bishop and his retinue. Afraid he will be hanged if the bishop captures him, Robin looks around desperately for some escape. He notices a small house and an old woman to whom he cries out for help. Recalling that Robin Hood once made her a gift of shoes and hose, the old woman agrees to exchange her gray coat and spindle for his green mantle and arrows. Dressed as a woman, Robin returns to his men, who fail to recognize him until he identifies himself by name. Meanwhile the bishop arrives at the old woman's house, takes her for Robin Hood, and arrests him/her. Riding through the forest with his captive, the bishop chances to see bowmen standing "under the green-wood tree." When he asks who they are, "Robin" replies that one of them is a man called Robin Hood. Who, then, are you, the bishop asks? An old woman, she answers, adding, "Lift up my leg and see." The bishop is then captured by the real Robin Hood, who steals five hundred pounds from him, forces him to say Mass, puts him backward onto a horse, and sends him riding off through the forest.[1]

Consider a second ballad.

Wearing "their gownes of grene," Robin Hood and Little John encounter a yeoman leaning against a tree, dressed in a "capull hyde." Upon quarreling, Little John and Robin Hood part ways, John going to Barnesdale, where he is captured by the sheriff and bound to a tree to await hanging. Meanwhile, once Robin learns that the yeoman is seeking the outlaw Robin Hood, he conceals his identity, promising to assist the stranger, but only after a contest of bow and arrows—which Robin wins. The yeoman turns out to be Sir Guy, whom Robin Hood kills and then decapitates, impaling Sir Guy's mutilated and now unrecognizable head on the end of his bow. Swapping clothes with the dead man, Robin Hood slips into Sir Guy's "skin" and rides off to Barnesdale, where he brandishes the disfigured head of Sir Guy, claiming to have captured the notorious outlaw Robin Hood. Having gained the sheriff's confidence, the disguised Robin Hood liberates Little John, who then shoots the sheriff in the back.[2]

The Robin Hood who appears in these two ballads is an antidisciplinary figure whose salient characteristic is a refusal to recognize the authority of cultural categories or the rule of accepted codes of behavior. As Peter Stallybrass has argued, the early ballads persistently transgress spatial, linguistic, and bodily bounds while inverting the hierarchies of gender, class, and religion.[3] This is certainly the case in the two ballads I have described, in which Robin Hood violates boundaries that are social (he consorts with a knight and a sheriff); spatial (he trespasses in the king's forest and invades towns); religious (he mocks the clergy); economic (he robs rather than labors); and sexual (he impersonates a woman). What is particularly striking about the transgressive acts in these and other ballads, however, and what catches my eye, is how frequently they are brought about through instances of cross-dressing in which Robin Hood disguises himself in someone else's clothing.

In recent years both Robin Hood and cross-dressing have attracted considerable scholarly and popular attention. Since the late 1950s articles published in the British journal *Past and Present*, as well as in collections and books by John Bellamy, Richard Dobson and John Taylor, Eric Hobsbawm, J. C. Holt, Stephen Knight, and Maurice Keen, to name only the most important, have contributed to what might be described as a Robin Hood cottage industry fueled by historians of medieval England.[4] As Kathleen Biddick has astutely argued, this infatuation of post-1950s scholars with Robin Hood can be understood as an instance of the "return of the pastoral," in which the pastoral becomes "an imaginary site at which historical contests over 'authentication' and 'truth' in public culture can be waged." Biddick claims that recent Robin Hood historiography reveals a strong desire to identify Robin Hood as a peasant hero, despite some three hundred years of cultural appropriation that effectively turned him into a gentleman, a desire that Biddick sees as a response to the problems of a postimperial Britain.[5] Although my own reading of the late medieval cultural performances involving Robin Hood is not interested in recuperating the historical Robin Hood, it has inevitably been to some extent shaped by this historiographic project, particularly in regard to my claim that the Robin Hood figure of late medieval performances offered a model of resistance to various forms of authority. I would, however, identify the desire motivating my own work less as a longing for the pastoral than as an attempt to imagine a cultural space for the contestatory and disruptive, although the two are by no means mutually exclusive.

At the same time that Robin Hood has become a magnet for historians, contemporary scholars working from a variety of theoretical perspectives— post-Foucauldian analysis of the discursive construction of sexuality, the poetics and politics of representation, materialist feminism, and queer theory, among others—have begun to explore cross-dressing as a cultural practice, especially in the theater. Much of this work ranges widely, reading forward from the Renaissance theater to the contemporary films of John Waters.[6] Yet what unites all these studies is a refusal to reach back to medieval theater, in which cross-dressing was also the standard practice, with male actors almost without exception playing all roles, both male and female. In recent Renaissance scholarship, in particular, the theater of medieval Europe is constructed as the ground upon which the Renaissance theater and, by extension, critics of it, work their dazzling refigurings. Medievalists, too, have tended to downplay the complexity of theatrical cross-dressing as a cultural practice in medieval Europe.[7] There are certainly many reasons for this critical blindness, including the unfashionableness of any search for origins. But a crucial factor is that the Middle Ages are often understood to have been shaped by a monolithic and homogenizing patriarchal regime that predates modern constructions of sexuality and otherness. Cross-dressing on the medieval stage, from this perspective, can be safely bracketed as standard and, therefore, unproblematic.

Even a casual acquaintance with the theater of the Middle Ages should reveal, however, that it was the site of intense cultural and ideological negotiations involving the testing and contesting of conventional social roles and cultural categories such as race, class, and gender. Likelier than not, the idea of a stable medieval subject is something of a modern fiction that conceals the complexity of subjectivity in the Middle Ages and puts in its place the naive idea of unconstructed identity. Such a fiction does not fit well with recent understandings that social categories were less fixed and determinate in the Middle Ages than is often thought and that the gender, status, and racial positioning of medieval subjects was a conflicted cultural process.

In this chapter, I examine Robin Hood performances as a significant instance of cross-dressing in medieval theater.[8] I argue that the use of a cross-dressing main character results in deviant moments that cannot be entirely undone by the ultimate return of culturally sanctioned social, sexual, and economic arrangements at the end of the performance, and further, that the deviance of those moments was certainly not lost upon medieval participants and spectators, even if my reading of those moments as deviant is, of necessity, a product of my own cultural milieu.[9] These acts of cross-dressing, which transgress taboos while also triggering complicated patterns of desire, cannot, I also argue, be reduced to one simple meaning, but rather perform a range of cultural work.

Cross-dressing is, however, often assumed to mean only one thing. Such is the case, for instance, in Lisa Jardine's claim that the Renaissance theater is by definition homoerotic and can be understood simply as men gazing at men and thus excluding women. In contrast, I wish to suggest that theatrical representations of characters who use dress to cross various boundaries are culturally complex acts that function on many different levels. Like Marjorie Garber, I take the cross-dresser to be a potential figure of category crisis that not only blurs boundaries between male and female but also undermines the whole attempt to construct stable binary categories of oppositional difference, a figure onto which irresolvable crises of boundary definition (man-woman, Orient-Occident, rich-poor, gay-straight) can at specific historical and cultural junctures be displaced and (not quite) contained.[10] Possessing permanent status "in between"—neither male nor female—the cross-dresser refuses to be pinned down and hence manifests a threatening lack of conformity to social norms. As pervasively liminal beings within Western cultures, cross-dressers can disturb the natural order of things, representing the cultural equivalents of chaos, disorderliness, and pollution.[11] Theatrical cross-dressing taps into this liminality, permitting immersion in its destabilizing qualities within the performance space.

Although largely unremarked upon despite this recent spate of interest, cross-dressing plays an important role in early Robin Hood ballads and performances. It is cross-dressing in the first place that enables Robin Hood to do his work of border crossing, providing him with a mechanism for evading and getting the best of his adversaries. Besides functioning as disguise, cross-dressing also has symbolic force as a device that allows the outlaw to tap into the cultural power associated with the figures he cross-dresses as. When he exchanges clothes with the old woman, for instance, Robin Hood wraps himself in the potent symbolism of the unruly woman, drawing on her transgressive force to escape the bishop. When he dresses himself in Sir Guy's clothes (in his "capull hyde" or "skin," which suggests that he puts on not just the clothes but more intimately the flesh of his enemy), Robin Hood steps into the body of the socially powerful and uses his new incorporation to dominate the sheriff.

While not losing sight of the varied cultural work of cross-dressing, I shall focus in this chapter on the destabilizing power of cross-dressing. My analysis takes up two central issues: how cross-dressing permitted Robin Hood to penetrate and infiltrate official spaces, gaining access to strongholds of orthodoxy from which he would otherwise have been barred, and how cross-dressing was used to symbolically incorporate others—whether characters in Robin Hood ballads (like the old woman who exchanges her clothes for the outlaw's) or actors and spectators at Robin Hood performances—into Robin Hood's band, giving them at least temporary access to his disruptive force.

In the end, however, in what can be seen as a covert acknowledgment of the threats of both of these forms of cross-dressing, Robin Hood ballads and performances repeatedly work to reinscribe Robin Hood within a normative system, using various recuperative gestures and strategies of closure in an attempt to arrest the havoc he has caused and to force a return to "real" identities. Although such strategies continually sought to contain the transgressive impact of cross-dressing, they could never entirely undo its subversive work. Somewhat paradoxically, in fact, considerable cultural energy went into maintaining Robin Hood as an anti-authoritarian figure adaptable to a variety of needs.[12] In this chapter, I examine cross-dressing's use as an agent of penetration into orthodoxy's inner sanctums; its ability to symbolically incorporate people into Robin Hood's band; the recuperative strategies employed to contain it; and, finally, the continued maintenance and protection of its rebellious potentialities. What I wish to sketch are the outlines of an antidisciplinary discourse in which the cross-dressed outlaw gestures toward forms of subjectivity, especially masculine subjectivity, that deviate from the normative subjectivities constructed by the discourses of fashion regulation discussed in the preceding chapter.

The historical materials available to explore this topic are themselves in an unstable and indeterminate shape. Despite the well-documented popularity in late medieval England of summer festivities featuring Robin Hood, precisely what took place at these festivities is uncertain. Only one fragmentary play-text from the time survives: twenty-one lines written on the upper half of a folio leaf dating to around 1475 that seem to represent a dramatic version of the ballad "Robin Hood and Guy of Gisborne," in which Robin Hood first competes with, then decapitates, and finally impersonates Sir Guy. Both E. K. Chambers and Francis Child assume that there is little doubt that this fragment refers to the play that William Paston mentions in one of his letters dated 16 April 1473. In this letter, Paston describes a man named Woode, whom Sir John Paston had employed "thys iij. yer to pleye Seynt Jorge and Robyn Hod and the Sheryff off Notyngham."[13] A play "Robin Hood and the Friar" and a fragment of another, "Robin Hood and the Potter," were printed by Copland around 1560. These three plays constitute the only scripts of early Robin Hood plays now known to be extant.

Archival evidence suggests that Robin Hood performances were primarily regional games and plays performed in communities in the south and west of England like those found in the N-Town manuscript or at Croscombe in Somerset: that is, they were parish-based rituals closely associated with summer king games, May ales, morris dancing, and other forms of popular festivity, probably including plays of the sort represented by the 1475 fragment and games or feats of strength.[14] Historical records indicate that Robin Hood performances also often involved "gatherings" designed to collect money for the parish, such as the one that took place at Kingston-upon-Thames in the early sixteenth century, and processions similar to the London procession on 24 June 1559 described by Henry Machyn. The procession Machyn saw and recorded in his diary included, he tells us, a "May-game . . . with a gyant, and drumes and gunes . . . and then Sant Gorge and the dragon, the mores dansse, and after Robyn Hode and lytyll John, and M[aid Marian] and frere Tuke, and they had spechys round a-bout London."[15] During the fifteenth century Robin Hood appears to have become an increasingly popular figure at summer festivities, where he often replaced earlier lords and abbots of misrule, as is implied by an entry from Aberdeen in 1508 referring to "Robert Huyid and Litile Johne, quhilk was callit, in yers bipast, Abbat and Prior of Bonacord."[16] What this evidence points to is a range of activities centering on Robin Hood that included games, plays, processions, and collections involving impersonation of the outlaw—activities that I shall consider under the general rubric of "Robin Hood performances."

Another valuable yet problematic source of information about early Robin Hood performances comes from ballads, collected for the most part long after the performances to which they are usually assumed to be related.[17] A line from Langland's *Piers Plowman* written around 1377 suggests that "rymes of Robyn hood" were already well known by the late fourteenth century, and the first of the extant ballads of the cycle known as *A Gest of Robyn Hode* was probably written around 1460, arguing for an early and widespread ballad tradition.[18] Moreover, British folk plays from the nineteenth and twentieth centuries often show considerable overlap with the Robin Hood ballads, drawing on similar themes and even using similar language. But if, as Michael Preston hypothesizes, incidents from the ballads were first written into traditional folk plays sometime in the eighteenth century, then extant folk plays would seem a suspect source of evidence about early Robin Hood performances, and in fact I have not relied upon them.[19] Although it is impossible to establish any direct link between the extant ballads and the early performances, I have followed the lead of Chambers in assuming that even in the absence of a direct link there is a connection between the two representational forms.[20] In his recent study of Robin Hood, Stephen Knight also argues that the ballads and plays are related, both representing a widespread popular discourse about the outlaw.[21] For the most part, I have confined my discussion to those ballads generally identified as belonging to the medieval tradition.[22]

In the discussion that follows, I shall first consider the role of cross-dressing in the ballads. Then I shall turn to cross-dressing's role in late medieval performances, focusing especially on the Kingston games, for which we have the fullest archival information. In both cases, I take Robin Hood as a culturally complex and polysemous figure, one that cannot be reduced to a unitary meaning, not even at one specific historic juncture.

## "Robin Did Off His Gowne of Greene"

A persistent feature of the ballads is the way Robin Hood uses cross-dressing to penetrate official spaces and, once inside, to poke holes in the social and economic structures they house. Crucial to this dynamic is Robin Hood's association with the forest, a place symbolically located outside the official order. In the ballads, the forest is usually identified as Barnesdale or Sherwood—one of medieval England's best-known forests and the site of Edward III's lavish hunting parties in the mid–fourteenth century—but it is also sometimes described in vaguer terms as simply the "grene-wode" where Robin lurks. In the Middle Ages, control of the forest was a central concern of the government, which fought what often amounted to a losing battle to retain exclusive use of the forest.[23] Since woodland districts, however, were often beyond the reach of church and manor and were vulnerable to price fluctuations, immigrations, dearth, and social instability, they were strongholds of popular justice.[24] Representing popular resistance and communal justice, the forest had become by the fifteenth century England's privileged place of collective criminal activity.[25] This cultural understanding of the forest plays a pivotal part in Robin Hood's invasive strategies.

What also matters for Robin Hood's penetration of authority's domains is not just that the outlaws live in the forest, but that they live in the forest near a town, which is usually identified as Nottingham, Barnesdale, or Doncaster.[26] This close proximity allows the forest to stand in symbolic opposition to the town and urban values; it is the free space where activities disallowed by civic authorities or urban convention flourish. At the same time, the forest's closeness to the town makes possible Robin Hood's easy movement between the two geographic territories and the cultures—outlaw and urban—each represents. This spatial logic also helps explain why Robin Hood is usually pitted not against the king or the higher nobility but instead against lower levels of officialdom, especially those representing urban and commercial values.

As an outlaw residing in the forest, Robin Hood lives where the norms of urban culture are negated by criminality.[27] His intimate connection with the forest is signaled by his trademark costume of green cloth. While dressed in green, Robin Hood's identity is clearly displayed on his body, effectively trapping him within the outlaw territory of the forest since it so clearly identifies him as a denizen of the greenwood. The extent to which Robin Hood is defined by his clothing is suggested by the fact that when he ventures outside the safe space of the forest wearing his own clothes, he is nearly always recognized for who he is and hence is apprehended by the authorities. In the ballad "Robin Hood and the Monk," for instance, Robin Hood enters a church in Nottingham dressed in his own clothes; he is immediately recognized by a monk who summons the sheriff's men, who then capture him.[28]

But when he takes off "his gowne of greene" and puts on someone else's clothing, Robin Hood is able to move about freely.[29] Although this might be taken as an obvious and not very remarkable demonstration of the fact that disguise works, something more complex is also going on with this cross-dressing. When Robin Hood gains his freedom by concealing his identity, he is liberated not just because he is no longer recognizable but also because he has draped himself with the cross-dresser's liminal powers. This is what happens in "Robin Hood and the Bishop" when Robin Hood appropriates the dress of the old woman in order to escape the bishop. While dressing like a woman might conceivably afford him some degree of concealment of his real identity, it also lets him adapt the symbolic force of the "unruly woman" to his own advantage.[30] In other instances, such as in the ballad "Robin Hood and the Butcher," where Robin dresses in the butcher's clothes and so disguised enters the town, cross-dressing is used more aggressively not just to conceal his real identity and so hide from authority but to acquire the power he needs to attack it on its own territory.[31] Dressed like a butcher, Robin Hood gains entry into the geographic and, more important, economic centers of the town, which he can then subvert from within. It is also what happens in the 1475 dramatic fragment, which contains the line "This knyghtys clothis wolle I were," presumably spoken by Robin Hood after he has cut off Sir Guy's head. Putting on the dead and headless knight's clothes, Robin Hood is able in some measure to *become* him and hence to muster a knightly identity in order to confront the sheriff. As a form of disguise, cross-dressing helps Robin Hood hide his identity; as a ritual act, cross-dressing allows him to make use of destabilizing forces.

Once enabled by cross-dressing to move from forest to town, Robin Hood sets to work to topple values linked to the town, disrupting its internal workings.[32] In this task, cross-dressing's powers assist him once again. Although what has attracted the most attention from scholars is Robin Hood's social transgressiveness, whereby he undermines various authorities—most prominently represented in the figure of the sheriff—and so subdues corrupt rule through the power of popular justice, his rupture of the economic and sexual orders associated with the town are perhaps even more insistently unruly.[33] That Robin Hood and his men live outside the economic order is signaled from the outset by the fact that they apparently live without property and without goods of any kind beyond what they wear, eat, and fight with. Moreover, their prototypical economic transaction—theft—is of course outside the authorized system of exchange.[34] In the ballads, Robin Hood steals large sums of money, horses, and other valuables—establishing himself as a successful highway robber.[35] But although theft, which Robin typically undertakes while dressed in his own clothes and still in the forest, must have evoked pervasive fears of highway robbery, it ultimately proves less disruptive than his other, less scrutinized, economic practices, especially those that occur when he invades urban space.

In "Robin Hood and Guy of Gisborne," to return to one of the most fascinating of the early ballads and one that seems to echo the 1475 dramatic fragment, we can glimpse traces of this economic subversion at work. When Robin Hood appears in town dressed in Guy's "capull hyde," he refuses the "knight's fee" the sheriff offers him as his bounty-hunting reward for (so the sheriff believes) decapitating Robin Hood. Instead, Robin Hood requests a nonmonetary form of recompense, asking to be allowed to strike the captive Little John. Although this request is in part driven by the narrative's need to find a way of freeing Little John from his bonds, it also functions as a deliberate rejection of a particularly corrupt, although officially acceptable, form of economic exchange. By rejecting monetary payment in favor of what looks like corporal punishment but turns out to be an act of loyalty, Robin Hood critiques the premises of the bounty system, in which money is paid for captured bodies. Robin Hood's next action after he rejects the sheriff's payment—that of cutting Little John free—can in this light be read not just as the liberation of his companion but more broadly as a removal of the body from a system that would treat it literally as a commodity to be bought and sold. When Robin cuts Little John's bonds, he returns his companion to the economic logic of the outlaw band, based on a system of personal loyalties and freedom of association in which bodies cannot be treated as commodities. His refusal of the bounty fee thus undermines the coherence of an economic order founded on the commodification of the body, a system visible not just in the workings of bounty hunting, in which bodies are directly equivalent to and explicitly disciplined by money, but also, although more subtly, in the workings of a wage-labor economy in which bodies are made to serve the interests of profit. The critique of the bounty system thus stands as a critique of the official economic order of towns, an order predicated on purchase of the body and its labor.

Since the 1475 play-text does not include these details of the freeing of Little John, however, it is difficult to say how much this theme of economic resistance might have figured into its performance. Where the play-text does involve economic subversion is at the end when Robin Hood liberates "thevys" from prison, thus suggesting if not an endorsement of their illegal economic practices, then at least a sympathy with them. In addition, if the 1475 fragment represents a play that was actually performed at a festivity like the one recorded at Kingston in the early sixteenth century, then other kinds of economic transactions, which I shall discuss later, would have been brought to bear on the events of the play, framing it in ways that might have encouraged a transgressive revision of certain aspects of the normative economic order.

The cross-dressed Robin Hood's subversion of urban exchange systems is also explored in the ballad "Robin Hood and the Potter," which has an analogue in a play-text of around 1560.[36] This ballad explicitly takes up questions of the market, including such issues as the fair pricing of consumer goods. After a potter complains that he is too poor to pay the toll that Robin demands, Robin Hood puts on the potter's clothes and goes to town to sell his wares. When he reaches the market, Robin sets out his goods and does a brisk trade, largely because he has priced the pots well below their market value: "The pottys that wer werthe pens feyffe, / He sold tham for pens thre" (lines 137–38). In one sense, he thus "outdoes" the potter, who, so the ballad hints, would not have been as successful as Robin is in disposing of his goods. In another sense, however, Robin Hood "undoes" the market system, since he intentionally undervalues his pots, thus challenging the profit-driven logic of the marketplace.

This underpricing can, of course, be taken as an economic form of popular justice that readjusts the exchange to favor the consumer, making goods available at low cost.[37] But the economic disruption at work here strikes even deeper and is more complex. Countering the theme of consumer protection that it in part espouses, the ballad makes it clear that populist pricing, however attractive in the short term, will eventually put tradesmen out of business: "Preveley seyde man and weyffe, / 'Ywnder potter schall never the'" (lines 139–40). And the consequence, left unsaid in the ballad, is that eventually the whole system of production and consumption will be undermined, since if goods are underpriced, there will soon be no more profit that might be spent for the production of more goods to sell to yet other consumers. In this light, Robin Hood's selling spree, undertaken while he is cross-dressed as the potter, comes to look like an urban version of highway robbery, a quasi-criminal form of economic activity that is appealingly populist but also ultimately deeply subversive in its implied deconstruction of the profit motive necessary to drive the market economy.[38]

Cross-dressing plays a role in another of Robin Hood's illicit forms of economic activity—the wager. Wagering, officially understood as an improper and "wasteful" use of money, especially when it involved an apprentice betting away his master's money, went against permissible economic transactions and as a result was frequently proscribed. Part of the trouble with wagering, from the standpoint of official economies, was that it evaded the controls of systematic pricing. It was below the table and off the books, unconnected to authoritative regulatory processes. As such, it thumbed its nose in the face of the elaborate rules devised by urban authorities to instill uniformity in market transactions and in wage payments.

Another problem with wagering was that it also engaged the body in "improper" work. In the case of the Robin Hood ballads this improper work is usually some sort of violent physical contest in which the wager takes the form of one-on-one combat presented as part battle, part game. This is what happens, for instance, at the beginning of "Robin Hood and the Potter," where Little John bets Robin Hood that none of them will be able to make the potter pay a toll and Robin then fights the potter to try to win the bet. Although perhaps desirable from a military perspective as a way of practicing for battle,[39] the "labor" performed in these contests could hardly have meshed well with understandings of work framed by the context of an urban market economy, in which the body's efforts and competitiveness alike were to be directed toward the ends of well-regulated production rather than toward violent bodily assault and destruction.

In the wagering that takes place in the ballads, cross-dressing helps conceal Robin Hood's identity and rig the bet in his favor. In "Robin Hood and the Potter," Robin disguised as the potter overhears talk of a forty-shilling wager that has been made on a shooting match among the sheriff's men, decides to compete, and wins. The sheriff's men "thowt gret schame, / The potter the mastry wan" (lines 209–10). In a similar act of deception at the end of "Robin Hood and the Butcher," Robin Hood (dressed as the butcher) lures the unsuspecting sheriff into the forest by claiming to know the outlaw after the sheriff says he would give a hundred pounds to catch him. Such acts of cross-dressing, which turn on deceit and trickery as Robin Hood maneuvers his opponent into a vulnerable position by hiding his identity, flout norms of honest and fair trade. A thief, a bettor, and a con man, the cross-dressed Robin Hood becomes a disrupter of the established economic order, who undermines the putative authority of accepted practices of labor, pricing, and payment for services. Given that Robin Hood performances themselves constituted a kind of labor undertaken to gather money for the parish—labor that could be seen as both legitimate because endorsed by the church and illegitimate because so closely resembling theft or begging—the economic transgressions found in the ballads might be taken as the working out of similar economic contradictions.

While assaulting the economic positioning of subjects, the cross-dressed Robin Hood also subverts the sexual order. Once again, "Robin Hood and the Potter" provides a good example. While at the market selling the potter's wares, Robin Hood packs up his last five pots and has them sent to the sheriff's wife. She "repays" him by inviting him to dine with her and her husband, the sheriff. When Robin Hood accepts her invitation, he begins a double dismantling of the managed sexual economy of the household. First, he undermines the sheriff's control of his wife by winning her affections for himself, giving her not only five pots but also a gold ring and saying to her, "'Dam, for mey loffe, and ye well thys were, / Y geffe yow her a golde ryng'" (lines 241–42). Having penetrated the sheriff's household in his guise of the potter, Robin Hood then dupes the sheriff into coming with him into the forest, where the sheriff is robbed and ritually humiliated. He further undermines the sheriff's authority at this point by sending him back to his wife with the gift of a white horse for her. This act, combined with the earlier gifts of pots and gold ring, symbolically stages Robin Hood's usurpation of the sheriff's role as head of his household and therefore controller of, and provider for, his wife. Revealing where her loyalties lie, the wife responds to her husband's humiliation with laughter, saying to him, "Now haffe yow payed for all the pottys / That Roben gaffe to me" (lines 305–6). With these words, she explicitly links the sexual economy of marriage to that of the market, calling attention to Robin Hood's breach of both.

In these instances, cross-dressing puts Robin Hood in a liminal position where he can attack the dominant culture.[40] Dressed as old woman, bounty hunter, potter, or beggar, Robin Hood is more disruptive than he could ever be in his "real" identity of outlaw, since in these guises he is unknowable, untrackable by official eyes, able to infiltrate places otherwise forbidden to him, and hence most free to do his damage. Cross-dressed, Robin Hood becomes the nightmare of all ordering regimes—a violator of all attempts to know, to regulate, and to control.

Like the chronically destabilizing transvestite described by Garber, Robin Hood's temporary cross-dressing has the effect of calling categorizing systems of all kinds—social, economic, sexual—into question. Perhaps the clearest evidence for the threat the cross-dressed Robin Hood poses comes from the persistence with which the ballads make sure that he is unmasked in the end and so exposed for who he "really" is. As these acts of unmasking reveal, the instability brought about by Robin Hood's cross-dressing demands the reassertion of normative order. At the ballad's end, he is made to step back into the forest, back into his true identity, and so back into the recognizable and hence controllable sphere of overt outlawry. In this way, the narrative reestablishes the parameters that seem necessary for the temporary and safe contemplation of the deviant and cross-dressed figure of Robin Hood.

## "Whan They Were Clothed in Lyncolne Grene"

I would argue, however, that Robin Hood's own acts of cross-dressing, as represented in the ballads and the plays that seem to treat similar topics, are in the end less transgressive than is the ritual cross-dressing of outsiders who were symbolically incorporated into Robin Hood's band by clothing themselves "in Lyncolne grene."[41] The reason for this has to do in large part with what incorporation into Robin Hood's band represented, culturally speaking. In exploring this act of incorporation, I start with the male body, since it is the male body that stands at the center of Robin Hood's fellowship. In the masculine community of outlaws that constituted Robin Hood's gang, the male body was constructed as aggressive, competitive, and physically fit. Strong, vigorous, healthy, and active, this body can be understood as at once both desired and feared by orthodoxy. On the one hand, it was the ideal fighting body, skilled in the techniques of warfare and eager for combat, whether in the form of competitive games or hand-to-hand battle.[42] It was also, in some ways, the ideal laboring body, whether for agrarian work or for the skilled production of goods. On the other hand, this body projected a violence that was not always in conformity with the needs of an orderly and regularized economic system. The bodies of Robin Hood's men might not, it could turn out, be fit for either war or work; instead these bodies might prove ideally shaped for murder and mayhem.

Concerns about the malleability of these bodies and the extent to which they could be controlled are revealed in the ballads' preoccupation with bondage. Played out in a running motif of capture and release, questions about how to contain the violent male body are frequently raised by the ballads. Fear of bondage in fact motivates many of Robin Hood's escapades, as he attempts to outwit and evade the authorities who would capture and subdue him, as is the case in "Robin Hood and the Bishop," when he cross-dresses to escape capture by the bishop. Typically, however, not Robin Hood but one of his men is seized by the sheriff or another agent of official culture and then is tied up to await hanging or some other punishment. As in "Robin Hood and Guy of Gisborne," Robin Hood's role within this scenario is to effect the release of his bound companion—which he accomplishes through physical violence—and then to reintegrate him into the fellowship of the outlaw band. Bondage is understood in these ballads to be the ultimate torment, signifying official culture's conscriptive power over the male body. The unfettered male body, in contrast, is held by the outlaws in the highest esteem. Authority's response to the hypermasculine body constructed within Robin Hood's band is to capture and bind it; the outlaw leader's function is to free it and return it to its unbound state.

Within the licensed space of the forest, this aggressive, unfettered male body is inscribed within a completely masculine community that allows it free play.[43] Within this masculine group, affinities based on familial and kin ties or on marital and domestic relations are replaced by same-sex, same-age alliances: Robin Hood's gang consists of no father-son or husband-wife groupings but is instead made up almost entirely of unrelated men, joined together in a nonhierarchical group (although Robin Hood is the leader of the band, his position is constantly open to challenge, especially by Little John, and the ballads show a seemingly endless fascination with the staging and restaging of Robin Hood's proving of his right to rule).[44]

From one perspective, Robin Hood's band harmlessly resembles other widely accepted masculine groupings. Like the craft guild, for instance, another homosocial masculine organization, the outlaw's band could be taken as a group of unrelated men gathered together for mutual social and economic advantage—a fellowship or company. Or, like royal and magnate households, the outlaw gang could appear to be a model of orderly rule—a well-organized social institution with nearly complete legitimacy.[45] From another perspective, however, the outlaw's band represents a warped image of idealized masculine communities like guilds or households, one that takes the basic homosocial organization of those institutions and distorts it in ways that implicitly critique their most basic assumptions about the value of "fellowship." Organized around violence, conflict, and crime, the outlaw social unit filled with "many a wilde felow" represents a very different sort of "company," one whose practices perhaps inevitably comment on more acceptable masculine social groupings.

Given this ambiguous construction of the masculine outlaw body and the fellowship of the outlaw band, incorporation into Robin Hood's company might not have been an insignificant event. Within the ballads, cross-dressing often acts as the mechanism whereby outsiders are made part of Robin Hood's band, whether willingly or by force. The fighting skills of the pinder (an official in charge of impounding stray livestock) in the ballad "The Jolly Pinder of Wakefield," for example, are rewarded by Robin Hood with an offer to let the pinder join his band and be dressed in his "livery." Robin asks him: "O wilt thou forsake the pinder his craft, / And go to the green wood with me? / Thou shalt have a livery twice in the year, / The one green, the other brown [shall be]."[46] Here the offer of incorporation into Robin Hood's band is seen as an act of largesse and the livery a mark of favor. In a more coercive instance of incorporation through costume, when the sheriff in "A Gest of Robin Hood" is captured by Robin Hood, he is forced to strip off his own clothing and sleep all night on the forest floor dressed like the other men in the outlaw's gang. Although this dressing of the sheriff in outlaw's garb has to do in part with humiliation and physical deprivation, since the sheriff, we are told, suffers miserably through the cold night without his own warm clothing, it also calls attention to the way in which a change of clothes can spark a change of identity. When Robin Hood forces the sheriff to put on his outlaw's clothing, he explicitly says to him: "I shall the teche, proude sheryfe / An outlawe for to be" (lines 223–24). In another instance from the same ballad, the king asks to be allowed to dress himself and his retinue in "Lyncolne grene." He then joins Robin Hood and his men in an invasion of Nottingham. Here royal patronage, manifested through an act of cross-dressing that makes the king one of Robin Hood's men, effectively legitimizes the outlaw band, valorizing the (deviant) masculine society it represents. In these instances, cross-dressing acts not only to incorporate outsiders into Robin Hood's gang, but also, and perhaps more importantly, to remove status inhibitions, mingling different social classes—king, sheriff, outlaw—in the inversionary world of the greenwood.[47]

Compelling though these instances seem in the ballads, in the Robin Hood performances incorporation through cross-dressing was even more culturally significant. Cross-dressing in these performances took two interconnected forms: that of actors, usually local young men, impersonating Robin Hood and his men; and that of onlookers who purchased and wore paper livery badges identifying them as part of Robin Hood's band. The churchwardens' accounts from Kingston record regular expenditures on material for both forms of cross-dressing. In 1516, for example, the accounts record the purchase of sixteen great liveries (consisting of "arrayment made in green and yellow"), presumably worn by the actors, and nine-hundred small liveries, which consisted of badges that could be pinned on the spectator-participant's hat or coat. During the festivities, which could last over a number of days, the young men playing Robin Hood and his men collected money for the parish by selling livery badges, both locally and in nearby towns. The number of people who were symbolically incorporated into the band by purchasing livery badges could be quite large. In the year 1520 in Kingston, when a great deal of money was spent on new costumes, two thousand badges were made.[48] Although the scale and duration of the festivities at Kingston were unusual, even the smaller numbers of liveries sold at other Robin Hood performances, such as the two hundred badges sold at Reading in 1501, suggest an impressive level of participation in the games.[49]

The reaction of Philip Stubbes to the sale of livery badges hints at some of the disruptiveness associated with this symbolic incorporation. Describing a gathering by the lord of misrule and his company, Stubbes writes: "They have also certain papers, wherein is painted some babblerie or other, of Imagery work, & these they call my Lord of Mis-rules badges, these they give to every one, that wil give money for them." People would then "weare their badges & cognizances in their hats or caps openly." Stubbes goes on to complain about how anyone who refuses to purchase a livery badge is "mocked & flouted at, not a little."[50]

What bothers Stubbes is, in the first place, the coercion he perceives being used to make people buy badges when they do not want to. Like the sheriff in "A Gest of Robin Hood," these onlookers would seem to be, at least in Stubbes's eyes, unwilling conscripts into misrule's band, forced there by fear of public scorn. (If Stubbes's perceptions are accurate, this public scorn of those few who refuse to be incorporated by purchasing livery badges attests to considerable support for the lord of misrule and his fund-raising activities.) Since the sale of livery badges at Robin Hood performances appears to have been endorsed by parish churches, for whom it was an important source of income, however, the symbolic incorporation effected by wearing these badges could have represented mass conformity as much as mass transgression. Given this possibility, Stubbes's outburst might seem to be motivated primarily by radical Protestant sentiments against forced conformity to Catholic traditions or, more generally, by any use of images or externals. At the same time, however, his words have the effect of constructing a social scene in which those who are reluctant to participate are aligned with the values of orderliness while the agents of and sympathizers with Robin Hood are seen as disorderly.

Stubbes is even more troubled by the way people allow themselves to be "openly" identified with the lord of misrule.[51] Worse than just buying the badges, some people then wear them visibly, Stubbes complains, thus flaunting their association with the outlaw band. This response seems to recognize that wearing a livery badge is a mark of membership in an identifiable group, that is, it equals incorporation. In this context it is worth noting that unlike heraldic symbols, which represented an individual and served to distinguish that individual from others, in the late Middle Ages livery and livery badges represented groups of people and served to join the individual with a larger social unit.[52] Linking individual with individual, livery constructed a network of horizontally rather than vertically organized social relationships and so created a relatively egalitarian grouping. Thus to put on the lord of misrule's badge might have been a sign not just that the wearer had caved in to social pressure but also that he or she was willing to be visibly linked with a particular social grouping and hence to enter into the whole panoply of meanings associated with it. Since the particular social grouping in question was that of an outlaw band, it is perhaps not surprising, then, to hear Stubbes deplore the public wearing of what he takes as signs of misrule and outlawry.

Issues of criminality, hovering in the background of Stubbes's complaint about the sale and wearing of the lord of misrule's badges, were in fact explicitly linked with the popular summer games featuring Robin Hood and the lord of misrule.[53] In addition to the coercion involved in gathering money for the parish—coercion that Stubbes sees as tantamount to highway robbery—ritualized theft and trespass were also a part of summer festivities centering on Robin Hood. In the common practice of stealing into the greenwood to cut down timber for use at these festivities, including for the maypole, participants joined in quasi-criminal activities that were only partially and grudgingly tolerated and that pitted wealthy landowners against commoners. Although the force of popular custom was strong, it did not always win out. The prioress of Clerkenwell, for example, complained to Edward I about damage inflicted on her fields by the crowds who came to watch plays and wrestling matches, some of which might have involved Robin Hood.[54] In 1480, in a later instance, the mayor of Coventry, siding with the wealthy, complained about "the people of every great city" who "yearly in summer do harm to divers lords and gentles having woods and groves" by taking their boughs and trees.[55] In light of the acts of trespass and poaching perpetrated by Robin Hood in the ballads, these ritual practices might well have been seen by both sides as iconic moments of class warfare in which taking boughs came to represent a populist form of social justice that asserted traditional, communal rights against the prerogatives and private interests of the rich. In this way, the Robin Hood performances can be said to have exercised an economic subversion that to some extent mirrored the themes of the ballads.

Questions of economic subversion are especially compelling for the Kingston games, which were celebrated at Whitsun in the context of the

Whitsun fair. As Sally-Beth MacLean has noted, the market was a key factor in Kingston's development as a borough, and among the borough privileges granted to Kingston were two fairs, one of which took place during the week of Whitsun. Moreover, the only church in Kingston was All Saints Church, which sponsored the games and which was next to the marketplace, a spatial organization that would have emphasized the importance of economic forces. The paying participants, which sales of badges suggest ranged as high as three thousand in 1536, would have been drawn from outside Kingston, since statistics from 1545 suggest that Kingston had in that year a population of just over one thousand adults. The fair would have been an attraction for these outsiders, luring them to the games and increasing income. At the same time, the games might have drawn people to the fair, boosting Kingston's economy. If this were the case, then the Kingston games must be seen as doubly supporting the economic status quo by collecting money for the parish church and by increasing sales at the market fair. But such undoubted collusion with official forces need not have wiped out entirely the latent economic message of the Robin Hood games, one that tapped into themes of theft, robbery, begging, and other subversions of a dominant market order. Although MacLean is undoubtedly correct in describing Kingston's Robin Hood games as an important investment in the life of the community, the return on that investment may well have taken unexpected forms.[56]

A subversive reading might have been aided by the fact that Robin Hood performances appear to have been the province of young men. If references in the Kingston accounts in 1515 to "leycroftes man" and "brenkerstes man" can be taken as representative, it was usually apprentices who played the role of Robin Hood, while their masters, fathers, sisters, and wives became the spectators. The performances' reliance on young males, who were usually expected to behave in subservient ways and who had little power, wealth, or standing in the community, suggests something about how and why the performances might have, on occasion, spun out of control. It must be noted, however, that the Kingston records detail consistent official support for the parish's Robin Hood performances, which received assistance from important officeholders like churchwardens, bailiffs, constables, and chamberlains. But although this official support describes a level of interest in the games that might be interpreted as evidence of the games' perceived utility in reinforcing parish and civic unity, as MacLean argues, the subversive nature of the characters being impersonated was apparently often hard to hide.

A particularly vivid example of the blurring of performance and criminal act that might have been encouraged by cross-dressing's ability to symbolically incorporate young men into the outlaw's band occurred in 1497 when the men of Wednesbury went to the nearby town of Willenhall to make a gathering for their Robin Hood festivities. Not only did they collect money but they also apparently used the opportunity to settle old scores. Precisely what happened is unclear, but legal records reveal that the man from Wednesbury playing Robin Hood was accused of ordering his hundred or more followers to strike down any inhabitant of the town of Walsall they might come across in the course of their collection. "Robin Hood," however, claimed that he was innocent of any crime, insisting that he had come to Willenhall according to tradition for no other reason than to collect money for his church.[57] Whatever the truth of this claim, the incident suggests how easily a group of young men roving about the countryside gathering money while pretending to be Robin Hood and his outlaw band might get caught up in their act— or, just as important, might be perceived by others as crossing over the boundaries separating performance and reality.

A fear that Robin Hood performances might lead to real criminal acts appears to be what motivated the Scottish Parliament to decree in 1555 that anyone impersonating Robin Hood would be banished and anyone electing a Robin Hood would be deprived of his or her freedom for five years. Giving substance to the Scottish Parliament's fears, this decree failed, however, to stop a crowd from electing a tailor as Robin Hood in 1561, naming him "Lord of Inobedience," and forcing open the jail to set free the prisoners. Perhaps evidencing the strong popular support that underwrote playing Robin Hood, the perpetrators not only went unpunished but the magistrates were imprisoned until they pardoned the rioters.[58] In this instance, the act of impersonating the lord of misrule apparently provided inspiration for real rebellion as the performance offered a route for social action.

As these examples suggest, the penetration and subversion of urban social and economic structures featured in the ballads were often played out within the real space of late medieval communities through Robin Hood festivities. Once symbolically incorporated into Robin Hood's outlaw band, men could cross over into an altered social imaginary where they could put on another, less orthodox, identity. It is difficult to do more than speculate about the psychosocial effects of these acts of impersonation on the participants, although incidents such as the one at Wednesbury suggest that playing at outlawry could be both seductive and de-inhibiting, opening the way to behaviors not usually permitted or performed. One likely outcome of this temporary impersonation of the arch-outlaw, however, was to make visible social and economic tensions normally kept under wraps. Acts of trespass, poaching, robbery, and riot, although limited by the ritual framework of the festivities, could hardly have failed to raise the specter of real insurrection—for all parties involved, both participants and spectators. Again, what can be seen here is the destabilizing work of the transvestite, of the one who crosses over, even in the transitory and seemingly innocuous guise of a parishioner wearing a Robin Hood costume or badge.

The transgressive cultural work of cross-dressing found in Robin Hood performances, with its simultaneous concealing and revealing of identities, relies on the observer's gaze as well as on the assumption that appearance and identity are in some way connected. As the body is veiled and unveiled, masked and unmasked in these performances, the viewer is invited to take outward appearance as a sign of identity. Thus spectators were asked—as theater audiences always are—to imagine that the actors dressed as Robin Hood and his men were the outlaw band. What makes this process particularly complex in the case of Robin Hood performances is that the performers and participants, who were not professional actors but ordinary young men from the community, would all have been well known to each other and to the spectators. Hence forgetting their everyday identities would have been, we might imagine, difficult. Yet ritual disguise is a symbolic gesture understood and respected in popular performances even as late as the twentieth century. When a morris-dance team performed in the 1930s in their English village, for instance, a local woman was heard to remark of the costumed performers, "I don't know who they be." Her companion exclaimed, "Why, Mrs. Johns, that's young Smith up to Longmean Farm," pointing out one of the dancers. To which the woman stubbornly replied, "I don't know who they be."[59]

For late medieval audiences of Robin Hood performances, a similar refusal to recognize might have played an important role in making acceptable rebellious behavior that otherwise would have been forbidden if the performers' "true" identities had been discerned beneath their disguises. At the same time, allowing neighbors to hide themselves completely under their costumes must have functioned as a strongly recuperative act. Whatever might happen during the performance—and the records suggest that real disruption was not an unknown consequence—the community could rest assured that when the festivities were over the "outlaws" would be banished and the "real" young men would take up their usual roles in everyday life. Like the recuperative strategies used by Robin Hood ballads, whereby Robin Hood's true identity is ultimately revealed and he is returned safely to the forest, such trust in the transformative power of costume might have helped contain the subversiveness of the festivities by promising that any disorder would be fleeting. At the end of the day, the costumes and livery badges would come off and the status quo would be reasserted, or so interested parties might have chosen to believe.

Despite these recuperative tendencies, such was the power of cross-dressing that licensed misrule always threatened to spill out of bounds. This is what happened with Kett's rebellion of 1549, which began when crowds who had gathered for the Wymondham games in midsummer started to pull down enclosures made by the gentry. A reported sixteen thousand commoners under the leadership of Robert Kett marched on Norwich and took the city; like Robin Hood, Kett held parliament beneath a ceremonial oak tree, and his followers carried green boughs to recognize each other.[60] The defiance authorized by the reversible world of the Robin Hood performances also seems to have inspired protesters like the Derbyshire rebels, who in 1497 donned Robin Hood clothing and "in manere of insurrection wente into the wodes." Similarly, imitating Robin Hood's men by buying livery badges might have spurred behavior such as that of one Piers Venables of Derbyshire, a criminal who helped rescue a prisoner being taken to Tutbury Castle, and who was described as having with him a band of men "beyinge of his clothinge" like Robin Hood.[61] Although spectators might take comfort from the thought that the normal order would be reinstated once disguises were taken off, ample room for disturbance could nevertheless be engendered by those disguises.

My point here is not just that licensed misrule could prove hard to contain, but also that cross-dressing of the sort involved in turning young men of the community into an outlaw band could provide a conduit through which the subversive activities associated with Robin Hood might break out of the performance space and invade the larger social terrain. It is suggestive that the historical record gives examples of festive cross-dressing providing the stimulus for more permanent cross-dressing, inspiring people who had begun by disguising themselves within the space of licensed misrule to take that same act of ritual cross-dressing and extend it into their daily lives. Rudolf Dekker and Lotte van de Pol claim that female transvestites in early modern Europe often first experimented with cross-dressing in this way, trying it at festivities and later adopting it more permanently.[62] This fluid line between theatrical performance and everyday life, between temporary cross-dressing and permanent, calls to mind Judith Butler's description of how a marginalized group can perform within a system that excludes or ignores it and, by performing, can change the boundaries it is fenced off by. As Butler suggests, a performance can in this way force a reexamination of hegemony and of the position of participants and spectators in relation to it.[63] Robin Hood performances of the fifteenth and sixteenth centuries might have similarly encouraged a remapping of boundaries and a reexamination of structures of authority. That they in fact did so is implied by the ecclesiastical and civic response to Robin Hood performances. For, as Alexandra Johnston observes, it was not the large-scale Corpus Christi plays that provoked the wrath of sixteenth-century bishops, but rather parish festivities such as Robin Hood performances.[64]

## "To Mayntene the Outlawes Stronge"

I have been arguing that one function of the cross-dressing in Robin Hood performances was to provide a means of acting out the subversion often associated with the figure of Robin Hood. I do not, however, wish to suggest that cross-dressing was in any way exclusive to these performances. Cross-dressing was in fact allowed, or even expected, on numerous other occasions, including at carnival festivities, during riots, while traveling or in flight, or for erotic stimulation.[65] Most carnivalesque cross-dressing involved men impersonating unruly, grotesque, or lascivious women—including such figures as Noah's wife and Maid Marian. And in many areas of early English popular culture the woman in masculine attire is a recurrent figure.[66] What these examples point to is a cultural familiarity with cross-dressing, especially cross-dressing that transgressed gender categories. The cross-dressing that took place in Robin Hood performances did not often cross gender boundaries, except perhaps in the character of Maid Marian or the old woman from "Robin Hood and the Bishop," if any performance ever enacted the events of that ballad. But it did cross social and economic ones, refashioning young men into transitory outlaws and allowing them to imagine themselves in alternative ways.

As an instance of queer play with dress and identity, this cross-dressing could not be completely undone by the recuperative gestures that sought a return to reality in the end. Nor could the cross-dressing in Robin Hood games and ballads be entirely overridden by attempts to limit, suppress, or co-opt it, although many such attempts were made. One official response to the threat of unlicensed misrule, including forbidden acts of cross-dressing, was simply to ignore it. The *Anonimalle Chronicle*, for example, describes how the convoy bringing the captive King John II of France to London in 1357 was attacked by a band of several hundred men dressed in green and equipped with bows and arrows. The French King was understandably alarmed but was reassured by the Black Prince that these were Englishmen living rough in the forest by choice, and that it was their everyday habit to dress in this manner.[67] In this instance, the Black Prince's pretense that these armed men are not dangerous outlaws but merely woodsmen roughing it looks like an outright denial of reality, especially given the language of a statute of 1360 that described similar groups of men in much more alarming terms as those who "have been plunderers and robbers beyond the sea and are now returned and go wandering and will not work as they were used to do before this time."[68]

Another official response to heterodoxy's tendency to spill beyond its licensed borders was to try to exclude it entirely. This is what occurs in a prohibition by Archbishop Grindal of York in the late sixteenth century in which many kinds of popular performances are banned from churches and churchyards (which were often the only suitable places for a performance).[69] Tudor authorities likewise deplored the "playes of Robyn hoode, mayde Marion, freer Tuck, wherin besides the lewdenes and rewbawdry that ther is opened to the people, disobedience also to your officers, is tought," and sought when possible to prevent "Assault Afrey or other disturbans" from spectators, to quote from the banns posted at Chester, 1539–40.[70] In the eyes of these officials, disobedience, tellingly, is what these performances teach, a disobedience presumably inspired by the roles being impersonated and extending beyond the confines of the performance.

Perhaps the most culturally creative response, however, was to co-opt misrule.[71] This is what happened to Robin Hood during the course of the late sixteenth and seventeenth centuries as he was transformed from a lower-class ruffian into a gentleman outlaw and was ultimately rewritten as a character in an Arcadian fantasy. This drastic transformation of the criminal of medieval legend can be understood as part of a process of neutralizing his transgressiveness and, not incidentally, of regulating popular culture. By rewriting the story of Robin Hood in this way, and particularly by reshaping the character of the outlaw himself, his subversive and antihegemonic power was effectively erased so that today few traces of it are left.[72]

This co-optation also reveals, however, a certain admiration for the transgressions associated with Robin Hood, which held appeal not just for the relatively powerless and disenfranchised but for the ruling classes, too. One reason why the ruling classes could co-opt the outlaw is that the early Robin Hood ballads limit their overtly antiauthoritarian attacks to relatively few and quite specific targets—sheriffs, monks, bishops—while not challenging ruling institutions, especially not royalty. The ballads are neither broadly anticlerical nor antiaristocratic, although they attack individual corrupt representatives of both groups. By singling out individuals as targets, the ballads personalize their attacks in ways that avoid condemning large social groups. And in at least one instance, the ballad "A Gest of Robin Hood," a more direct opening for aristocratic co-optation was made available in the scene in which the king is symbolically incorporated into Robin Hood's band, making him an honorary outlaw. The ballad ends by bringing Robin Hood to live at the court.[73] In this ballad, we can see royals and outlaws assuming allied positions. Records for Kingston suggest that royalty could have been among the spectators of the Robin Hood performances held there: a Household Book of Henry VII records payments in May of 1505 to "the players at kingeston towardes the bilding of the Churche stiple."[74] Thus Henry might not only have watched Robin Hood and his men at play but also have witnessed at first hand the power of incorporation into Robin Hood's band.

The results of these acts of co-optation could be almost fantastically strange. Edward Hall, for example, describes how Henry VIII in 1509, the first year of his reign, along with "therless of Essex, Wilshire, and other noble menne, to the numbre of twelue, came sodainly in a mornyng, into the Quenes Chambre." According to Hall, Henry and his men were "all appareled in shorte cotes, of Kintishe Kendal, with hodes on their heddes, and hosen of thesame, euery one of theim, his bowe and arrowes, and a swORde and a bucklar, like out lawes, or Rokyn [sic] Hodes men." The effect on the queen and her ladies was such that they "were abashed, aswell for the straunge sight, as also for their sodain commyng, and after certayn daunces, and pastime made, thei departed."[75] Although this cross-dressing, in which king becomes outlaw, seems in large part to con-stitute an elaborate aristocratic sex fantasy, as Stallybrass has suggested, flirting with the danger of inversionary symbolism on a deeply personal level must also have been part of the appeal as Henry experimented with what it would be like to be an outlaw.[76]

Another, less erotic and more obviously political, co-optation of Robin Hood took place on May Day in 1515, when Henry VIII and his court rode to Shooter's Hill, the woodland outside London that was a site for popu-lar games. According to *Hall's Chronicle*, there they were "ambushed" by two hundred "yeomen" clothed in green led by "Robin Hood," who invited the king and queen to come into the greenwood and see how the outlaws lived. The royals accepted this offer and were served venison by "Robin" and his men; soon after, Hall adds, Henry "took his progress Westwards and heard complaints of his poor commonality, and ever as he rode he hunted and liberally departed venison," playing the role of Robin Hood before his subjects.[77] Once again, a frisson of danger seems to be part of the desired effect, as rulers are exposed to possible bodily peril, even if it is only ersatz peril, in transgressive play with the outlaw. Al-ready we can see here in Henry's acts the transformation of Robin Hood into a figure of gentlemanly largesse and royal patronage, a transforma-tion that puts the outlaw to other political uses than those played out in popular festivities.

These examples suggest that there were important reasons—sexual, social, economic, and political—to "mayntene the outlawes stronge" and so to preserve and reshape, rather than suppress and abandon, older sto-ries and performances about him.[78] In its adaptability, the figure of Robin Hood proved to be a polyvalent cultural representation, one that had dif-fuse uses and was taken up by different social groups. In the figure of Robin Hood, subordinate groups could challenge the values of orthodoxy;

in the same figure, ruling groups could seize for themselves the powerful symbolics of popular culture and misrule. As the complex and lengthy cultural history of Robin Hood reveals, the outlaw was—and still is—exceptionally moldable, open to appropriation in any number of ways. The 1994 Winter Olympics offer a recent example of how resilient the figure of Robin Hood continues to be. At the Olympics, the German figure skater Katarina Witt dressed herself as Robin Hood for one of her skating routines. When asked by sportscasters why she had chosen this particular costume, Witt—invoking both the gender- and status-based subversion associated with cross-dressing as the outlaw—replied that she was drawn to the figure of Robin Hood by the freedom implied by masculine dress and also by the social justice associated with him. Since Witt was making a final, comeback appearance at the Olympics and was skating as an older, underdog contender, her act of cross-dressing—which was particularly striking given the hyperfeminized costumes usual in women's figure skating—might also be construed as an unconscious attempt to co-opt the outlaw's power, a power that Henry VIII had also recognized centuries before. What all of these appropriations of the outlaw show is not so much that the discourse of Robin Hood itself changed as that the conditions of that discourse's emergence, insertion, and dispersion have been, and may well continue to be, transformed within specific historical contexts.[79] What is worth noting is that the various transformations of that discourse, whatever their differences and discontinuities, so often feature cross-dressing as a mechanism by which individual subjects can seize Robin Hood's power.

By way of closing, I would like to return to a feature of cross-dressing that I have not explicitly addressed thus far: the gap that it opens up between the body and its clothing. From the perspective of embodied subjectivity, cross-dressing can be thought of as a mode of performance that deliberately brings to the center of attention—and critiques—the socially constructed nature of sexual and social difference. Playing on the disjunction between clothes and body, cross-dressing provocatively exposes what appears natural as artifice, revealing how what would seem to be innate and essential differences of class and gender are in fact anything but.[80] As Butler has said: "The replication of heterosexual constructs in non-heterosexual frames brings into relief the utterly constructed status of the so-called heterosexual original. Thus, gay is to straight *not* as copy is to original, but, rather, as copy is to copy. The parodic repetition of 'the original' . . . reveals the original to be nothing other than a parody of the *idea* of the natural and the original."[81] Exposing through its parodic play the constructedness of identity, cross-dressing in Robin Hood performances and ballads reveals embodied identity as something that is constantly in flux, capable of being changed as easily and as often as clothes are put on and taken off.

This recognition of how clothes construct selves, challenging the biological body's power to define identity in a fixed, once-and-for-all way, is explored most fully in "Robin Hood and the Bishop," where once Robin and the old woman exchange clothes each becomes the other so thoroughly that everyone is completely taken in. Even Robin Hood's men fail to recognize who he is until he tells them his name. In such moments, the question of how we know "who he is" is raised up for deliberate scrutiny. Although the old woman attempts to reassert the primacy of innate, bodily difference as a sign of identity—offering to "prove" to the bishop that she is really a woman by telling him to "lift up my leg and see"—her offer has precisely the opposite effect, recalling how effectively the marks of biological sexual difference have until this moment been hidden by her masculine garb. Until she chooses to reveal herself to the bishop, by pointing out the real Robin Hood and by offering to display her naked body, she has become the outlaw so completely that her own female identity has been displaced, veiled by the signifying power of clothing. Although this particular ballad cannot be linked directly to an early Robin Hood performance and is generally considered to be a later ballad, one that was circulated in seventeenth-century broadsides and seems geared toward humiliation of Catholic clergy,[82] accounts from Kingston show that there was a Maid Marian figure, who was probably played by a cross-dressed young man. It is likely that this character more closely resembled the carnivalesque and buffoonish Marian of the morris dance than the romanticized love interest of the later versions of the Robin Hood legend.[83] If this were the case, then the Marian role might have provided a space for the performance of concerns about the gendered body similar to those expressed in "Robin Hood and the Bishop." In both ballad and performance, as a sign of identity the naked body represents too little, too late.

In contrast to the repressive discourses considered in the previous chapter, which attempted to discipline identities precisely by denying their constructedness and controlling the differentiating signs available in clothing, theatrical play with dress of the sort found in Robin Hood performances did just the reverse. In these performances, theatrical cross-dressing not only rejected the disciplining code that sought to limit individuals to one fixed, knowable, determinate, and determining identity but also worked to *unmask* the constructed nature of identity.[84]

CHAPTER 3

✛

# Conduct Books and
# Good Governance

*Se þi body vnder þe, þat it be euenly gouernyd in penaunce fro Lustys, in
mesure, in þat hym befallyth, in mesure of clothyng, of etyng, of drynkyng.*
—*Jacob's Well*

*Bodies are objects over which we labour—eating, sleeping, cleaning, diet-
ing, exercising.*
—Bryan Turner, *Body and Society*

Social theory asks that we think of conduct as a form of practice centering on the body. As practice, conduct is made up of what Marcel
Mauss has called "techniques" of the body—movements, gestures,
postures, and other corporeal behaviors. Not only do these bodily techniques vary from person to person, but they also change shape, Mauss argues, "between societies, educations, proprieties and fashions," carrying
different meanings in different local and historical contexts.[1] In this
view, conduct is shaped by the society that produces it, as the body is invaded by hierarchies and rules that it enacts in accordance with the symbolic systems of that society. If conduct represents one important way in
which social relations are inscribed on our bodies, then to examine individual conduct is to scrutinize what Pierre Bourdieu calls "the arbitrary
content of the culture," which the body reveals in its techniques.[2] As
Mary Douglas observes: "The care that is given to [the body], in groom-
ing, feeding and therapy, the theories about what it needs in the way of
sleep and exercise . . . correlate closely with the categories in which society is seen in so far as these also draw upon the same culturally processed
idea of the body."[3]

To theorize conduct as social practice is to view it as an activity, event,
or performance, rather than as a structure, system, or code. Viewed as
something individuals actively participate in, rather than as a static codi-
fication of rules, conduct becomes at once more central to social life and
more resistant to analysis. Difficult to freeze into place or to pin down,
conduct must be apprehended, insofar as it can be grasped at all, through
oblique glimpses that catch practice at work in the complex and dynamic

processes of everyday life. As Bourdieu forcefully argues, any theory of practice has to confront the gap between interpretation and use, between analysis and participation. Practices are never entirely logical or coherent, never completely meaningful or functional. Social agents are often unaware of their daily practices, which can be inconsistent with larger systems of meaning and perversely at odds with patterns of social or cosmological order. But such unawareness, Bourdieu contends, should not be seen as ignorance that can be resolved by external and detached observation, undertaken in the name of a social science that purports to understand the meaning of cultural practices by submitting them to analysis and critique. Instead, Bourdieu insists, any logic of practice has to take account of the fact that practices may sometimes be just "things that are done" and hence may resist or exceed the parameters of critique and analysis.[4]

Although practice is part of an essentially nondiscursive domain, as Bourdieu recognizes, it has at various historic junctures been submitted to discourse. This submission of practice to discourse has taken place most notably in the form of conduct books, written texts that in a variety of ways seek to convert the dynamic and flexible activities of human behavior into more or less systematized sets of rules and advice. As deliberate codifications of practice, conduct books are located midway between the individual body and the culture that produces it, thus embodying cultural practices that are deflected and refracted through them. Tools of the social construction of the self, conduct books work to establish and disseminate preferred bodily practices as part of their project of offering advice on appropriate behavior. In conduct books, where codes of behavior are explicitly laid out for the use of the reader, we can glimpse the inner workings of the *habitus* as we observe the processes whereby history is embodied in individual subjects.[5]

The historical connections between conduct and the social have been most thoroughly investigated in regard to early modern European culture, especially in the work of Norbert Elias, Mikhail Bakhtin, and Michel Foucault. In *The History of Manners*, Elias charts how the notion of *civilité* arose in the early modern period as an expression of new standards of bodily decorum joined with new social and political formations, particularly the growth of the absolutist state.[6] Social purity and the segregation of elites from the lower classes were achieved, Elias argues, through an emphasis on bodily purity and the notion of a self-contained, "clean"— especially in regard to bodily orifices—and controlled individual subject. Elias shows how certain socially undesirable bodily functions such as eating, spitting, touching, and yawning gradually became associated with fear, shame, and guilt, leading to a rise in what he calls the "threshold of shame and embarrassment." As a result, socially desirable behavior was made a matter of automatic self-control. This social conditioning, which Elias associates with the rise of the middle class, served to separate the socially undesirable from their betters. An emergent ideology of bodily refinement and self-control was thus linked to social and, as others who have elaborated on Elias's work have shown, gender differentiation. The "open," unbounded, "grotesque" body that in Elias's view had been unremarkable and unconflicted in the medieval period thus became a sign of baseness, disorder, social inferiority, and political powerlessness.[7] In this way, according to Elias, signs of social stratification and political power came to be explicitly written onto the body of the individual through internalized rules of conduct.

Elias's argument about how canons of bodily refinement and self-control underwent a major shift in the early modern period, becoming self-reinforcing mechanisms of social differentiation, meshes with Foucault's argument that in the early modern period, self-discipline was for the first time located within the individual social agent when discipline and punishment were removed from an open, public, collective space to hidden, private, interiorized zones. This argument, developed most fully in *Discipline and Punish*, depends, like Elias's, on the construal of a Middle Ages during which public control over the individual body was absolute and unquestioned.[8] As Foucault sees it, when the early modern period shifted control of the body from a public to a private sphere, it both produced and recorded a changed attitude toward embodiment and so formed part of a historic rupture.

Similarly, Bakhtin's distinction between the grotesque and the classical body assumes that a momentously new sense of embodiment arose in the early modern period. In *Rabelais and His World*, Bakhtin contrasts the grotesque body (open, unfinished, and transgressive) with the classical body (opaque, finished, and closed off). For Bakhtin, the grotesque and the classical bodies function primarily in terms of class conflict, with the former representing a plebeian culture that rebels against "official order and official ideology" and the latter representing the official language of the ruling classes. The terrain of the grotesque body is public, located within the marketplace, while the classical body is private, lodged within "palaces, churches, institutions, and private homes."[9] Although the grotesque body theorized by Bakhtin is partially understood in ahistorical terms as an antidisciplinary instrument that can be deployed at any time, he also links it specifically with a collective medieval culture fast disappearing circa 1500–1550. Thus in Bakhtin's reading the grotesque, undisciplined body represents the experience of a collective, plebeian, medieval culture being squeezed out by early modern civilizing forces linked with the state, church, and family.

Compelling though these stories about the disciplining of early modern bodies are, they unfortunately derive their power from a misleading construction of the medieval period as a time when identity was unconflicted and notions of bodily decorum as well as social and political differentiation were lacking—a time when conduct was not yet grist for the mill of the civilizing machine.[10] But within the divisive, rivalrous, and contentious societies that made up medieval Europe, codes of conduct were an important resource in the construction of identity and the distribution of power from at least the twelfth century on.[11] Through such rituals as ceremonies, feasts, tournaments, and processions, guildsmen, the aristocracy, and the clergy all used elaborate forms of bodily decorum to display their power and prestige. Similarly, religious rules and monastic customaries dictated standards of bodily control that served, among other things, to make the individual conform to the norms of the religious collective.[12] Moreover, starting in the thirteenth century, books explicitly devoted to describing appropriate patterns of behavior for lay people began to be written in all of the European vernacular languages.[13] These conduct books, which developed out of a long tradition of advice on manners and behavior drawn from such sources as the Latin *facetus* literature, especially Cicero's *De officiis*, mixed with folk belief, church doctrine, and political precepts, focused explicitly on the self-construction of subjects. In their emphasis on *ars hominem format*, these conduct books concur that nurture, not nature, fashions subjects and that, to a large extent, the individual is in charge of his or her own self-fashioning.[14] Despite the assumptions of Elias, Bakhtin, and Foucault about medieval bodies, these conduct books reveal that long before the sixteenth century the "civilizing" work of bodily discipline was already well under way.

What chiefly interests me in this chapter is not just the kinds of cultural work conduct books performed while regulating bodily behavior but also *how* they did it. My analysis therefore focuses on the methods late medieval conduct books adopted in order to school their readers in a self-created subjectivity, encouraging them to participate in their own construction as well-governed subjects. As part of the process of making this schooling persuasive, conduct books equated bodily control not with repression and subjection—as Elias, Foucault, and Bakhtin all do—but with opportunity and fulfillment. The body constructed by conduct books was seen as an object over which the self could productively labor, with real social and economic rewards waiting in the end. The well-governed body was in this way presented as something the individual could—and would want to—work to achieve and hence was taken not as the product of repression of desire but rather as the means to desire's fullest satisfaction. This willing conscription of the individual into the cultural work of social conformity and bodily control undertaken by conduct books is my focus in this chapter.

## Laboring over the Body

As recent scholarship has emphasized, the intersection of new cultural needs among readers, especially bourgeois readers, and changes in commercial publishing were important stimuli for the proliferation of conduct literature in the late Middle Ages.[15] As paper replaced parchment, books became cheaper and more widely available over the course of the fifteenth century; the advent of printing in England in 1476 significantly speeded these processes of wider dissemination of written texts. At the same time, those who had learned to read for business purposes now sought other kinds of reading material, especially works offering entertainment and education. The market for books in England during the late Middle Ages thus included a socially broad buying public to whom publishers provided ever cheaper and more readily available books.[16] A flourishing trade in secondhand books also made expensive and relatively scarce manuscripts accessible to a wider range of readers.[17] What this implies is a close connection between commerce and publishing as the production of books came to be a profit-making activity and books began to be marketed in ways that appealed to a largely urban readership, which often had a vested interest in commercial activity and self-enhancement.

In the fifteenth and early sixteenth centuries manuscript and printed conduct books brought financial profit to book distributors, who discovered and undoubtedly helped to increase a public eager for such works. It is no coincidence, but rather a mark of shrewd business sense, that Caxton, de Worde, and Pynson all included conduct poems among the output from their presses. Although it is difficult to judge from the available evidence precisely how popular English conduct books were and with what readers, the relatively large numbers of extant manuscripts and printed editions as well as some information about ownership suggest that even in manuscript form conduct poems were popular among bourgeois readers. For example, a manuscript containing *Stans puer ad mensam* was owned by Walter Pollard, a member of a mercantile family; *Richard Hill's Commonplace Book*, which contains three conduct poems, was compiled in the early sixteenth century by a grocer; and a manuscript drawn up as a code for freemasons around 1377–1401 contains a copy of the conduct poem *Urbanitas*. Such evidence has led Jonathan Nicholls to conclude that "the majority of the extant manuscripts of the English poems more often imply that it was to the merchant/trader class that they appealed rather than to the children of the land-owning class."[18]

Whatever their actual audience, conduct poems pitched themselves as a source of financial and social profit for their readers. Part of the success of conduct books as commodities is in fact attributable precisely to their ability to *market* conduct. Conduct books sold themselves by selling decorum as a useful tool for socioeconomic mobility and personal happiness. Adopting a typical stance, the *Babees Book* of around 1475 stresses that "governaunce" will lead to "lastynge blysse" and "self auaunce,"[19] promising that self-discipline will pay off handsomely and that the reader should therefore eagerly employ the advice conduct books offer. Similarly, the popular *Stans puer ad mensam* views desires for success and popularity as logical motives for good manners, while also assuming that the individual can use good manners to achieve those desires.[20]

The simultaneous marketing of bodily conduct and conduct books points to one of the most important consequences of the late medieval submission of the body to norms of decorum: a reification and commodification of the embodied subject. When conduct was marketed as a useful discipline that could be learned and self-imposed, the body was turned into an object over which people could labor. The well-governed body was thus constructed as a valuable commodity that could be acquired through good advice and hard work. Even before printed versions were disseminating their message to a wider bourgeois readership, conduct books had already begun to commodify the body. *The Book of Vices and Virtues*, a fourteenth-century English translation of an earlier French text, offers a good example. It also, however, expresses lingering doubts about the ultimate value of this process. *The Book of Vices and Virtues* classes manners as "myddel goodes," which are better than "smale goodes" such as the ephemeral gifts of Fortune and explicitly material items, but not as valuable as "verrey goodes" such as the grace of God, virtue, and charity. In this schema, manners are seen as "goodes of kynde and of techyng," that is, goods made up of both natural traits and acquirable characteristics, including such things as bodily beauty, strength, wit, understanding, memory, and manners.[21] Making apparent the commodification that underlies this discussion of behavior, the passage is prefaced by an extended metaphor in which the world is imagined as a fair full of merchandise, wherein many foolish merchants are deceived by false goods, taking glass for sapphires or copper for gold, whereas the good merchant knows "what a þing is worþ and þe vertue of euery þing."[22] As this comparison of the world to a market suggests, conduct is here treated in explicitly commodified terms; it is a "good" that can be "purchased" by study and hence is subject to the logic of economic exchange.

But *The Book of Vices and Virtues* is also troubled by certain aspects of this understanding of manners as commodities—troubled in ways that are tied to the double meaning of "good." Most problematic is the fact that despite what is seen as their real, material value as "goods," manners cannot define true goodness. Why not? First, because they do not necessarily help their possessor to avoid damnation; second, because they may often do harm, especially when they cause people to become proud and scornful of others who lack such gifts. Moreover, manners cannot be equated with virtue because they sometimes fail just when they are most needed and, most important, because people do not always use them to serve God.[23] Thus they are "myddel," not "verrey," goods.

Manners may be desirable, acquirable, and profitable, but they are also suspect in many ways, especially since they can be misused; that is, in the terms set up by *The Book of Vices and Virtues*, manners can be used to the nonvirtuous, nonspiritual ends of gaining social and economic advantage. As conduct is turned into a commodity, sold through the advice offered by conduct books, it is placed with a different financial and symbolic economy than in its traditional equation with virtue, and is subsumed under a new logic of representation. Once commodified, conduct was disturbingly open, as *The Book of Vices and Virtues* seems to understand, to all the uses and abuses of any item of commercial transaction as it escaped from the determining system of morality that had previously circumscribed it.

Caught up in processes of commodification, conduct books sold readers a set of ideas about self-determination, self-construction, and self-performance. In conduct books, the embodied self was explicitly recognized as a *product*, shaped by the individual in active collaboration with the advice the book offered. The ideal self, the one best poised to find happiness as well as earthly and spiritual rewards, was the self that most successfully put to work the processes of self-governing described by conduct books. To a large extent, then, the individual was free to shape the final social product as he or she chose. As this suggests, conduct books ask to be taken not as coercive discourses but rather as tools offered to the reader to be used voluntarily and in the reader's own best interests.

Yet conduct books were highly prescriptive texts that functioned in powerfully determining ways. Although promising personal satisfaction as a reward for following their advice, conduct books were engaged in a repressive control of bodily impulses that was allied with the construction and maintenance of specific cultural categories and hierarchies. Like other disciplining discourses, conduct books formed their subjects by embodying them, in Bourdieu's sense of "embodiment" as an education process or a way of inscribing bodies into culture.[24] Using codes of bodily behavior, conduct books constructed a cultural order and placed subjects—willingly or not—within it. For this reason, the program of voluntary self-governance championed by conduct books has to be seen as complicitous with forces of social control, indoctrination, and subordination.

The complex relationship between these two projects of voluntary self-production and coercive cultural inscription has, however, often been treated in a way that erases individual happiness entirely. In Foucault's understanding of bodily discipline, for instance, discipline is directly opposed to desire, set up as its negation through institutionalized power and rational surveillance.[25] This is the case, in Foucault's view, especially where sexual desire is involved. In the classic Foucauldian view, bodily control is an absolute expression of social control. From this perspective, regulation of the body is a key part of the symbolic enactment of power, and the well-behaved subject is seen as precisely that, the *subject* of repressive discourses that interpellate him or her into a particular social order.

But in late medieval conduct books desire is made to serve discipline, as the subject is persuaded to participate in his or her own embodiment into the social order. I would not want to deny that conduct books certainly are strongly authoritarian discourses that carefully disguise their own self-interest by trying to make compliance with their rules seem to be in the best interests of the governed subject. But to ignore their persuasive tactics, to overlook the compelling mechanisms they use to get people willingly to play the roles they offer, is to miss the logic of their operation, which turns on the voluntary, the desirable, and the profitable. Conduct books work ideologically to make bodily control something the rational subject *wants*, even as they position that subject within the social order, working to create categories and hierarchies based on the marketing of acquirable traits such as manners.

## Disciplining Bodies

To concretize the assertions I have been making about the regulation of the body and the construction of an enthusiastically self-disciplining subject, I wish to turn to two closely connected late medieval conduct poems: *How the Wise Man Taught His Son* and *How the Good Wife Taught Her Daughter*, which appear side by side in a late-fifteenth-century manuscript, Ashmole MS 61, the versions I shall use here.[26] The smallish size and inelegant handwriting of this 161-leaf paper manuscript suggest that it was an inexpensive copy made for the burgeoning book trade at the end of the fifteenth century and was probably aimed at prosperous urban readers—perhaps of the mercantile or possibly artisanal classes—who had a taste for didactic works that promised self-improvement. The manuscript has the tall, narrow format of an account book, leading Felicity Riddy to believe it was used by a household manager to train not just children but also servants.[27]

Although one recent editor claims that nothing except the title links the two poems, they nonetheless resemble each other in several key ways.[28] In the first place, they share a similar preoccupation with how parental advice can ensure the child a happy and prosperous life, bespeaking an interest in exploring the role of nurture (or discipline) within a familial setting. Both poems also adopt a highly personalized and intimate voice—that of the wise and loving father or mother who wishes the best for the child—which carries, on the surface at least, no hint of the detached, abstract, and prescriptive inflections of the institutional authority it echoes. Finally, the poems have in common a generalized bourgeois focus, grounding their advice within a well-to-do urban milieu, wherein self-discipline is defined in explicitly material terms. Although overt class or status markers are lacking in the poems, their emphasis on correct consumption suggests a social and economic level that meshes with the mercantile or prosperous artisanal classes.

The most striking difference between the two poems would seem to be that they offer gender-specific advice on behavior. But in fact the degree of gender difference is deceptive. Despite the pretense in the *Good Wife* poem that we are being shown a mother giving advice to her daughter, the poem represents a thoroughly masculine perspective on female behavior, as is signaled by the use of "Wife"—a term that implies an androcentric position—rather than "Mother" in the poem's title.[29] Both poems are therefore probably better taken as attempts by an official male culture, particularly urban civic culture, to embody male and female bourgeois subjects than as advice deriving from and reflecting genuine differences in male and female experience. In this section, I consider the disciplining work of these texts, examining how they produce officially acceptable male and female selves, reserving discussion of their persuasive tactics for the next section.

*How the Wise Man Taught His Son* is a short, hundred-line poem that understands self-discipline of the male body to involve primarily discipline of others rather than of itself. In the poem, the son is taught not how to control his body's gestures, physical processes, and movements but rather how to use his body as an agent of control of other things and other subjects. This lack of concern with controlling the male body's unruly processes suggests several interesting things about the poem's construction of a masculine bourgeois subject. Although we might imagine that the lack of attention to controlling the unruly male body means that the male body is culturally licensed to be unruly and hence to act in a free and unrestrained manner, that turns out not to be the case. Instead, the poem begins by assuming that the male body, far from being by nature unruly and so in need of control, is instead innately docile and well governed.

Not needing to be disciplined by culture, the male is set up in the poem as already tamed by the soft hand of nature. The son, the paradigmatic male described in this poem, is young—fifteen years old—we are told, and "meke and myld" in manners as well as "Gentyll of body and of vsage" (11–12). He is already gentled by nature, with a body predisposed for good behavior. The impression the poem gives is of a malleable, disciplined male subject, an impression borne out by the tone, which is less imperative than cautionary. For instance, the father twice asks his son to "thinke one thys" advice rather than insisting that he obey it (18, 97). Instead of showing us the father ordering his son how to behave, the poem presents the parental advice as an almost rueful listing of life's inevitable disappointments, which the father must caution the son to expect and, where possible, to avoid.

Because the son's bodily behavior is understood to have been appropriately prefashioned by nature into a docile, well-mannered shape, the poem spends little time inculcating the methods of bodily self-control. In line with medieval teaching about masculinity, the male is seen as by nature reasonable and controllable, linked innately with rationality. The disciplining hand is therefore light in this poem, since the son's body is pre-scripted into the realm of the already disciplined.[30] Only the son's tongue threatens disruption and so needs restraint: "tell not all thynges þat þou maye," his father warns, "For þi tonge may be thy fo" (34–35). But the other parts of the male body are understood to be already orderly and well-governed; hence, the issue of self-control of the male body is largely ignored.

Instead, the male body is fashioned here as an agent of discipline. What the poem's advice aims to do, then, is to teach the young man how best to act in the role of discipliner, his assigned cultural position. Deflecting self-rule into rule over objects—especially the symbolically central object of the wife's body—the poem describes the pivotal problem facing the bourgeois male subject not as control of himself but rather as control of the rambunctious world of goods surrounding him.[31] In this poem, possessions are imagined as much more ungovernable than bodies and are seen as the source of widespread disorder, unhappiness, and social and economic ruin. Property management thus becomes the chief skill the son must master in order to achieve success and happiness.

The poem teaches its lessons in object control by carving out a manageable space within which masculine power can be shown to operate effectively—the household. Perhaps surprisingly, given our modern tendency to equate the domestic with the feminine, *How the Wise Man Taught His Son* positions the male firmly within a domestic stronghold, giving him an enclosed territory over which he can rule and from within which he can safeguard his interests in respect to the larger social sphere. His daily routine as sketched out in the poem is grounded within the home, and his position within the household is seen as the source of his identity. But the poem also assumes that the household requires detailed care, and the son is given extensive advice on how to labor over it and so make it submit to his will.

While the household is constructed as an unruly but ultimately governable realm, the public sphere is treated with suspicion. Sociability is figured as dangerous for the male, especially in terms of its threat to his property. The poem warns the son against holding office, against inviting the envy or enmity of neighbors, and against male rivalry—all dangers associated with the social terrain beyond the household. Public spaces such as taverns are seen as dangerous, and social relations, especially with other men, are imagined as destructive of personal happiness.[32] Aside from advice about avoiding all social contacts, the son is given little information about how to act in the public sphere; he is merely told that if he attends to God's business, goes to Mass, and says his prayers, then he can go about the "werldes besynesse" (24) assured that God will "send þe all þat thow hast nede" (29). Otherwise, everything in the poem is focused inward on the household and on the male's authority within it. The son is thus encouraged to retreat into the household, which functions as a more controllable alternative to the larger social order.

In his assigned role as property manager, the biggest obstacle the son faces in learning to govern his possessions is his wife. Perhaps not surprisingly, how the son should subdue his wife occupies a large part of the father's advice. In line with the poem's attempt to make the domestic order stand as a microcosm of the political order, the father's advice eschews tyranny, stressing instead a benevolent rule over the wife that will prevent possible insurrection. The son is advised to punish his wife lightly, using the medium of language rather than physical blows ("late feyre wordes be þi ȝerd," 42). Moreover, the son is warned not to revile her since "To call hyr wykyd, it is thy schame" (48), because as his property, her reputation is linked with his. He is also cautioned not to be jealous, or if he is, not to let his wife know it, since that would give her the upper hand.

As these examples suggest, the potential for the wife to disrupt the domestic order has to do primarily with her linchpin role in the whole project of masculine control of the household economy: if she gets out of line, the entire system—and the masculine identity built on it—falls apart. Good governance of the wife thus becomes a crucial part of the production of a satisfactory masculine identity. If she is controlled, so too is the rest of the son's property, and the well-oiled domestic machine will produce his promised happiness. That so much rests on discipline of the wife helps explain why this poem, not to mention *How the Good Wife Taught Her Daughter*, spends so much time fencing in female behavior, even though the advice is here explicitly directed to males.

Despite its attempt at constructing a well-behaved domestic sphere wherein masculine identity can be ratified, the poem is ridden with anxieties. The male subject produced by the poem is everywhere faced with threats of the dissolution of his domestic fiefdom and hence of himself. What is most disturbing, the poem suggests near its end, is the ultimate lack of control over the domestic that will inevitably come as a consequence of the son's death, when another man will step in and take his wife as well as his goods. "An oþer schall comme at þe last ende, / And haue hys wyfe and catell than," the poem threatens (74–75). And at this end point, all his good governance over wife and property—"all þat euer A man doth here" (77)—will be undone.

The poem tries to mitigate this final loss by framing it within a homily about the universality of men's conditions, leveling social difference and constructing "man" as a universal category. In death, the poem argues, both king and prince are brought down to the same position as a poor man, since not even the richest or most powerful man can take his wealth with him to the grave. So, the father tells his son, do not strive for high estate or riches, but rather "purchasse paradyce" (92), since nothing is so certain as death. Despite the conventional description of death as a social leveler, the poem leaves a lingering sense that social and economic differences in fact cannot be erased, competition cannot be made to disappear, and control of goods cannot be assured. By the end of the poem, the bourgeois masculine subject figured as confident ruler of his domestic realm has become riven by anxieties and has lost more control of his object world than he might imagine, his home at best a temporary shield against a hostile outside world that threatens to fracture his tenuously constructed and only temporarily well-guarded self. If the poem uses consumer goods to create a domestic kingdom over which the bourgeois male holds sway, then it also opens that male subject up to the depredations of commodity culture.

In *How the Good Wife Taught Her Daughter*, which is twice as long as *How the Wise Man Taught His Son*, female subjectivity is less a source of anxiety and the female body is more in need of vigorous disciplining than in the poem directed to the son, neither of which should be surprising given the masculine perspective informing the poem.[33] In contrast to *How the Wise Man Taught His Son* and despite the pretense of a mother speaking to her daughter, the tone of the female version is uniformly authoritarian and imperative, as the daughter is rigorously instructed in how to regulate her bodily behavior. Unlike the advice given the son, the daughter's instruction is grounded in control of her body, reflecting the common medieval equation of woman with body and man with spirit. Foucault has explicitly associated self-control of the body with the development of capitalism, arguing capitalism's dependence on "the controlled insertion of bodies into the machinery of production."[34] Within late medieval England, however, early capitalism's regulation of *the* body usually meant regulation of the *female* body, especially mastery of her sexuality, in the interests of household authority, property accumulation, and distribution of wealth under a patriarchal system of primogeniture. Within the urban world that formed the immediate context for the poem, "ungoverned" women, especially young women, were seen as trouble-makers, their sexualized and commodified bodies a danger to the household values and the masculine authority that underpinned civic life.[35] Revealing this sexual economy at work, in these two conduct poems self-control of the male body takes the form of control of property, while self-control of the female body is seen as a pacification of the unruly world of goods that is represented most potently in the female body as object or private property.[36]

In line with this project, the daughter is presented as by nature unruly, possessed of and by a transgressive body. As a consequence of her innate unruliness, she has to be ordered to be "meke and myld" (20) and to be "of gode berynge and of gode tonge" (24), unlike the son who is by nature predisposed to bodily restraint. Mary Douglas has argued that the socially constructed body is especially vulnerable, and therefore dangerous, at its margins, at boundary areas where social meanings shade into ambiguity and uncertainty and where social stability can be threatened with upset and disruption.[37] In *How the Good Wife Taught Her Daughter*, the socially constructed female body is dangerous primarily at its boundary area of the mouth, which must be aggressively controlled. By way of regulating her speech, the daughter is told to "make no Iangelynge" (22) in church, not to scorn anyone, to answer suitors courteously and her husband meekly, and to be in general "Suete of speche" (53). "Windy words" blasting from the ungoverned female body can pierce and disrupt the social fabric, so must be held back by regulated speech.[38] In another version of the poem, the daughter is even warned to beat her children when they do wrong rather than "curse hem . . . [or] blowe," presumably because angry words are more harmful than physical assault.[39]

The daughter is also ordered to control her facial movements and so to be "fayre of semblant" (45). She is warned not to change her countenance by laughing and not to gape too wide. This prohibition against gaping calls to mind Caroline Bynum's observation, in her description of women's bodies as portrayed in medieval devotional works, that "the good female body is closed and intact; the bad woman's body is open, windy and breachable."[40] Since, as Bakhtin says of the grotesque body, it is "unfinished, outgrows itself, transgresses its own limits," the female's by nature unruly body must be constantly put under surveillance and mastered by vigilant and unceasing control that shuts its orifices, restrains its movements, and generally renders it closed, contained, and harmless.[41]

Open female mouths—whether giving vent to gusty laughs, wide yawns, or unrestrained speech—carry a double threat, as late medieval court cases involving improper female speech make clear. They breach corporeal boundaries, making the woman's body dangerously open, while also disrupting social relations by launching the dangerously open body into the social realm. For this reason, advice aimed at closing the female mouth can be seen as working to produce a safely enclosed female subject, one that is less of a threat to the masculinist social order.[42]

The female body is, in addition, both vulnerable and dangerous at its social boundaries, that is, as it moves through urban space. When the daughter is cautioned to control her body's movements, not to walk too fast and not to toss her head or swing her shoulders as she walks, this advice suggests an omnipresent social gaze that watches and remarks the way a woman moves in public. She is also instructed to control the range of her movements, not going from house to house, to market, to tavern, or to cockfights, but rather staying safely at home: "Byde þou at home, my douȝter dere" (77). Governing her bodily movements as she walks, the female subject is taught to be conscious of herself as an object of public regard, as a performer closely watched by spectators.[43] The social space is here envisioned as highly theatrical, requiring a nuanced, self-aware, and highly guarded performance. In this performance the natural female body has to be constantly monitored and regulated, its basic impulses restrained and reshaped in socially acceptable ways so as to hem in its potential transgressiveness. It is worth emphasizing how this differs from the figuration of urban space in *How the Wise Man Taught His Son*: in that poem, the public sphere is a threat to the man; in this one, however, it is the woman herself who is a threat when let loose in public. This reversal makes a certain sense given that, as historians have shown, the public sphere in late medieval towns—the space of guild, craft, and governance—was exclusively male.[44] The son may be warned to avoid public life, but that warning is grounded in the assumption that it is there for him should he desire it.

As this constant monitoring suggests, control of the female body's movements effectively indoctrinates the woman as to her social position and fixes her in it. She is taught first that her natural bodily processes are suspect and that continual self-vigilance is necessary in order to play her proper role. More crucially, through emphasis on bodily self-regulation she learns that it is her social lot to be disciplined, and she is encouraged to join in that disciplinary project herself: "Thes poyntes at me I rede þou lere, / And wyrke þi werke at nede, / All þe better þou may spede" (78–80). Recalling Bourdieu's remarks that "when the properties and movements of the body are socially qualified, the most fundamental social choices are naturalized,"[45] we can here see the female subject helping in the naturalization of the social choices allowed her. As her body is hemmed in, constrained, and controlled, it mirrors the social role she is expected to play—one precisely of enclosure, subjection, and submission.

Since her body is seen as her husband's property and is therefore linked to him as his chattel, in his absence she is expected to take on his role as overseer of his possessions within the domestic economy. Within the household, the daughter is instructed in proper domestic labor. The emphasis is on work—her own and that of her servants—within the household. She is expected to put workers to work while also pitching in when necessary: "Amonge þi seruantes if þou stondyne, / Thy werke it schall be soner done," the poem advises her (151–52). Leisure, she is told, is something she cannot have if she wants to thrive (169–70). Here her body is subjected to the discipline of domestic work from two positions—manager and laborer. In order to be a "hous-wyfe gode" (123), the daughter has to internalize rules of behavior that make her both her husband's designated agent, who acts as an extension of him, and his property.[46]

As part of the process of controlling her body, her sexuality is also restrained. She is first warned against being alone with a suitor—"Syt not by hym, ne stand þou nouȝht / Yn sych place þer synne mey be wroȝht" (31–32)—and then is quickly married off, thus making sure her sexuality is placed safely under her husband's control. Similarly, prohibitions against going to public places like taverns and cockfights are directed chiefly at issues of sexual control. She is warned not to act like "a strumpet oþer A gyglote" (75) and is cautioned not to "A-queynte" herself with every man whom she meets in the street (83–84), a semantic choice that reveals the poem's concern with the sexually charged nature of these encounters. Similarly, when warned against tavern-going, she is cautioned through a sexual pun that makes clear what the real prohibition is: "Ne go þou nouȝht to þe tauerne, / Thy godnes forto selle þer-Inne" (65–66). Again, what is at issue is her status as her husband's well-governed property, a status that consorting with other men, especially sexually, threatens to disrupt.

Control of female sexuality spills over in the poem into broader control of sociability in general, whether with men or women.[47] The daughter is instructed not to talk in church with her friends, not to make "maystry" in anyone's house, and not to chide her neighbors. In part, sociability represents a threat to female virtue, as is made clear in the advice to avoid sitting or standing alone with a suitor where there could be any chance of falling into sin (23). But female sociability also represents a threat to social relations that goes beyond the specifically sexual. Envy, gossip, borrowing of money, scorn, miserliness, covetousness, and other sins against the social economy are to be avoided because they rupture social relations. Too much social contact, including homosocial contact, is dangerous, because it pulls the wife away from the close control of her husband and threatens to undermine his power. Fears of female sociability were probably connected to the high proportion of "surplus" women in late medieval towns, since the sex-ratio imbalance common in urban environments meant that many women never married and thus could be perceived as threats to the male-dominated family-household unit that provided an important structuring mechanism for urban social and economic relations.[48]

As threats to the husband's rule over his wife, uncontrolled female sexuality and sociability have economic repercussions, and both are explicitly coupled in the poem with the improper use of goods. The proper use of goods or, more broadly, wealth is set out in the opening when the daughter is instructed to pay her tithes and give to the poor (11–14); it is implied as well in the well-oiled running of the household, such as in the command that after her servants are done she should pay them (194). Improper use of goods is proscribed when she is ordered not to dress out of rank and not to envy the success of neighbors. The daughter is also warned not to borrow or spend other people's money (185–92). The importance of the right regulation of property comes to a head in one single stanza that moves through a series of related meanings of "gode," advising her to thank God for all her "gode," that is, all material goods including food, and then she will live a "gode lyfe" and be a "gode hous-wyfe" (157–60). The stanza ends by driving the point home that misuse or loss of wealth and property leads to unease and discontent: "At es he lyues þat Awes no dette" (161).

One of the most interesting aspects of the cultural work of this poem is the way that it locates accountability for self-discipline within the female subject herself. Thus the balancing of "thrift" against "unthrift" is made the daughter's own responsibility, as in fact is all of the behavior laid out in the poem. While *How the Wise Man Taught His Son* taught the son to govern his goods, *How the Good Wife Taught Her Daughter* encourages the daughter to govern herself. And in what seems to be a deliberate ideological move, she is instructed to labor over her own body for her own profit, since bad conduct "thy-selue it wyll vn-do" (175). Emphasizing the daughter's responsibility for her own behavior, the poem repeatedly uses the phrase "loke þou," as in "Gladly loke þou pay thy tythes" (11), to advise the daughter, encouraging her to engage in self-surveillance. The phrase also recalls the public gaze to which the female body is subjected and which is always "looking" at her as she "looks to" her own bodily control. To perform her role properly, the bourgeois female must therefore watch herself as she herself is always watched by others.[49]

To the extent that it assumes bourgeois female identity is performed and shaped in the public eye, *How the Good Wife Taught Her Daughter* prefigures Erving Goffman's *The Presentation of Self in Everyday Life*, which also conceives of subjectivity as something that is constructed through public "presentations." For Goffman, the self is essentially performative, established and maintained through a series of roles played by social actors before ever-changing audiences. Goffman is careful to point out that these roles are by no means freely or individually chosen by the performer, but rather incorporate and exemplify "the officially accredited values of the society."[50] We might thus say that social performances are to a large degree scripted by the *habitus*, whose inchoate processes can be witnessed on the bodies of the individual social agents who act in accordance with its inarticulate but nonetheless pressing demands. As Goffman has said, the ultimate goal of any social performance is "to sustain a particular definition of the situation," hence to represent a particular claim as to the nature of reality. In this way, social performances can be said to make visible the inner workings of the *habitus* in accordance with which they act.[51]

The operations of the *habitus* are especially apparent in what Goffman terms "social mobility performances." In Goffman's view, upward mobility not only depends upon rising income, but also "involves the presentation of proper performances . . . and the maintenance of front," using the requisite sign equipment made available by the culture.[52] Goffman argues that status or social position is not primarily a matter of material conditions; nor is it a fixed category or thing to be possessed, but rather a more or less coherent pattern of appropriate conduct. "Performed with ease or clumsiness, awareness or not, guile or good faith," social status, he says, "is none the less something that must be enacted and portrayed, something that must be realized."[53]

The implications of these claims for behavior and subjectivity are made clearer in a relatively unknown essay entitled "The Nature of Deference and Demeanor," in which Goffman explicitly takes up the question of conduct, especially conduct pre- and proscribed by spoken and unspoken social rules. In this essay, Goffman defines a rule of conduct as a "guide for action, recommended not just because it is pleasant, cheap, or effective, but because it is suitable or just."[54] As a consequence, breaking a rule of conduct usually leads to feelings of uneasiness and to negative social sanctions. Not surprisingly, Goffman explicitly links rules of conduct with the performance of a self, remarking, "When an individual becomes involved in the maintenance of a rule, he tends also to become committed to a particular image of self . . . he becomes to himself and others the sort of person who follows a particular rule, the sort of person who would naturally be expected to do so."[55]

Like social performances, rules of conduct are seen by Goffman as acts of communication that represent ways in which the self is confirmed (both the self for which the rule is an obligation and the self for which it is an expectation) within public space. Rules of conduct are thus for Goffman less objective codes than persuasive suggestions whispered by the *habitus*. Whether an individual keeps or breaks a rule, the rule effectively transforms both action and inaction into expression. Goffman is chiefly concerned in this essay with the category of rules that he calls "ceremonial," that is, rules of etiquette, especially rules governing rituals of deference and demeanor. Deference, according to Goffman, is a ceremonial means of conveying appreciation of a participant to that participant; in deference performances, actors "promise to maintain the conception of self that the recipient has built up from the rules he is involved in."[56] Through rituals of avoidance and rituals of presentation, a social dialectic is constructed wherein actors establish and maintain relational differences between one another. Demeanor, the second term in the essay's title, depends on such technologies of the body as deportment, dress, and bearing, which allow the actor to create an image of him- or herself meant for others' eyes.

Goffman's assertions about how subjects are publicly constructed and performed are particularly relevant to *How the Good Wife Taught Her Daughter*. In the world of this poem there is no privacy; instead everything takes place publicly, before the eyes of watchful onlookers whose presence is always acknowledged and whose gaze must be considered in any successful performance of a self. In essence, the female reader of *How the Good Wife Taught Her Daughter* is being schooled in a collective, visible performance of her own subjectivity. She must learn how to behave on the public stage where she is the object of the social gaze. Her task, as presented in the poem, is to shape her behavior in accordance to the preferences and values of the collectivity, but to believe that she is doing so voluntarily and for her own personal benefit.

Useful though Goffman's work is in shedding light on the ideological work of these conduct poems, his theory of the publicly performed self lacks an adequate recognition of the way in which relations of domination reproduce themselves. Although social performances are, Goffman claims, tied to a larger system of values, as understood by Goffman that value system seems problematically detached from material relations and from power. It is here that a return to Bourdieu's theorizing of the operations of the *habitus* is especially necessary. In an important note to his discussion of structures, *habitus*, and practices in *The Logic of Practice*, Bourdieu argues that in social formations in which relations of domination are not reproduced by objective mechanisms, hierarchical relations of dependence would be impossible to maintain without the permanence of the *habitus*, which is "socially constituted and constantly reinforced by individual or collective sanctions." Where there are no objective mechanisms, the social order relies on the order that exists in people's minds; the *habitus* then acts as a materialization of the group's collective memory, assuring the maintenance of the imagined order. In such cases, it is thus the *habitus* that reproduces structures of domination and that, even in new situations, can invent ways of maintaining old functions.[57] Late medieval conduct books offer a compelling instance of how the *habitus* maintains old functions and structures of domination, especially in terms of gender, even in a new situation (an urban bourgeois environment) and through a new cultural form (the conduct book).

What made conduct books particularly successful in achieving these ends was the way that they conflated external control with individual desire. In both of the conduct poems I have been discussing here, discipline is configured as something that the individual subject must be willing to impose on the self. But discipline is also seen as negation—of sexual urges, of social interactions, of movement through the world, and of opportunities for increasing wealth or status. Discipline involves concealing one's true feelings, as in the case of the jealous husband forbidden to show his jealousy sketched out in *How the Wise Man Taught His Son*; it involves repression of desires, as in the case of *How the Good Wife Taught Her Daughter*'s strictures against going to taverns, cockfights, or other entertainments. Self-discipline demands constant vigilance and continuous labor, with no chance to indulge in idleness or relax one's guard. It is hard work and little pleasure. But in the social world described by these poems, self-discipline is nonetheless overwhelmingly presented as the route to self-creation and self-fulfillment—the only option, in fact, for the bourgeois subject whose social situation imposes high demands for bodily control.[58] Discipline in these poems is thus figured as desirable, a step toward the attainment of happiness and success.

## Desiring Discipline

We might imagine that only the most abject of subjects would voluntarily submit to the self-discipline demanded by these poems, especially in the case of the repressive measures urged on the female in *How the Good Wife Taught Her Daughter*. But the poems are careful to provide a number of inducements for willingly adopting their advice and hence the subject positions they map out. In an ethnography of contemporary English working-class culture, Paul Willis has shown some of the ways in which subjects can be encouraged to locate themselves more or less uncomplainingly where hegemony wants them, however much that might be against their best interests.[59] In Willis's study, it is the subtle hand of culture, rather than the brute foot of economic might, that keeps individuals in the social class they have been born into, and, moreover, it is culture eagerly embraced, not unwillingly yielded to. Willis's study shows cultural forces to be far more pernicious than pure economics in maintaining structures of domination. The subjugating work of late medieval conduct books may be more explicitly focused and more overtly controlling than the impersonal and decentered cultural forces that Willis identifies as making working-class youths want working-class jobs, but it was nonetheless just as effective in getting individuals to participate in their own social inscription, whether or not such inscription was in fact in their best interests.

The strategies used by conduct books to make their readers desire to reproduce themselves in socially sanctioned ways are both rhetorical and ideological. Through a combination of voyeurism, scare tactics, and the promise of reward, conduct books sought to present sufficient reason for bourgeois subjects to adopt, wholeheartedly, their disciplining formulas.

Offering behind-the-scenes glimpses of domestic life, these conduct poems use the inducements of storytelling to paint intimate pictures of ordinary yet model lives in order to encourage the willing internalization of rules of behavior. Like a number of other late medieval conduct books, *How the Wise Man Taught His Son* and *How the Good Wife Taught Her Daughter* are structured as narratives that tell stories. They are in fact short fictions with plots and characters, rather than merely lists of precepts or prohibitions. Both poems tell a relatively detailed and engaging story about the protagonist's life, focusing on the individual engaged in ordinary life. We see the son and daughter getting up in the morning, saying prayers, going to church, and then carrying out their daily household routines. Going beyond just giving us a catalog of the daily routine, the poems also sketch out a *cursus vitae* of each protagonist, thus expanding the narrative's scope to reveal the individual at various stages of life, from adolescence through courtship and marriage, the raising of a family and running of a household, up to the approach of death. By adopting the form of a story, the poems manage to capture the reader's attention and to involve him or her in the poems' concerns. Moreover, the narrative form also brings into play the powerful dynamic of identification whereby the reader is encouraged to identify with and take up the same subject position as the fiction's protagonist or narrator. Although I would certainly not wish to discount the possibility of a resisting reader, it seems likely that many readers would have readily fallen in with these proffered subject positions and so have become more open to the poems' advice.

The poems also gain persuasive power by seeming to offer privy information, promising an insider's look at intimate father-to-son and mother-to-daughter relations: "Lyst and lythe A lytell space," *How the Good*

*Wife Taught Her Daughter* begins, "Y schall ȝou telle A praty cace" (2). Using the enticements of voyeurism and the lure of a juicy story—"a praty cace"—the poems attract the reader's interest to what they have to say. The reader is encouraged to spy on the normally hidden world of bourgeois domestic life. By welcoming the reader into the private household, these poems stake out new discursive territory by narrating fictions of bourgeois life within the traditional genre of advice literature, which is typically far less narrative in structure.

In both poems, the son and daughter are depicted in action, leading their lives within a deftly sketched-out domestic background. The rhythms of their daily routines are effectively evoked: they are shown at Mass, doing domestic chores, interacting with husband or wife, and raising children. Moreover, the reader is encouraged to look into the household's interior, to peer into the bedchambers and kitchens that define the private space of marital and familial relations. As readers are invited to become voyeurs, the desire to see into hidden rooms is made to serve the poem's concern that the characters in the poem be taken as exemplary, as models of correct behavior. Readers not only get to see for themselves how good conduct pays off, but they are also goaded on with titillating glimpses of private life that urge them to pay attention to the poem's message.

Narration is also used to avoid overtly coercing the reader, framing the advice obliquely as a story about a specific parent and child. The poems refrain from demanding that the reader behave in a particular way, deflecting their prescriptions for good governance onto the son and the daughter, who are the objects of the advice given not by the poem, but by the parent. Thus it is the father or mother who becomes the nominal voice of authority, not the anonymous author or the cultural strains he represents, and it is the son or daughter who is the ostensible target of the advice, not the reader. Both poems nonetheless shrewdly implicate the reader in what unfolds, opening with the call—explicitly framed by a personalized "I" speaking to "you"—that the reader listen and learn from what follows. In this way the instruction is filtered through the device of a story about a parent instructing a child. The ideological work of the poems is as a result undertaken with subtlety and indirection, operating as suggestion rather than exhortation. "Take god hede to þis matere, / And fynd to lerne it yff ȝe canne," *How the Wise Man Taught His Son* encourages the reader (3–4).

Once narration has encouraged the reader to identify with and possibly seek to imitate the subject described in the conduct book, then other persuasive tactics come into play. Both poems frame their advice within a social world that is figured as hostile and threatening. The weapon to use against that dangerous world, the poems promise, is the well-governed body, which helps protect the vulnerable self and offers safety. Although female sociability, for instance, is a danger primarily to the masculinist regime, sociability is carefully presented in *How the Good Wife Taught Her Daughter* as dangerous to women themselves; thus women are encouraged to give up a social life outside the household without a struggle on the promise that they will be safer if they remain within the confines of the household. In a similar vein, in *How the Wise Man Taught His Son* good conduct is seen largely as an armor for the male subject against the world, a first line of defense against the hazards of urban life. Once again, good governance—seen not as repression of desires but as a rational response to a hostile external environment—is marked as an effective antidote to social perils and hence something any reasonable man would want to adopt without further compulsion.

What also makes these poems so persuasive and so ideologically effective is their insistence that conduct is not something imposed from outside the self in the form of a set of constraints to which the hapless individual is involuntarily subjected by larger powers, but rather something controlled and manipulated from within the individual, who is construed as at all times free to shape his or her behavior as desired. The poems show no overt coercion at work and leave no sense of the heavy hand of subjugation. Self-governance is instead presented as the mechanism by which an individual can, through personal initiative alone, attain success and happiness. The optimism and confidence of this position are breathtaking. Potential barriers—such as lack of wealth, absence of employment opportunities or marriage prospects, low social standing, or poor health—are never mentioned. Instead, the assumption is that learning to control one's own behavior is the definitive factor in determining happiness, with the individual's own enthusiastic participation as the only requirement. This notion of complicitous self-discipline whereby rules are internalized and then voluntarily imposed on oneself for one's own supposed benefit comes across with particular vividness in the Ashmole version of *Stans puer ad mensam*, which calls on Christ to be "to chylder A bodely leche," and then claims that the courteous child will learn to be able to be a "leche" to himself in difficulties.[60] Manners are here strikingly figured as literally a way to *care for* the self. By implication, then, submission to rules of conduct becomes a form of self-medicating; to refuse to take one's medicine would put the body at risk and would be foolishly self-destructive.

Finally, it must be said that despite these convincing rhetorical moves, the persuasive task of conduct books was undoubtedly made considerably easier by the material context within which they were produced and consumed. As historians have argued, late medieval urban life—the milieu within which conduct books seem to have most widely circulated and which is captured within the narratives of *How the Good Wife Taught*

*Her Daughter* and *How the Wise Man Taught His Son*—offered new op-portunities for social mobility and economic success. The relative fluidity and complexity of urban life at all levels brought about by steady migra-tion from the countryside, combined with a high mortality rate, which undermined urban family structures, not to mention the public visibility that arose as a consequence of a higher population density, encouraged a reliance upon manners, fashion, and consumption as important mecha-nisms for acquiring and displaying status and identity, rather than on fixed signs of social standing such as birth-determined rank or legal sta-tus.[61] In such a climate, little coercion would be needed to encourage adoption of what were presented as socially and economically useful codes of bodily behavior that could be used in crafting an identity. Here in the urban, commercialized, display-oriented context that produced and consumed so many conduct books, perhaps more powerfully than any-where else, desire was made to join in with the project of self-discipline and social inscription, as subjects were promised tangible rewards for willing participation in a regimen of bodily control and self-regulation.

## Discipline Undone

Although I began this chapter by taking issue with the construction of medieval subjects in the work of Elias, Bakhtin, and Foucault, I would not disagree with their insistence that the institution of a cultural regime of bodily self-governance—which they, however, would locate in a later historical period—represents an important moment in the construction of subjects. As the individual is schooled in regulating his or her own body's activities, exteriorized authority is translated into an interior, pri-vate space and individuals are made responsible for their own control. This process of the internalization of codes of behavior and instruction in self-discipline produced subjects who were intensely self-conscious about their behaviors and who were encouraged to see themselves as self-fashioned rather than as subjected to external controls. This is, of course, a vivid instance of the naturalizing action of ideology at work, using a spurious freedom of choice and sense of "rightness" to powerfully under-write notions of bodily propriety and to screen from scrutiny the way that, as Bourdieu notes, the control of conduct allows the culture to in-culcate its values.[62]

Medieval conduct literature such as *How the Good Wife Taught Her Daughter* and *How the Wise Man Taught His Son* demonstrates a sense of personal identity based not on God-given attributes such as birth into a particular rank but on processes of self-creation. Defining identity as something that is based on cultural behaviors rather than on natural essences, it stresses nurture over nature. This is the ideology underlying

Caxton's *Book of Curtesye*, for example, which encourages the reader to be aware that manners are not fixed (not *nature*) but always changing (part of *nurture*); hence new guides to behavior are constantly needed since there is no one standard that can always be applied in every situation.[63] Caxton here acknowledges that social roles, and hence the self they perform, are always shifting, adapting to the demands of new stages and new audiences. At the same time, he is certainly also speaking as a businessman, concerned to create a continual market for his ever-changing products. Whatever its motives, Caxton's recognition of the changeability of manners reintroduces serious cultural problems accompanying the idea of a changeable, self-disciplining subject that uses imitation as its strategy for learning how to act.

One of these problems has to do with the question of nature versus nurture, of inner being versus outer. Although a supposed congruence between inner and outer forms of behavior was a commonplace of medieval writings on behavior, this congruence was threatened by the assumption of conduct books that the subject is self-governing. Hugh of Saint Victor, for example, describes *disciplina* as an inner mode of reining in instincts and passions as well as an outer way of regulating appearance, speech, gesture, and public behavior.[64] For Hugh, *habitus, gestus, motus corporis, locutio, cibus,* and *potus*, that is, comportment, gesture, bodily movements, speech, and ways of eating and drinking, are signs of inner virtue. If, however, the outer guise, which is supposed to mirror the inner, can be easily changed by adopting whatever manners are currently fashionable, as Caxton assumes, then what does that do to the relationship between inner and outer? And what then happens to the subjectivity created out of their supposed unity?

A second problem develops from conduct books' reliance on learned behavior, which in their discursive universe is coded as positive and desirable. But as John Metham's *Physiognomy* points out, learned behavior can also be seen in a negative light, as counterfeit conduct assumed as a form of disguise in order deliberately to mask true, inner nature. Metham in fact attacks people who try to disguise their "true" dispositions by assuming a "false" and unnatural gait and movement. Metham is here arguing, following his sources, that a person's inner nature can be discerned through external appearance; hence dissembling external appearance is a form of falsehood that conceals what it should reveal.[65] But dissemble is exactly what conduct books ask subjects to do when they urge the putting aside of natural, instinctive behaviors in favor of more socially acceptable learned (in Metham's terms "false") ones.

Finally, a more serious problem has to do with the issue of imitation. Conduct books assume that behavior can and should be self-fashioned following exemplary models, thus putting considerable faith in the powers of imitation. But by investing so much confidence in modeled behaviors, conduct books raise the possibility of the imitation of the wrong models, hence possibly leading to bad conduct and unruly subjects. This potential predicament is recognized by Caxton's *Book of Curtesye*, which specifically advises readers to be sure to imitate only good examples and to avoid bad ones, like the "vnthryft Ruskyn galante / Counterfeter of vnconnyng curtoisye," whose "tacchis ben enfecte with vilonye" and who is a bad role model for young men—uncouth, loud talking, too tightly laced.[66] Within the social patterns of bodily control structured by conduct books, such out-of-control and misbehaving bodies must be proscribed, since they represent the antithesis of the socially well-regulated and submissive body. At the same time, however, the misbehavior of these bodies operates as a tactic in struggles to change the basic distribution of power.[67] Although Caxton tries to rule out the chance that the bad behavior of the "galante" will be copied by self-disciplining subjects, he cannot entirely prevent that from happening. In the end, then, as Caxton's remarks reveal, conduct books' own persuasive tactics work against themselves, unwittingly making a space for imagining the attractions of misbehavior. As the next chapter will show, imitation can prove much too powerful to be conscripted—as conduct books would have it be—into the service of only one master.

# CHAPTER 4

✛

# Mischievous Governance:
## The Unruly Bodies of Morality Plays

*To commit al kinde of sinne and mischief you need to goe to no other*
*schoole, for all these good examples, may you see painted before your eyes*
*in enterludes and playes.*
                    —Philip Stubbes, *Anatomie of Abuses*

Philip Stubbes's famous attack on playgoing, written in 1583 in the context of increasing suspicion of the theater, complains with special vehemence about the "bawdy, wanton shewes & uncomely gestures" used in plays and interludes.[1] Although some might argue that plays and interludes are as valuable as sermons and teach good examples of behavior, just the opposite is the case, Stubbes contends. These plays in fact encourage idleness, draw people away from sermons and lectures in churches, and lead to lust, whoredom, and uncleanness. Instead of offering good examples, they teach spectators how to "playe the vice," instructing them in the arts of murder and theft and revealing how to be a bawd and how to scoff, act arrogantly, and condemn God. Inspired by what they have seen on stage, Stubbes fears, spectators return home "and in their secret conclaves (covertly) they play ye Sodomits, or worse." In short, Stubbes concludes, every socially reprehensible vice that should be avoided is alluringly portrayed in plays and interludes, which offer their blandishments to unsuspecting and susceptible viewers.

Although responding to specific religious and political developments of the late sixteenth century, Stubbes's attack echoes earlier attitudes toward theatrical performances, especially those expressed by the *Tretise of Miraclis Pleyinge*, written sometime between 1380 and 1425.[2] Recent criticism has stressed that although the *Tretise* does not represent a wholesale condemnation of all drama, as is sometimes assumed, it does voice harsh complaints about theatrical activity.[3] Of particular interest in light of what Stubbes says, the *Tretise* condemns certain kinds of theatrical performances, which it lumps under the rubric of "playing miracles," for reasons similar to Stubbes's. Part of the critique centers on the fact that, according to the *Tretise*, "miraclis pleyinge reversith discipline" (116). More specifically, playing miracles "makith to se veine sightis of degyse, aray of men and wymmen by yvil continaunse, either stiring othere to leccherie and debatis as aftir most bodily mirthe comen moste debatis, as siche mirthe more undisposith a man to paciencie and ablith to glotonye and to othere vicis" (118–23). The *Tretise*'s charge in this instance is that by "reversing discipline," especially discipline over the body, playing miracles encourages an unwelcome self-indulgence that is induced by the "bodily mirthe" of the performance. The result is a dangerous loss of self-control that has the effect of leading spectators into vice. For the writer of the *Tretise*, as for Stubbes, theatrical activity has at least the potential to act as a spur to misgovernance, reversing discipline and inciting improper behavior.

This construal of drama as potentially antidisciplinary has to do with complex attitudes toward play, mimesis, and impersonation. In a recent article, Glending Olson has argued persuasively that at least some people in late medieval communities thought of plays as a kind of play; as a result, they "conceptualized performance, including religious drama, in accord with their ways of thinking about forms of social play generally, and judged it as they evaluated those other forms, by applying essentially ethical criteria having to do with motive, purpose, and propriety."[4] Thus, although the Wycliffite tract, "Ave Maria," allows some forms of recreation, it condemns the man who plays in "a pagyn of þe deuyl, syngynge songis of lecherie, of batailis and of lesyngis," arguing that lords and ladies should not allow their servants to participate in such entertainments.[5] Similarly, the relatively tolerant *Dives and Pauper* allows plays and entertainments that are done "principaly for deuocioun & honeste merthe" but not those involving "rybaudye."[6] In these and other instances discussed by Olson dramatic activity involving mimesis and impersonation is situated within a broad context of other forms of social play and is judged in terms of its social and ethical functions.[7]

Several aspects of the *Tretise* are of particular interest for what they reveal about late medieval dispositions toward theatricality understood as continuous with other kinds of social play: the association of dramatic performances with the body and with money, the evocation of relations of domination in order to attack "miraclis pleyinge," and the question of audience reaction. The *Tretise* consistently links "miraclis pleyinge" with the body, emphasizing how dramatic activity caters to the bodily at the expense of the spiritual. Playing miracles is, according to the *Tretise*, "of the lustis of the fleyssh and mirthe of the body" (112–13). As a consequence, it leads to bodily sins like gluttony and lechery while encouraging neglect of spiritual activities like penance and contemplation (118–28). Unlike other representational forms that do not involve impersonation, plays "ben made more to deliten men bodily" (378) and so in them "the fleysh is most meintenyd and the spirite lasse" (492–93). In a telling phrase that sums up its understanding of the relationship between bodies and drama, the *Tretise* succinctly describes playacting as "fleysly pley" (480).

While concerned about the connection between playacting and the body, the *Tretise* also raises questions about the explicitly material side of dramatic activities and their position within the economy. One charge that the *Tretise* makes against the playing of miracles is that it represents improper expenditure, directing the flow of money away from legitimate ends, which in the view of the author of the *Tretise* include charity, basic living expenses, and payment of debts. Thus the *Tretise* complains of the supporters of plays that what "they shuden spendyn upon the nedis of ther negheboris, they spenden upon the pleyis" (598–99), and then "to peyen ther rente and ther dette they wolen grucche" (599–600). Moreover, in order to acquire money to spend on these miracles, people "bisien hem beforn to more gredily bygilen ther neghbors in byinge and in selling" (607–8), a charge that seems to suggest that the plays incite greedy and dishonest commercial activity. The *Tretise* ends with a call to spend "nouther oure wittis ne oure money aboute miraclis pleyeng, but in doinge hem in dede, in grette drede and penaunce" (717–19). For the *Tretise*, as these examples imply, playgoing resembles many other forms of undesirable social play, such as dicing or gambling, which divert money from its appropriate uses and thus pervert proper modes of spending and getting.

When the *Tretise* mounts its attack on certain kinds of theatricality it does so by employing a series of analogies, all of which turn on class and gender subordination. Although these analogies are entirely conventional, they nonetheless express a characteristic set of beliefs that have a bearing on the antitheatricality of the *Tretise*. As the argument is being laid out at the beginning of the *Tretise*, the author sets up a comparison between the playgoer and God on the one hand and servants and their masters on the other, saying, "Sithen an erthely servaunt dar not takun in pley and in bourde that that his erthely lord takith in ernest, myche more we shulden not maken oure pleye and bourde of thos miraclis and werkis that God so ernestfully wrought to us" (30–33). Another similar relationship is called to mind when the *Tretise*, describing how drama "reversith dissipline" (76), relates how a "scoler" trembles "seing the yerde of his master" (80–81). A third example involves the jealous husband who, "seeinge his wif to japun with his kindnessis, and to lovyn by hem another man more than him," chastises her (567–70). In another instance, the naturalness and appropriateness of patterns of domination and subordination are asserted when playing with God's miracles is likened to the inappropriate and unseemly "felawchip of a thral with his lord," which "makith his lord dispisid" (501–2). In all of these cases, what is assumed is an inevitable and just hierarchy of domination that is destabilized by theatrical activity.

To turn to my final point about concerns raised by the *Tretise*, the author is also troubled by what impact plays have on their spectators. This theme is developed in the section of the *Tretise* that cites six arguments that are often advanced in order to defend "miraclis pleyinge." The second of these arguments is that watching miracle plays makes "men commited to gode livinge" (150–51) by showing them the evil workings of the devil and so encouraging them to "leeven ther pride" (158–59) and turn toward Christ. In this way, it might be said by supporters that playgoing "turneth men to the bileve and not pervertith"(160–61). In the following section, which refutes these six defenses of playacting point by point, the longest refutation is devoted to demolishing the second point about the way negative examples in plays supposedly encourage spectators to reform their own behavior. The argument that the author mounts turns on the fact that since "miraclis pleyinge" is "sinne," although it occasionally converts men it is far more often the occasion of perverting men rather than saving them. Moreover, plays are dangerous because they draw not just individuals but whole communities "fro dedis of charite and penaunce into dedis of lustis and likingis and of feding of houre wittis" (293–94).[8] As Olson points out, it is not just the content of these plays that is under attack here but also the circumstances of their performance.[9] This seems to be the thought behind William Melton's proposal to have the York plays moved to a day other than Corpus Christi, since the revelry and excessive behavior of the spectators was inappropriate for a religious holiday even though the plays were not necessarily evil in themselves.[10]

These concerns expressed by the author of the *Tretise* usefully sketch out some of the attitudes toward theatricality held by at least some members of late medieval communities and therefore provide a context for considering how the morality plays that are the subject of this chapter might have performed destabilizing and transgressive cultural work, as I wish to suggest they did. Whatever the truth of the *Tretise*'s fears about the effects of theatrical performances and however much the *Tretise* might try to control dramatic activities, the cultural life of late medieval England was rich in dramatic performances, and those performances were often fascinated by the theme of bad behavior. And although defenders of theatricality might wish to believe that evil characters in plays would inspire spectators to abandon their own vices, the fear expressed by the *Tretise* that the dramatic representation of misbehavior engenders more, not less, misbehavior has to be reckoned with.

The obvious late medieval performance to look to in order to see bad behavior—especially bad behavior in which standards of bodily conduct and socioeconomic boundaries are transgressed—is the carnival. Since the 1970s, the most widely used model for the analysis of medieval and early modern popular culture has in fact been the notion of the carniva-lesque, which has been construed as the privileged site for antiauthoritar-ian acts and lower-class rebellion. Developing out of a loose synthesis of symbolic anthropology and the writings of Bakhtin, the carnivalesque, with its irreverent, exuberant, and irrepressible play with and against the codes of the dominant culture, has been taken as the definitive popular cultural activity of preindustrial society. Carnival, so the argument goes, represents the purest moment of popular cultural expression. More broadly, carnival has come to be seen not just as a ritual feature of early European culture but as a mode of understanding, an epistemological cat-egory or indispensable model for the analysis of dissident culture, litera-ture, and symbolic practices.[11]

Whether seen as cultural safety valve, as an exercise of power and sur-veillance, or as an opportunity for genuine revolt, the basic principle of carnival is understood to be a downward transformation in which every-thing socially and spiritually exalted is represented on the bodily, mate-rial level.[12] This process of transformation includes irreverent speech, such as cursing and blasphemy; symbolic and actual violence, such as thrashings and beatings; and inversionary images, both cosmological (the underworld, hell, devils) and anatomical (the buttocks, genitalia, excre-ment). Carnival is seen as flaunting the sins of the flesh, including glut-tony and lubricity. Carnival glorifies feasting and the release from sexual inhibitions, embodying unbridled pleasure, abundance, excess consump-tion, noise, misrule, and disorder. In the carnival, as Bakhtin has argued, the "grotesque" body—unruly, excremental, rude, and unregulated—is al-lowed unrepentant freedom of expression while the regulated, enclosed, orderly, and pure body is banished from sight. Carnivalesque play is thus seen as unleashing the body, freeing it from its civilizing constraints and licensing it to misbehave in a variety of crudely rebellious ways.[13]

Although we have learned to look for its disruptive work in the car-nival, the misbehaving body appears in another performance site as well, in late medieval morality plays, where we might least expect it.[14] The morality play is on the face of it an odd venue for the display of the bodily grotesque and its subversive work. Commonly understood as didactic drama stressing mercy and forgiveness of sins, moralities are usually thought to be motivated by the social and ecclesiastical purpose of urging spectators to confession and hence to be actively engaged in the staging of examples of virtuous behavior. Populated by personified abstractions who engage in ritualized battles of good against evil, moralities would seem to be unlikely dramas in which to find exuberantly unruly bodies of the sort that might move spectators to the misbehavior feared by Stubbes and the writer of the *Tretise*.

But despite the modern tendency to read moralities as monologic representations driving heavy-handedly toward full expression of a moral message about human sin and divine salvation, a tendency that has condemned many of the moralities to go unread and unperformed, these plays are in fact full of flamboyantly bad behavior—bad behavior that is by no means entirely subordinated to the plays' themes of repentance. "Mischievous governance," as a character in the early-sixteenth-century moral interlude *Hick Scorner* is called, crops up in a variety of guises in moralities. Whether known as Mischief, Titivillus, Moenen, Sloth, Avarice, Riot, or World, such tempters, tricksters, vices, and devils all represent disorderly behavior grounded in the misuse of bodies and commodities. In these moralities, the grotesque body is linked with the world of goods to produce a potent model of misbehavior that could hardly have avoided the notice of various interested parties.

A conventional reading of the morality play as didactic drama aimed at encouraging repentance and confession tends to see the role of the vice characters as being to lead the protagonist into sin, thus setting him or her up to reap the rewards of ultimate repentance.[15] In this reading, the vices are clearly framed as evil and hence are readily rejected by both protagonist and spectator in favor of the salvation and redemption staged at the conclusion of the play.[16] The bad behavior of the vice characters in this drama of redemption is assumed to offer no real temptation to spectators and thus to have no corrupting effect.

But this reading is too summarily dismissive of the appeal of misbehavior, especially as dramatized in these characters. Morality plays invest their vice characters with remarkable energy, interest, and vitality, so much so that the vices are, as Stubbes says, very seductive examples indeed. At the dramatic level, the vices are often the most engaging characters in the play. They are typically given the wittiest speeches, the boldest personalities, and the best opportunities for slapstick and buffoonery. In contrast, the protagonist and the characters representing virtue often seem dull, colorless, and lacking in interest. Their speeches frequently take the form of sermonizing monologues and they are permitted almost no physical actions that might more effectively dramatize their roles. This discrepancy between dramatic interest and moral message—between lively vices and dull virtues—is often assumed to resolve itself in favor of the latter: the greater the temptations, the stronger the salvation. In this way the vitality of the misbehaving characters is seen as furthering the moral message. Yet this reading of the triumph of virtue over vice is achieved at the expense of full acknowledgment of the power of representation, especially the powers of dramatic representation in which the complex processes of impersonation and imitation intermingle.

Conduct books, as the previous chapter argued, place considerable faith in the strength of imitation. Examples of proper behavior held up for public contemplation will, they assume, inspire imitation, especially if such examples can be linked with the promise of social and financial reward. But imitation is a more complicated phenomenon than conduct books imagine. As the Brigittine monk Richard Whitford advises in a section of *The Boke of Pacience* called "An Instruction to avoyde and eschewe Vices and folowe good maners," which was written in the early sixteenth century, imitating good and holy people is helpful in becoming virtuous. Therefore, he advises his readers: "Drawe ever unto the beste, and unto the moste vertuous / and beste manered persons, and so shal you have good maners."[17] But if "with the good & holy persons you shalbe good and vertuous," then it also follows, Whitford states, that "with the pervers & yvel persons, you shalbe, as they be."[18] Whitford suggests that if behavior is so susceptible to the dynamics of imitation, then it is necessary to avoid all bad examples in order to eschew vice. The dilemma of the moralities, then, turns on precisely this: how to present sin without counteracting the didactic purpose.[19] As the morality *Impaccyente Povert* reveals when it presents itself paradoxically as "a mirrour vice to exclude," the dilemma moralities faced was not easily resolved, not least because all forms of representation prove problematic for the exclusion of anything.

Although moralities, like conduct books, may have sought to model appropriate behavior, their project was complicated by the prominent role disruptive behavior plays in them. In the readings that follow, I focus on misbehavior in three plays: *Mankind* (ca. 1475), *Interlude of Youth* (ca. 1514), and *Mary of Nemmegen* (ca. 1516). Each of these plays follows the morality pattern of dramatizing the story of a vulnerable protagonist who imitates bad examples, falls deeply into sin, and is ultimately redeemed. But the theatrical representations of misgovernance found in these three plays do not, I argue, unproblematically and unilaterally lead to the ratification of virtue over vice by the end of play; instead, these models of misbehavior—especially misbehavior grounded in the symbolic disorder of the body out of control—provided a way of exploring the relationship between violation of norms of bodily propriety and transgression of social and economic norms. Using the unruly body as a resource for resistance, these dramas of misbehavior and ultimate repentance provided a way of performing and hence negotiating complex relations between individual desire and social control. In the process, these plays demonstrate how seductive mischievous governance could be and how difficult to control.

## Open to Vice

One thing the protagonists of these three plays have in common is that they are drawn from marginal groups that were often viewed as particularly vulnerable to misgovernance. As representatives of communities that in many ways troubled the social imaginary of late medieval England, the protagonists of these plays—disgruntled laborer (*Mankind*), reckless youth (*Interlude of Youth*), and loose woman (*Mary of Nemmegen*)—were thrust into social conflicts the moment they stepped on stage. Although it is difficult to chart the extent to which such individuals might have constituted real threats to power in late medieval England, they certainly loomed large as perceived sources of disruption, as a variety of legal, cultural, and representational efforts to keep them in line suggests. Framed within the plot of the morality play, the sin and redemption of these characters provided a way to express and then neutralize fears about these marginal groups, by staging the dramatic conversion of the character from dangerously bad to safely good. Part of the ideological work of these plays seems to have been precisely to raise fears about the repercussions of allowing marginalized groups to pursue their desires, but then to use the theme of repentance and salvation to recuperate these characters, reintegrating them into their subordinated positions within the social whole and so erasing their threat. Look how terrible it would be if a laborer refused to work, a wealthy young man rejected marriage and the responsibilities of his social position, and a young woman were allowed complete sexual license, these plays say. But they then calm this terror by returning the laborer to his fields, the young man to his patrimony, and the woman to a convent.

Given their marginality, these protagonists were recognized as both highly susceptible to temptation and likely to become seriously disruptive once seduced away from socially acceptable behavior. Their fall into sin might often look unmotivated and hastily contrived, precipitated by trivial actions such as, in the case of Mary of Nemmegen, her aunt's refusal to give her a night's lodging. But the plays do not need to waste time creating plausible temptations, since the protagonists' marginality sets them up from the outset as by nature unable to resist even the slightest of nudges toward sin. Since they are culturally constructed as marginal persons in constant need of authority's oversight, it is no surprise when such protagonists are almost inevitably drawn into vice.

Significantly, their seduction into sin takes place within the same two arenas that are so assiduously policed by conduct books: the world of bodies and the world of goods. In these morality plays, the ungovernable processes of the body are seen as places where temptation can gain a foothold and then carry out its work. Bodily unruliness, whether figured as Mankind's idleness, Youth's thievery, or Mary's adultery, is dramatized in these plays first as opportunity for and, later, as a sign of sin. Control and subjugation of the body are therefore required in order to achieve the closure promised by the salvation staged at the end of the play. To be successfully redeemed, the protagonist will have to subdue his or her raging body, converting it into a sanitized, docile, well-behaved container that can house a similarly docile self.

In a similar fashion, commodities also are figured as providing openings for sin and so must ultimately be controlled and regulated. As the protagonists are tempted, they are shown succumbing to acquisitive desires and illicit ways of obtaining goods—through theft, consorting with the devil, or other forms of deceptive and deviant behavior. The plays stress that while living in sin the protagonists are surrounded by material comforts, enjoying abundant food and drink, fashionable clothing, and plenty of money to spend on dicing and other disreputable games. Part of what the protagonists must learn in order to be redeemed is the proper use of commodities. In all three cases, this involves complete rejection of material goods in favor of spiritual rewards. These plays set up a system of symbolic exchange in which desire for consumer goods equals sin and damnation while rejection of goods equals salvation and spiritual profit. Misconduct is thus made to represent a surplus of consumption and a deficit of spiritual value.

The imaginative work these plays perform is to take marginal and therefore already potentially disruptive characters, sink them into misconduct and depravity, then "save" them and through them the social order. Since misconduct in the moralities is viewed as sin—behavior that leads the individual away from God and salvation toward evil and damnation—the most powerful of ideologies is thus brought to bear on the rejection of misconduct. But the memory of the pleasures of misbehavior, of the satisfactions that come from unruly bodies allowed free rein and from material comforts lavishly used, lingers even after the plays force redemption onto their protagonists. In fact, when examined closely the attempts made by these plays to bring misbehavior to a halt look highly unsatisfactory and incomplete. Staged against the captivating possibilities for self-expression that have been so vividly enacted throughout each play, the reassertion of a controlling order at each play's conclusion seems at best an insufficient response. In the end, the inability of these three morality plays to negate the charms of misgovernance suggests just how little these theatrical representations were equipped to "exclude vice."

The following discussion moves chronologically through these three plays—from *Mankind* to the *Interlude of Youth* and then, finally, to *Mary of Nemmegen*. This order is also meant to reveal a progression in which the kinds of misgovernance enacted in each play become increasingly more disruptive and hence require increasingly greater methods of containment and stronger reassertions of a normative order. Thus, by *Mary of Nemmegen* the work of the disciplinary machine, which operates

smoothly and relatively gently in *Mankind*, is revealed brutally strug-
gling to wrench the unruly female body back into line. These three plays
also raise important issues of performance context, including questions
about who was watching the performances and for what reasons, that I
shall try to address while exploring their ideological valences.

## Disgruntled Laborer

Although the play's title encourages a universalizing reading uninflected
for socioeconomic or gender differences, *Mankind*'s subject is in fact
fairly specific. The protagonist, also named Mankind, is an impoverished
male agricultural laborer, apparently hardworking but with little in the
way of material or spiritual satisfactions to show for his efforts. This lack
of satisfaction opens the door to Mankind's abandonment of the two socially acceptable activities the play leaves open to him, work and piety.
"Of labure and preyer," says Mankind, "I am nere yrke of both" (585).[20]
Within the world of the play, labor and prayer stand as quintessentially
proper uses of the agricultural worker's subjugated body, the ends to
which its movements should be directed. When Mankind is tempted by
the vices, it is to abandon these approved uses of the body, replacing
them with their opposites, idleness and impiety. Bodily impropriety thus
operates within a restricted sphere in this play, seen not as a tempting
array of possible behaviors but rather as the negation of the proper uses of
the body, proper uses that are equally restricted, given Mankind's low social standing.

Despite its reputation among modern readers as an abstract, allegori-
cal drama, *Mankind* is fully grounded in corporeality, emphasizing bodily
functions, movements, activities, and gestures.[21] The importance of embodiment to the play is stressed in Mankind's first speech, in which he
identifies himself as made up of the two contradictory parts of body and
soul (195–96). Mankind laments that his soul is ruled by his body and,
using the analogy of a disorderly household in which the wife is master,
sets up his abandonment of bodily control for bodily misrule: "Thys ys to
me a lamentable story / To se my flesch of my soull to haue gouernance. /
Wher þe goodewyff ys master, þe goodeman may be sory," Mankind says
(198–200). Corporeality is the trigger for Mankind's fall, guiding the vices'
choice of methods to tempt him. Once he has fallen into sin, Mankind
demonstrates his depravity through lack of bodily decorum and control.
The vices and Mankind are repeatedly shown using their bodies for ends
other than labor or prayer, giving in to unrestrained bodily movements,
reveling in the excremental processes of the body, and engaging in loud
and obscene speech. All of these instances of bodily indecorum are figured as agents and signs of Mankind's fall.

In *Mankind*, improper control of the mouth is played out through the theme of "jangeling."[22] On one side is Mercy who represents the voice of goodness; as a spokesman for divine truth, he preaches "doctrine mony-torye." His speech is presented as wise, pointing to doctrinal truth, and sensibly modulated, if somewhat dull. Mischief, Titivillus, and the other tempters, in contrast, are masters of evil and inappropriate, though lively, language. Well-schooled in techniques of oral mischief, they are adept at such verbal arts as "ydull language," "japyng," and "fablys delusory." As part of their entrapment of Mankind, the vices Newguise, Nought, and Nowadays deliberately employ disruptive speech—chattering, singing, and other forms of uncontrolled utterances, including obscenities. In a central scene, Nought leads "all þe yemandry þat ys here" (333) in a scato-logical song, joined by Nowadays and New Guise singing: "Yt ys wretyn wyth a colle . . . He þat schytyth wyth hys hoyll . . . But he wyppe hys ars clen . . . On hys breche yt xall be sen" (335–42). Once Mankind succumbs to their blandishments, he too forgets the proper use of the mouth, join-ing in with the vices' sins of the tongue.[23]

As Mankind's fall through and into verbal sin suggests, unruly mouths are explicitly linked in the play to disruption of social norms. The peni-tential manual *Jacob's Well* makes clear that verbal misconduct—includ-ing blasphemy, grumbling, swearing, idle talk, bad counsel, cursing, flat-tery, and boasting—constitutes a serious violation of social as well as bodily propriety.[24] Recalling the admonishments against gossip and chat-ter in *How the Good Wife Taught Her Daughter*, uncontrolled tongues are taken as threats to social harmony because they unleash emotions better kept hidden, thereby provoking antagonisms and increasing social tensions.[25] In recognition of the dangers of unbridled tongues, various late medieval mechanisms of speech surveillance ranging from defama-tion trials to proscriptions of gossip sought to close noisy mouths both male and female, channeling speech into acceptable forms such as prayer and confession.[26]

The unbridled tongues of the vice characters are what entice Mankind into sin and so are responsible for disrupting the social order into which he had previously been appropriately positioned. Mercy warns Mankind against the vices, saying, "In language þei be large" (295), and advising him not to give them "audience" (299). Their socially disruptive power is dramatically staged in the play through the sheer volume and amount of their wordplay. Interrupting each other, joking, swearing, singing, and chattering to Mankind, the flow of their speech seems unstoppable. Volu-bility in all its excessive display here becomes a mark of social disarray, the tumbling confusion of their speech mirroring the effect they have on Mankind.[27]

Like the mouth, other orifices are seen in the play as potential sources of misgovernance. New Guise approaches Mankind at the start of the play by proposing a marriage between Mankind's mouth and "hys ars þat þis made" (346–47), linking them as agents of transgression. This transgressiveness is most dramatically displayed in a scene of onstage defecation that flouts standards of bodily decorum while also suggesting how far beyond socially normative behavior Mankind and the vices have moved. In another scene, the three vices sing a comic rhyming song in which excrement is the recurrent theme (335–43).

Rejecting all bodily constraints, Nought, New Guise, and Nowadays revel in uncontrolled motion. They leap about and dance, even encouraging Mercy to throw off his clothes and join them: "Anon of wyth yowr clothes, yf ȝe wyll play," Nought says (88). "Nay, brother, I wyll not daunce," Mercy replies (90), holding to more seemly codes of bodily decorum. As with unruly mouths, these unconstrained bodily movements are set up in contrast to bodies that move restrictedly and are decently clothed, bodies that willingly submit to discipline.

Unrestrained bodily movements are in fact constructed by the play as the antithesis of the proper use of the body, which is in Mankind's case understood to be unceasing and uncomplaining labor.[28] Mercy makes this clear when he cautions Mankind to do his labor and not be idle in order to avoid falling into sin (308). When first confronted by New Guise, Mankind makes the correct response, telling him to leave since he has to work (349). Later in the play he asks the vices, "Why stonde ye ydyll?" and chides them, saying, "Yt ys pety þat ȝe were born!" (364). As the vices continue to make fun of him for being "a goode starke laburrer" (368), he—still operating within the world of bodily movements geared toward labor—calls to them, "Go and do yowr labur!" (376). Finally, when Mankind succumbs to the vices' wiles, he signals his capitulation by saying, "I se well by tyllynge lytyll xal I wyn" (548), gives up his spade, and stops working. As this suggests, the definitive sign of Mankind's abandonment of his former life is his rejection of his spade.

This rejection makes sense, given that proper use of the body for labor is symbolized by Mankind's spade and the work it performs—the hoeing of the ground. But this iconic representation of agricultural labor is presented in a conflicted way in the play. In one sense the spade stands as a symbol of Mankind's class identity as a peasant tiller of the soil—perhaps the most powerful and purest representation of labor for medieval audiences—and operates as a safeguard against sin: Mankind uses his spade to beat back the three vices (377) and also hangs onto it in the face of their temptations as a reminder of who he is. To some degree this treatment of the spade as sign of peasant identity that recalls the value of manual labor is part of a mythologizing and fetishizing of the peasant that had begun well before the late fifteenth century.[29] But at the same time the spade also points to class conflicts by calling attention to the fact that peasant labor, although frequently sentimentalized by manuscript illuminators and poets alike, was often unproductive and unrewarding, bringing profits less often to the individual worker than to landowners.[30] In stressing the class inflections of Mankind's spade I am departing from interpretations that see his implement not as a sign of class affiliation but as a universal mark of the Fall of Man (spade and distaff being the two symbols of Adam and Eve's fall).[31] Despite the heavy biblical overtones of Mankind's spade, it need not be seen in entirely universalizing terms that are beyond socioeconomic conflict. In the scene where Mankind spades unwittingly into a board hidden under the ground, socioeconomic discontent seems to be brought to the surface when attention is directed to how hard and futile his work is, even when undertaken under more normal circumstances and without deliberately planted obstacles. The vices play on precisely this issue when they taunt Mankind with the poor return he is likely to get for his efforts at tilling the soil (352–59), reminding him, and perhaps spectators as well, that farm work is hard work.

In contrast to Mankind's lot of unceasing and seemingly unprofitable labor, the vices represent game and play, dancing and idleness, theft and deception—and money and goods flow easily through their hands.[32] A key scene shows the vices at "work." As Mankind sleeps, Titivillus whispers in his ear, urging him to join with New Guise, Nowadays, and Nought and to abandon his wife for a lover. When Mankind wakes up, he immediately heads to a tavern to find the three tempters. New Guise arrives first, complaining that his neck aches from just having escaped hanging. He is soon followed by Mischief, who has broken out of prison, killing his jailer in the process, and has had sex with ("halsyde in a cornere") the jailer's wife. When all the vices are assembled, Mischief holds a mock court in which Mankind is "tried." Mankind is then ordered by the vices to visit all the wives in the country when their husbands are out, to rob and kill, to avoid church services, and to take men's money and cut their throats (595–716).

Although the vices' labor is here presented as overtly criminal activity, complete with an inverted trial and punishment scene, it cannot completely avoid looking attractive in its promise to fulfill material and sexual desires, particularly in contrast with Mankind's hard, barren life. Illicit though their behavior is, it apparently brings the vices satisfactions, material comforts, and pleasure. Moreover, the delight of New Guise, Nought, and Nowadays in their own evil is undeniably infectious, seducing Mankind to join them. If exuberant misbehavior attracts Mankind, what does it do to spectators?

It has usually been assumed that *Mankind* was performed by a company of itinerant players acting on a booth stage in a provincial innyard

before a paying audience whose social standing corresponded with the social standing of the protagonist, in other words, by "a low-class company
of strolling players, players whose appeal was to the uneducated and the
vulgar."[33] But this view has recently been challenged. Mankind's exit line
"I wyll into þe ʒerde" (561) makes little sense if he is already in an innyard; the play's witty and sophisticated use of Latin would not seem to be
directed toward a rural peasant audience; and the repeated use of the
term "gathering" to describe the collection of money from the audience
by the vices, a term often used in relation to parish festivities such as the
Robin Hood plays, suggests not professional but amateur performers. Such
discrepancies have led to the hypothesis that *Mankind* was acted indoors
in a private performance, most likely in a large household, a college, or a
guildhall.[34] Elaborating on this hypothesis, Tom Pettitt has recently argued that *Mankind* was performed within such a venue in East Anglia
specifically on the occasion of Shrovetide.[35] In a persuasive rereading,
Pettitt draws significant parallels between *Mankind* and the mummers'
plays, both of which include such features as house visits, collections of
money, ritual animal disguise, combat-slaying-cure plot sequences, and
an emphasis on pre-Lenten seasonal license that looks forward to Lent's
themes of penance and austerity. Pettitt makes a convincing case for
viewing *Mankind* as an English *Fastnachtspiel* that would have been performed at Shrovetide as part of seasonal household or institutional festivities.[36] In an argument that to some extent supports Pettitt's claims,
Gail Gibson has noted that the inscription at the end of *Mankind* in the
Macro manuscript points to monastic ownership. She has also identified
various local references in the text that have led her to the conclusion
that the play was performed to raise money for Bury Saint Edmond's. But
since Gibson also argues for joint lay and monastic sponsorship of drama
at Bury, observing that the abbey of Bury closely resembled not monastic
life as depicted in Benedict's *Rule* but rather the great households of East
Anglian magnates like the dukes of Norfolk, and that the abbot had close
ties with affluent laity, her claims about the auspices of the play do not
necessarily contradict Pettitt's.[37]

Pettitt's conjectures are persuasive, but their construal of an elite and
self-contained audience for *Mankind* might be misleading. A somewhat
greater degree of audience heterogeneity is implied in a line that Pettitt
does not address: at one point Nought says that he will lead in song "all
the yemandry þat ys here" (333). In a discussion of the meaning of the term
"yeomanry," Richard Dobson and John Taylor define yeomen as "minor
landholders, not gentry, but a cut above the ordinary peasant husband-
men." While broadly endorsing this definition, Paul R. Coss has also
pointed out that the term has to be understood not just as a social grada-
tion between the armigerous and the peasantry "but also in relation to

the confusion of status and status terminology that was a feature of late fourteenth-century England."[38] In this sense, "yeoman" is a marker not so much of a specific class identity as of class confusion and indeterminate social standing. If the class indeterminacy suggested by the term "yemandry" is combined with Pettitt's hypothesis about the auspices of *Mankind*, then the play comes to look like a kind of mummers' play undertaken on the significant seasonal occasion of Shrovetide, featuring the iconic character of "the peasant," and performed before a household audience whose social makeup was perhaps not exclusively elite, especially since large English households usually included not only servants but also dependents and poor relatives. In this context, the misbehavior so exuberantly displayed by the vices, whose own class standing is unclear but whose deeds seem enabled by a degree of wealth and freedom that bespeaks something more than subsistence living, might have been less remote than if we imagine *Mankind* being performed before an exclusively elite audience who could hold at arm's length both the peasant protagonist and his tempters. And if the play were performed not by professionals but by members of the household, then the actions would have been even less distanced. Similarly, the Shrovetide context of festive revelry might have encouraged an openness toward the licentious themes of the play, an openness not entirely precluded by the solemnities of the upcoming Lenten season.

One way to foreclose the allure of the bad behavior in the play would be to argue that this audience enjoys vicarious pleasure in the vices but then, recognizing its own implication in sin, rejects vice. In this way, the seductions of misgovernance lead to a sense of collective guilt that ritually affirms the power of repentance.[39] While this reading resolves the problem of what to make of the vices, it not only slights their powerful appeal but also privileges resolution over process, the last moments of the play over all the rest of it. Although Mercy, having driven the vices offstage, ends by telling Mankind, "ȝour body ys ȝour enmy; let hym not haue hys wyll" (897), the body has already had free rein and its antics have proven both entertaining and fascinating, despite what happens in the end.

## Reckless Youth

The difficulty of obliterating the allure of misbehavior is intensified in the *Interlude of Youth*, written some forty years after *Mankind*. More overtly playing out social fears—in this case, fear of rebellious youth—the play features the struggles of Charity and Humility to win Youth away from his disreputable companions Pride, Riot, and Lady Lechery, and to direct him toward salvation. Like Mankind, Youth is presented as a universalized figure, but once again that universalizing masks important socioeconomic and gender issues. Organized around the familiar sin-redemption plot, the play nominally features a contest for Youth's soul in which Charity plays a Mercy-like role; "There may no man saved be / Without the help of me," Charity proclaims (8–9).[40] But despite the focus on redemption, the *Interlude of Youth* exudes anxiety about unruly and uncontrollable young men. In the end, this play also has more trouble than *Mankind* did in convincingly returning its protagonist to a vice-free state and satisfactorily rejecting the offers of his tempters.

In late medieval society, patriarchal authority operated in large part as a system of domestic or household regulation extending over youth as well as over women, both groups being similarly removed from control of property and hence relatively lacking in autonomy, social standing, and political power.[41] Young men, whether second- or third-born sons of aristocrats and gentry destined not to inherit property or apprentices and lesser tradesmen in urban crafts, were often effectively shut out of competition for positions of social standing and economic prosperity. Their presence within urban and household economies, however, could not be overlooked and was frequently a source of social tension.[42] And their behavior—which was complained about across a wide range of cultural texts from civic ordinances to satiric poems—when deviating from a narrowly defined ideal of conforming deference, was invariably seen as "unruly." As Charity says in an aside to the audience, "Youth is not stable, / But evermore changeable" (551–52).

It is also worth noting that "youth" were defined not just by age, but by the absence of binding commitments to the dominant social order. This recognition of the dangers of a lack of approved social ties that could lead to social affiliations deemed undesirable by dominant cultural forces figures in *Mankind*, where Mercy warns Mankind against the fellowship of the vices and tries to win him over to a fellowship based on friendship by calling him "my own frende" (277). But the theme of friendship as a structure of unwanted social relations is much more thoroughly developed in the *Interlude of Youth*, where Youth is shown forming social ties with his (bad) friends and where the severing of those ties once Youth is "saved" becomes a moment of ideological rupture in the play. When the play begins, Youth is already situated in a marginal social space, detached from familial or other authorized social connections: lacking brother, father, or governor of any kind, he has already "fallen" and is engaged in riotous living, unlike Mankind who has to be tempted by the vices. Mankind may be teetering on the edge of despair and revolt, needing only a push to send him over, but Youth is defined as lost to orthodoxy from the outset. "Are you so disposed to do," Charity asks him early in the play, "To follow vice and let virtue go?" "Yea, sir, and even so," replies Youth (60–62).

When we first meet Youth, he is flaunting his disregard for social norms. The play shows him shoving his way through the audience and boasting about his body, loudly proclaiming his disregard for all rules or constraints and planning to run through his inheritance with the help of riotous living. "I am a goodly person" (42), he gloats, "My body pliant as a hazel stick; / Mine arms be both big and strong; / My fingers be both fair and long" (49–51). "My legs," he adds, "be ful light for to run, / To hop and dance and make merry" (53–54). At first Youth thinks of virtue in terms of his vital, youthful body, rejecting Charity's argument that anyone trusting solely in his body will be damned while also ignoring Charity's ominous warnings about what old age will do to his body. His bodily vigor has the effect of motivating indifference to regulations—"By the mass, I reck not a cherry / Whatsoever I do!" (15–56)—as does the fact that he is heir to his father's lands (57). In short, the play's protagonist represents the epitome of healthy, vigorous, unfettered, and well-financed masculine youth, poised, as Charity recognizes, to follow vice, not virtue (60–61). What unfolds in the play is an extended attempt to force Youth to submit to the demands of authority and to come back under the sway of normative social structures.

Much more so than in *Mankind*, the protagonist here is the master of his own misrule, needing little coaxing to swerve from the sanctioned route. As a mark of his proclivities for vice, Youth himself takes on the mocking role of Mischief and derides all of Charity's warnings, particularly that age will soon undermine his vigor, while also belittling Charity's promise that heavenly bliss will be his if he follows the proper path. Living for the moment, Youth rejects all concerns for the future, whether earthly or heavenly. More significantly for the theme of submission to authority, Youth assaults Charity with a battery of nonsense questions, attacking him where it hurts most by challenging Charity's claim to be an authority figure justified in offering advice. This challenging is then developed into a full-blown fight as each side leaves to marshal support: Charity to enlist Humility to help him, and Youth to find his companions Riot and Pride.

In the ensuing battle between the opposing sides, the chief issue is whose counsel Youth should take. Throughout this long scene, although Charity tries to frame the action as a battle between virtue and vice in which his own part is to "convert" Youth, the real point is who has the right—and the power—to control Youth. Co-opting the language of instruction found in conduct books, each side in turn attempts to persuade Youth to obey its precepts. "Do by our counsel and our rede," Charity pleads (607). Riot counterattacks by telling Youth that if he follows Charity's "school" he will be a fool, then lists for Youth everything that he can "teach" him, including dicing, card games, and "many sports mo"

(679–89). Impressed by this advice, Youth thanks Riot and promises to "guide me after thy learning" (693). In this scene, the question of good counsel and of the suitability of the counselor—a question never raised by the hyperconfident textuality of conduct books—is brought to the surface as doubts about the social utility of advice and the motives of advisers are explored.

The argument between Riot and Charity over who should "rule" Youth turns on two important issues: the problem of sociability and the question of proper use of wealth. Sociability is understood by the play to be intricately connected with behavior, standing as one of the most crucial factors in determining how an individual will act. It is no surprise, then, that one of Charity's tactics is to try to undermine Youth's loyalty to his companions, urging him to "forsake them and do after us" (633). (This theme of "forsaking" will be evoked again at the end of the play with unsettling effects for the normative social system the play endorses.) Assuming that personal behavior is largely dependent upon social affiliations and fearing the individual's susceptibility to bad influences, Charity's words echo the warnings against socializing found in conduct books while also taking up the widespread fears against public assemblies and gatherings that find expression in so many late medieval civic regulations. The behavior of young men was, needless to say, a source of particular concern, not least of all because they were often only tenuously tied to sanctioned social networks. Banded together in same-age and same-sex groups, young men could hardly avoid looking like a challenge to hierarchically organized social relations, especially those revolving around age-based deference and heterosexual marriage.[43]

What is unusual about this play, however, is the perhaps unwitting sympathy it shows toward the desire for illicit forms of sociability. Although the dominant thrust of the play is to sever Youth's ties with the peers who are seen as leading him astray, the play also, and more conflictingly, pits loyalty to companions—however disreputable they might appear—against obedience to authority, highlighting the clash between the two in a way that does not entirely endorse the position of authority. Charity tells Youth that he must forsake Pride and Riot, speaking in terms that treat the two characters as abstract vices, but Youth's response frames them as real companions: "I will not him forsake," Youth replies, "Neither early ne late. / I weened he would not forsake me" (744–46). When in the end Charity, rather abruptly and unconvincingly, wins Youth over to his side, Riot and Pride berate Youth for forsaking them. Although this scene is intended to represent a conventional conversion from evil to good in which Youth must reject the abstract vices of riot and pride, it is infused with enough realistic emotion to be open to another reading. The protests by Riot and Pride, who sound more like real young men than abstract vices, that Youth is forsaking them conjure up the image not just of pernicious vices that refuse to be shaken off, but also of friends who are hurt by his rejection of them. When Riot says to Youth, "Once a promise thou did me make / That thou would me never forsake" (757–58), he calls attention to the fact that Youth's conversion requires that he both break his promise and cast aside his friends— neither of which the play is capable of treating as unambiguously virtuous acts. Unlike *Mankind*, where the vices are scuttled by Mercy with little ado and a singular lack of conflicting emotions, the *Interlude of Youth* has difficulty denying the vitality and value of affectional ties, no matter how socially proscribed. In the end, Youth is persuaded to abandon his companions and embrace his officially sanctioned social position, but that action is not seen as entirely without negative consequences.

The question of the proper use of wealth is similarly conflicted, once again being resolved in favor of an orthodox position but again without erasing some lingering doubts about the whole process. Since Youth has an inheritance, he is freed from the necessity of laboring, unlike Mankind; hence, economic questions in the play focus not on the proper getting of money but on the proper spending of it. The lesson Youth has to learn is not how to be a good, docile producer like Mankind, but rather how to be a good consumer. Avoiding exploration of the complicated problems of consumption that a wealthy young man might face and what might constitute "proper" consumer behavior for such a person, the play chooses instead to take the unproblematic position of complete rejection of all materiality not tied to spiritual ends. Correct consumption is thus defined in the play as the spending of money in pursuit of the pious life. When Charity "saves" Youth at the end of the play, he gives him new clothes and a rosary—consumer goods that are understood here as spiritual, not material, items—as aids for his new life of prayer, devotion, and preaching (767–75). Youth promises that he will devote himself from now on to mourning for his sins and turning other men from vice. In contrast to the loose spending that he engages in while under the influence of Riot and Pride—figured as drinking, gaming, and the buying of other pleasures— these pious acts reject all consumption, thereby turning Youth into the ultimate innocuous consumer, one easily integrated into a network of normative relations. By purchasing him an idealized social role as devout penitent, consumption would be channeled toward the necessary end of inserting Youth into the community, nullifying the danger he poses as a free and unattached social agent with an excess of money to spend; at the same time, however, portraying "good" Youth as a devout penitent fails to tackle the question of acceptable kinds of consumption for affluent young men.

As they argue over who should rule Youth, Riot and Charity address the question of consumption in terms of the profitability of virtue. From the start, Youth rejects the notion dear to conduct books that virtue is profitable. Instead, he boasts that he has been "promoted to high degree" (591) above dukes, lords, barons, and knights, who are "subdued to me by right, / As servants to their masters should be" (595–96). Casting aside socioeconomic standards and norms of virtue, Youth relies on bodily vigor, wealth, and freedom from constraints to create for himself an exalted social position. As Pride advises him:

> Above all men exalt thy mind.
> Put down the poor, and set nought by them.
> Be in company with gentlemen.
> Jet up and down in the way,
> And your clothes—look they be gay.
> The pretty wenches will say then,
> "Yonder goeth a gentleman,"
> And every poor fellow that goeth you by
> Will do off his cap and make you courtesy.
> (344–52)

Although the play means to suggest that Youth is deluded in this understanding of his own status, it never shows any of the detrimental effects his delusion has. At the same time, the play fails to offer a convincing alternative model of virtuous behavior leading to the presumptive pleasures of the same high status. Instead, the play tends to affirm Youth's own self-image, hence valorizing his circumvention of the normative system—intentionally or not.

In these ways *Youth* shows itself unable, or unwilling, to impose the orthodox line with complete success. Having created an image of the fun-loving, vigorously free, and wealthy young male, the play itself seems somewhat seduced by that image, incapable of erasing it entirely in the end. Although Youth is made to come around to the demands of authority, to accept the conditions of virtuous behavior imposed upon him by Charity, the play's ending raises both questions about what Youth is being asked to give up and doubts about how desirable the virtuous life is. It is especially telling that we are left in the end with Youth launched on a career of incessant proselytizing in which he promises to become a good counselor to all "misdoing men" (778), whom he will exhort to change their ways. Having shown us pure unfettered desire, the play leaves us with its eternal repression. The upshot is that the play's representations of misbehavior remain enticing, evading satisfactory recuperation into social norms.

Pettitt argues that, like *Mankind*, *Youth* was probably written for

household Shrovetide revels. Like *Mankind*, *Youth* is indeed full of festive revelry and shows a number of parallels with mummers' plays. And
the vices in *Youth* challenge Charity, the messenger of virtue, in a way
that suits the transitional season of Shrovetide much as the vices in
*Mankind* worked against Mercy.[44] Ian Lancashire has posited that *Youth*
was associated with the household of the earls of Northumberland,
whose servants performed plays at the seasonal intervals of Christmas,
Easter, and Shrovetide.[45] More specifically, Lancashire argues that *Youth*
was originally acted at the household of Henry Algernon Percy, the fifth
earl of Northumberland, possibly for the benefit of his eldest son Henry,
whom the father apparently thought ungovernable. According to Lancashire, the play is a kind of dramatic conduct book that "can be understood as prudent advice to a landed heir of noble blood and class."[46] If this
is the case, however, one wonders how effective the play was in inculcating its advice, given its inability to dismiss completely the misbehaviors
it attempts to proscribe. Moreover, what would young Henry have
thought, watching servants of his father's household playing these mischievous roles presumably for his benefit? This uncomfortable reversal of
power relations might have further undermined whatever coercive force
the play was supposed to have.

Although its original auspices seem to have been as part of Shrovetide
revels in a noble household with an unruly young heir, the play quickly
entered the repertory of sixteenth-century interluders and was acted up
to Elizabeth's reign, suggesting that its theme of youth in rebellion was a
popular one that played well to other audiences. *Youth* also proved successful when revived in the early years of the twentieth century and was
staged in England by Nugent Monck in numerous productions from 1905
to 1907.[47] This continued popularity says something about the resilience
of the play's concerns as well as its dramatic vitality.

## Loose Woman

The inability to contain the allure of transgressive behavior, which I have
been arguing is a formative feature of *Mankind* and, to a greater extent,
the *Interlude of Youth*, is at its most extreme—and bears the most significant consequences—in *Mary of Nemmegen*, a fascinating female Faust
story. The story exists in two early versions. One is a Dutch text of dramatic verse interspersed with prose passages, known as *Mariken van
Nieumeghen*, which was printed by Willem Vorsterman of Antwerp
around 1515; the other is an English prose tale printed around 1518 by Jan
van Doesborch of Antwerp, who apparently kept a shop in London. Although the precise relationship between the two versions remains uncertain, both are assumed to derive from an older, no longer extant

Dutch prose version, which the English narrative is usually taken to follow more closely than the existing Dutch text.[48] The prose and dramatic verse sections of the extant Dutch version appear to be the work of two different writers, the dramatic verse composed by a *rederijker* (rhetorician), who was a member of one of the *Rederijkerskamers* (Chambers of Rhetoric) popular in the Low Countries in the late Middle Ages. The *Rederijkerskamers* were cultural guilds that wrote poetry and performed plays in competitions around the country, in the process disseminating such texts to a wider public.[49]

In the discussion that follows, I will focus on the English prose version, referring to the Dutch play when relevant. In doing so, I am not trying to argue that the English version was ever performed; indeed there is no evidence to suggest this. Instead, I take *Mary of Nemmegen*, like the extant Dutch version, which frames its dramatic verse sections within expository prose narrative, to be a narrative that represents in printed form the plot, characters, and themes that were staged in the Dutch play. As such, *Mary of Nemmegen* can be seen as a reading version of the enacted play, and in fact it has a distinctly dramatic flavor, particularly in its vivid and effective use of dialogue and its many woodcuts, which provide visual cues for the reader. In addition, given the close commercial and cultural ties between England and the Low Countries, it is possible that some of the English readers of Van Doesborch's book, who might have been drawn from the merchant traders who frequented the Low Countries' fairs and their attendant festivities, including plays, might have seen *Mariken van Nieumeghen* performed there, as also might the English travelers and pilgrims who passed through the Low Countries. At any rate, Van Doesborch apparently had reason to assume that his book would find a receptive audience among English readers.[50]

Moreover, although there is no evidence to show that *Mary of Nemmegen* was ever performed in England, there was a close connection between the popular drama of England and the Low Countries that is only now beginning to be explored. The Dutch morality play *Elckerlijc*, which was also a product of the Chambers of Rhetoric, has been shown to be a precursor to *Everyman*; *Eerste Bliscap*, a play on the life of the Virgin, has been linked with the N-Town Virgin sequence; and other ties between the drama of the two countries have recently been identified—for example, civic pageants sponsored by English merchants resemble the Flemish *ommegang* (processions, tableaux, marching giants, and other figures) they might have seen on trading trips to the Low Countries.[51] If the pattern of transmission of *Everyman* is typical, then plays from the Low Countries reached England through the printing presses that flourished in both countries, were translated, sometimes made it to the stage, and in either case became part of a shared culture, especially in London and other trading centers. In discussing the printed narrative version of *Mary of Nemmegen* as a morality, I am assuming that although it takes a representational form different from that of *Mankind* and *Youth* and so has somewhat different cultural functions, particularly in terms of audience dynamics, it nonetheless shares with them similar concerns.

Unruly wives show up in a number of late medieval performances in England, such as *Johan Johan*, Lydgate's *Mumming at Hertford*, and the "Noah's Flood" pageants from the Corpus Christi dramas. Less frequently represented is the unruly *girl*—a story whose plot and characters could easily be created, however, out of the proscriptions in *How the Good Wife Taught Her Daughter*. *Mary of Nemmegen* is thus a rare late medieval exploration of the social phenomenon of the unruly girl, one that features anxieties about parenting as well as about the parameters of young female behavior—anxieties that were explored from a masculine perspective in the *Interlude of Youth*. Focusing on the powers and dangers of the young female body, as well as on the dynamics of female desire within a consumer culture, the narrative takes on risky cultural material.[52] Much more so than *Mankind* or the *Interlude of Youth*, *Mary of Nemmegen* reveals the ideological cracks that cannot be papered over by the attempt to recuperate the sinful protagonist and reinscribe her within the dominant social order. In the end, the narrative shows itself remarkably unable to contain the desirability of the loose female behavior it wishes to proscribe, except by applying the most viciously repressive measures whose brutality undermines the recuperative effort.

The story begins with Mary located in the safe space of her uncle's house, where she is sheltered from the dangers of the world. But, in a move that can be interpreted as a lapse in good parenting, the uncle launches his niece on her misadventures. Sending her alone to Nemmegen to the market, he warns her that if she is delayed she should go to her aunt's house for the night. Mirroring the glimpses in *How the Good Wife Taught Her Daughter* of the pitfalls of the public sphere for women, a landscape of danger faces Mary as soon as she leaves her uncle's house. Unbeknownst to Mary, her aunt is an ill-tempered political partisan and scold who on that same day "had chyd ayen .iiij. or v. women" in defense of the young duke of Guelders, whom she supported.[53] Innocently following her uncle's advice, Mary shows up on her aunt's doorstep, where she is greeted "knapysly and angerly" by her aunt, who accuses her of both drunkenness and sexual license: "For I knowe well that the yonge men of vyllages can teche maydens the nygght daunses in the corne," the aunt says (34–35).[54] Through these lapses in guidance and nurture on the part of the uncle and the aunt, the play probes an issue never entertained by the untroubled self-help world of conduct books: what happens if parental advice is bad or if an authority figure is evil? Mary's downfall is thus set up as the direct result of the inappropriate behavior of those who are authorized to protect and control her, raising questions about the late medieval assumption that women and girls are to be policed by fathers and husbands.

Driven away by her aunt, Mary sinks into despair and in this vulnerable state is approached by the devil in the form of a one-eyed man named Moenen. Making clear the gendered nature of the temptation and sin that will follow, Moenen promises her that if she will give in to his desires, he will make her "a woman aboue all other women" (73). This exaltation above other members of her sex involves giving her knowledge, in the form of Moenen's pledge to teach her the seven sciences as well as many languages, in addition to wealth: he promises her "manye other costely iewelles and also money" (91). Importantly, Moenen also offers her self-governance and the freedom to do what she wants—"you shall haue all your owne pleasure to do that thynge that ye wyll desyre" (92–93)—so that no other woman will have the pleasure she will have. The terms of this temptation are important. Mary is presented not only with wealth and worldly pleasures but also, like Faust, with knowledge. More crucially, she is also promised what is tantamount to an escape from the female condition in which subjugation is the norm. In contrast to the glimpses we get of her previous life with her uncle where, we are told, she "dyd all yt was to do" (8) in his house, suggesting a round of endless domestic drudgery and subservience, what Moenen holds out to her looks distinctly appealing.

Agreeing to Moenen's offer, and fully aware that he is the devil, Mary goes with him to a tavern—the spatial antithesis of the household—where, in a symbolic act of conviviality that marks Mary's changed state, they "made good chere with reuelynge and daunsynge and payde for euery man that cam in theyr company" (150–51).[55] At this point her uncle rather belatedly starts to worry, expressing his concern "that she shulde myscarye nowe, synes I haue browght hyr vp of a chylde" (159–60). As these lines suggest, however, her uncle seems more concerned about how Mary's behavior might reflect upon his own reputation as a guardian rather than about Mary's safety. Meanwhile, Mary and Moenen go to Antwerp where they "reuell and playe and spare for no coste" (199), making "reuell and mysse rule" for a long time (250).

As in *Mankind* and the *Interlude of Youth*, a connection between pleasure, play, and consumption is developed in these scenes in the tavern where Mary revels in misrule with Moenen. Having substituted prostitution for marriage and so having entered into an unnatural form of female sexual relations, Mary plays out her subversive role as devil's house-wife.[56] In a perversion of the proper domestic economy, she uses her knowledge and skills to aid Moenen in entrapping men, duping them out of their money through various con games. Once again, the threat to the dominant economic order that is posed by free spending with no productive labor is a focal point, here underscored by the many men slain through Mary's doing. The work Mary is engaged in, located within the tavern rather than the household, framed by prostitution rather than marriage, and featuring lavish expenditure rather than housewifely thrift, is clearly set up as a devilishly deviant form of female labor. But the narrative cannot entirely conceal the fact that Mary leads a life of freedom and pleasure with Moenen. These scenes make overt the central paradox of the play in terms of female desire: satisfaction of female desire is by the definition of masculine rule criminal and sinful, leading men to their deaths, yet it brings women pleasure. The price of female submission to masculine authority is thus brought to the surface at this point.

After six years, Mary becomes aware that she has been living "vycyouselyy & synfully" (270). Despairing that it is too late for her to repent, she nevertheless convinces Moenen to go back home with her. They arrive in her town on the day of a church dedication when a play is being performed. Recalling her uncle's words that a play is often better than a sermon, Mary goes to watch the performance, which turns out to be about "synfull lyuynge" (331). Recognizing the play's relevance to her own situation, she begins to repent "hyr mysse lyuynge" (335). But Moenen, not willing to let her go, takes her in his claws and carries her up into the air, then casts her down, hoping to break her neck. Her uncle, who happens to be at the play as well, witnesses this spectacle and then recognizes Mary. Unhurt by Moenen's tricks, Mary gives her uncle an abbreviated story of her life with the devil, omitting the murders and other crimes, saying only that in that time "haue there many wonders be done" (388). The two then set out in search of someone who will absolve Mary, ending up eventually in Rome before the pope.

At this moment, when the story must do its work of redeeming and recuperating Mary, the ideological stresses are most obvious. In order to bring Mary back into the acceptable pattern of female behavior, the story first downplays what might be seen, especially from a female perspective, as the positive aspects of Mary's life with Moenen, particularly the attractions of freedom and knowledge that figured so prominently in Moenen's seduction of her. To this end, when the pope asks why she went with the devil, Mary replies that his gifts of gold and silver and also the pleasure she had with him, dancing and playing, made her do it (453–56). Through this recasting of her temptation as based on money and pleasure—not knowledge and freedom—she herself is made to participate in the restructuring of her fall that is necessary for her reintegration into the social fabric, denying that anything beyond mere greed induced her to agree to join Moenen.

The brute force required to effect Mary's reintegration into a normative social order is most starkly revealed when the pope gives Mary three
iron rings to bind herself with, promising her that when they fall off her
sins will be forgiven. Mary then enters a nunnery of the order of Mary
Magdalene, full of converted sinners who like her had also been "mysse
women" (508–9). For twenty-four years she fasts and prays until at last
God has mercy on her and undoes the rings from her neck and arms. She
falls on her knees, thanks God, and asks people to "take a ensample of
me" and amend their wretched living. The narrative ends with Mary's
death two years later.

As this summary suggests, the problem of containing the seductive-
ness of unruly behavior is full-blown in *Mary of Nemmegen*. Salvational
closure may be handled fairly convincingly in *Mankind*, shutting off the
appeal of the life offered by Mischief and the vices and, to a lesser extent,
in the *Interlude of Youth*, but it falls short in *Mary of Nemmegen*. The
advantages of Mary's life of freedom, adventure, and knowledge combine
with the narrative's inability to make her "salvation" look like something other than bondage and punishment to undermine the logic of the
morality play wherein bad behavior is punished while good behavior is
rewarded. When Mary first falls into sin, she is leading a life of what appears to be absolute female virtue—chaste and obedient—but her virtue
proves no protection and perhaps even increases her susceptibility (if she
had been less docile and more worldly, the play leads us to suspect, she
would have been more immune to her aunt's invective). Her life of sin,
once she falls into it, looks highly desirable—full of ease, freedom, and
comfort. And her salvation, after she repents, seems more imprisonment
than release from sin. Given these narrative twists, the story simply cannot succeed in its intended project of single-mindedly impugning Mary's
years with Moenen and valorizing her salvation through life in the convent. It has been argued that *Mariken van Nieumeghen* reveals cultural
tensions between Dominican thought and traditional rhetoricians' ideas
about salvation, on the one hand, and humanist notions about art and
knowledge on the other.[57] Certainly this offers a partial explanation of
the problem the English version of the story has with imposing satisfactory closure, but I suspect much more is going on.

I would argue that the problem of closure has to do with the clash between female desire and the social needs of a masculinist order, a clash
that cannot be successfully resolved within the structures of late medieval culture. Like Mary Magdalene, Mary of Nemmegen is constructed
at the dangerous intersection of sexual license and knowledge, of feminine and masculine. Moenen seduces Mary through the offer of knowledge, although he also offers to furnish her with material wealth. But her
knowledge, linked as it is to sexual abandon and hence unrestrained by

proper gender and social hierarchies, is figured as literally destructive of the masculine order—it kills men. Just as her aunt's unbridled tongue is associated with political disorder, so too is Mary's unbridled body connected with a breakdown of social order.[58] Late medieval English society was preoccupied with norms of sexual behavior, if court cases can be taken as accurate evidence of social attitudes: marital and sexual issues account for a majority of the business of the church's lower courts.[59] It was equally concerned with regulating speech, particularly female speech, which like the open mouth posed threats to an imagined social harmony. Both the scold's tongue and the wanton's body are seen in this play as sins against patriarchal communal ideals of peacefulness and orderliness. By giving rein to her desires, Mary moves out of the sphere of order into disorder, pleasing herself but disturbing normative relations. In this way, the satisfaction of female desire—whether understood in sexual terms or as the attainment of intellectual and material goals—is cast as invariably at odds with (masculine) communal needs. The class as well as the gender bias of these communal needs is suggested by an oral version of the story of Mary of Nemmegen, recorded in the nineteenth century, which ends with her uncle's triumph over the devil and leaves out the harsh confession and penance segments.[60] This version perhaps represents a more popular, that is lower-class, perspective, for which unruly females pose less of a threat.

The only way Van Doesborch's narrative, which was probably aimed at the prosperous urban commercial classes and perhaps at male readers, can recuperate the unruly girl, however, is by rejecting her dangerous sexuality entirely. Too potent to be reintegrated into the social order in the role of niece, which she had once occupied, or of wife, which she might once have aspired to, Mary can in the end only be safely housed within the fenced-off territory of the nunnery, where along with other women like her she can be lodged in a socially secure space.[61] The three iron rings that she is made to wear point to the enormity of the danger she represents, one that requires physical bondage to prevent her from wreaking havoc. Breaking the code of domesticity through her illicit sexuality, her perversion of nurture, and her usurpation of male prerogatives of freedom and knowledge, Mary subverts both family and community, becoming an enemy of society who is figured as an enemy of God.[62] As a dangerously unruly woman, Mary has to be doubly subjugated, first through physical bonds and then by enclosure in the socially walled-off space of the nunnery. The result of this highly overdetermined closure in which authority is brutally and literally reimposed on the female body is to make unavoidable a confrontation with the mechanisms of domination. In the figure of Mary we can see the operations of masculine power on the female body, binding it and walling it off from the social realm, all in the name of salvation.[63] The most lasting impression of *Mary of Nemmegen* is, then, an awareness of the heavy-handed repressiveness of orthodoxy played out against the undeniable desirability of female misbehavior—especially from the perspective of the woman who might contemplate engaging in it.

## Lingering Desires

In their emphasis on sin and salvation, these three moralities drive home a definition of individual behavior in which the body is carefully controlled for the ends of proper labor and acceptable consumption. By ritually exorcising antisocial tendencies—whether portrayed in the body of the discontented worker, the rebellious youth, or the wanton woman—these moralities work at the behest of the existing social order. In this process, misbehavior is defined as vice or sin, something to be immediately and thoroughly rejected for the most compelling of reasons, the ultimate salvation of one's soul. But, as I have endeavored to show, misbehavior in these moralities constantly escapes this normative reading. Even at their moments of greatest transgression when they would seem to be least susceptible to a sympathetic reading, Mankind, Youth, Mary, and the vices and devils who tempt them look less like cautionary examples whose behavior is to be avoided at all costs than like symbols of the satisfaction of personal desire whose escape from social control offers many inducements for imitation.

As Foucault's work on discipline suggests, late medieval England can be said not merely to have identified misbehavior but also to have produced and then used it in its drive toward social control of the embodied subject.[64] Misgovernance of the kind found in the moralities was indispensable to the construction of the late medieval social order, required as a way of marking subjects with the signs of their social positions. In this way, the refusal to behave in a socially sanctioned manner could be both a sign of power and of resistance to it. As instances of resistance and despite their conscription into the service of orthodoxy, the unruly bodies of characters in moralities also act out alternate, less socially acceptable models of subjectivity. In so doing, they shift the boundaries of permissible behavior, however slightly, redrawing the lines for normative identities.[65]

What makes this enactment of alternate identities so significant is its potential effect on spectators, an effect that is admittedly hard to discover. Although modern cinema involves a rather different technology of looking than that informing medieval drama, studies of film spectatorship nonetheless offer some useful suggestions for reconstructing late medieval audience-actor dynamics. Recent film theory argues that viewers of the cinema are adept at negotiating complex and seemingly conflicting patterns of identification. When watching a film, spectators alternately identify with representations of themselves (as victims or heroes) and then with apparent antagonists (killers or villains). Although screen killers or villains—evil characters who seem to be set up as socially unregenerate and hence nothing like the viewers—would appear to block rather than encourage audience identification, that is not always the case; instead, viewers can move back and forth between heroes and villains, continually taking up different subject positions and alternately identifying with one or the other.[66]

These patterns of shifting and conflicting identification posited by film theorists argue that spectators—and readers, in the case of *Mary of Nemmegen*—might have felt an affinity not just for Mercy, Charity, and other representatives of obviously virtuous behavior who were supposed to be the plays' most virtuous and hence sympathetic characters, but also for Mischief, Riot, and Moenen, not to mention the protagonists who waver between the two extremes. Although moralities sought to make their misbehaving characters perform as antimodels that, in the words of one critic, would "serve the serious parts by illustrating the allegory and by underlining the moral teachings through parody and negative example,"[67] spectators were free—and in many cases were encouraged by the text and perhaps even more so by the actors' vivid dramatization of their misbehaving characters' roles—to respond empathically to them. In this way, the misgovernance of these characters might well have escaped the ideological limits placed on them by the plays, functioning as Stubbes feared they would—as attractants rather than repulsants. In the end, their unruly bodies linger as imaginative undoings of normative standards of bodily control and social coercion, embodiments of desires that refuse to be repressed.

CHAPTER 5

✣

# Devoted Bodies:
## Books of Hours and the
## Self-Consuming Subject

*How shulde I rede in þe book of peynture and of ymagerye?*
*—Dives and Pauper*

S ometime in the early sixteenth century in what was probably a per-
fectly ordinary transaction, the Tourotte family of northern France
came into possession of a luxurious book of hours. One of their first
acts upon acquiring this devotional book was to stamp it with the signs
of their ownership, which they did by commissioning two new illuminations of themselves for insertion into the book and by arranging to have
two existing illuminations emended.[1] In the first of the new illuminations, the Tourotte family—father and son, mother and daughter—are
depicted kneeling in prayer within what looks like a room, possibly a
chapel, in a private house (see figure 1). On tapestry-covered tables in
front of their kneeling figures lie open books of hours. The wall in the
background behind the family is covered with an elaborate floral design,
and they are benevolently watched over by Saints Anthony and Peter,
who stand shelteringly near them. In the second illumination, which appears across the page from the first, Tourotte and his wife—dressed in the
same costumes that they wear in the first picture—kneel outdoors on
desolate ground in a barren landscape beneath a larger-than-life grinning
death's head; God floats above their heads, while Jesus and the Virgin
Mary intercede on their behalf. The scene is bleak and comfortless (see
figure 2).[2]

What is most striking about the Tourottes' decision to mark possession of their book of hours by painting into it images of themselves is in
fact its conventionality. Although this act of self-inscription might strike
us as extraordinarily narcissistic and possessive, it was a fairly ordinary
occurrence within the representational form of the book of hours, especially in its more luxurious manifestations. From royalty to anonymous
bourgeois owners, those with the means to do so routinely had themselves painted into the books of hours they commissioned, claiming the
book as their own and projecting themselves into its sanctified devotional space.[3] In so doing, they left for us alluring traces of their subjec-

Figure 1. The Tourotte Family Praying with Saints Anthony and Peter. The Tourotte Hours. The Walters Art Gallery, MS W. 222, fol. 1v. France, Poitiers, ca. 1465; fol. 1v added in the early sixteenth century. By permission of the Walters Art Gallery, Baltimore, Md.

Figure 2. God with Christ and the Virgin Interceding on Behalf of the Tourottes. The Tourotte Hours. The Walters Art Gallery, MS W. 222, fol. 2. France, Poitiers, ca. 1465; fol. 2 added in the early sixteenth century. By permission of the Walters Art Gallery, Baltimore, Md.

tivity, identity markers on painted vellum that convey complex attitudes toward a self bold enough to intrude upon sacred territory.

The two owner-portraits added to the Tourotte Hours deserve a closer look. In the first illumination, the Tourottes are shown praying together *en famille* in a comfortable domestic interior where they are sheltered by the protective embrace of Anthony and Peter. The image exudes calm, stability, and security. Surrounded by material comforts and kneeling peacefully before their open prayer books, the Tourottes look serene, self-satisfied, and content—the very picture of prosperous and stable domesticity. In the second self-portrait, the mood is quite different. Here mutability and fear, not stability and contentment, are the focal points. In this illumination, *père* and *mère* Tourotte kneel alone on either side of a leering skull; the Virgin Mary and Christ appear behind them, not offering protection or shelter, but looking away from the Tourottes up to the imposing figure of God overhead. The landscape is desolate, empty, and rock-strewn. There is no security, no safety, no peace here, but only the ominous signs of immanent death and bodily decay. It is as if the Tourottes have been snatched away from bourgeois bliss into a landscape of perpetual loss.

The contrast between these two illuminations, I wish to suggest, points to an important concern that lies at the heart of the subjectivity constructed by owner-portraits in books of hours—the topic of this chapter. Safety versus danger, permanence versus decay, enclosure versus rupture, docility versus threat—in these oppositions we are shown a visual testimony to the themes of permanence and change as projected onto the embodied subject positioned within devotional space. In the one portrait, we see a domesticated, stable subject secured against the vicissitudes of time by a comfortable interior space. In the other, however, we can discern a vulnerable and anxious self, a subject kneeling precariously in an apocalyptic terrain, exposed to the mutability of time and the body, where domesticity offers no safeguard. The contrast between these two portraits provides a useful opening into some of the cultural processes that, I wish to argue, are at work in owner-portraits. These portraits, on the one hand, can be read as important moments in the construction of a docile, self-contained, and devoted subject; they also, however, as the second Tourotte portrait so dramatically reveals, undermine the very stability and permanence of the subject they create and display.

One of the most remarkable aspects of these owner-portraits is the way that they insert the self into the highly charged and exalted sphere of the devotional image. Owners are commonly shown in the presence of saints and other divine figures, witnessing and even participating in sacred events from the birth of Christ to the crucifixion. In at least one instance, the book's owner actually becomes a holy figure: in the Sforza

Hours, originally made for Bona Sforza in the late fifteenth century but inherited by Margaret of Austria, a portrait of Margaret is used for the face of Saint Elizabeth in a Visitation scene.[4] In such depictions, the self is made an equal of the holy subjects it worships, so that the act of devotion comes to involve self-worship as well, creating thereby a spectacular subjectivity in which the self is made the object of intense scrutiny. This scrutiny would have been all the more significant if the book of hours were used as it was intended to be, on a daily and even hourly basis as part of a ritualized devotional routine, in which the owner would return repeatedly to self-contemplation as part of the act of devotion, looking at him- or herself inhabiting the same plane of representation as saints and holy figures. Even if the book were not used on such a routine basis—if it were kept instead as an heirloom or prized investment, as the expensive format and pristine condition of some extant books of hours suggest was sometimes the case—extreme self-consciousness and valorization of the individual subject would nonetheless still be likely hallmarks of these portraits.

The subjectivity staged in owner-portraits was part of a general commodification of devotion in the late Middle Ages.[5] As commodities that were bought and sold, bequeathed and inherited, books of hours were more than just devotional texts. Conspicuous consumption in fact figured prominently into their popularity as they became desirable props in a social drama of public exhibition and status display. One fascinating consequence of this commodification of devotion was that owner-portraits also became implicated in the dynamics of consumption. In these owner-portraits the devout worshiper's body is taken as itself an object of consumption, something that could be contemplated—consumed without ever being used up—over and over again whenever the owner wished. One result of treating the owner's body as an item of consumption was a reification and commodification of the individual akin to what Roland Barthes has seen in certain seventeenth-century Dutch group portraits, which he describes as still-life paintings wherein the human body is fetishized as a material object annexed to "the empire of things."[6]

In the remainder of this chapter, I explore more fully these interrelated processes whereby the self in owner-portraits, immured within the trappings of its domestic interior and valorized by its position within the sanctified space of the devotional image, is taken as a commodity available for inexhaustible private consumption and scrutiny. These illuminations extend the project of conduct books, encouraging not only a self-controlled but also a self-conscious subjectivity in which individuals are asked to regard themselves as selves, thus, as happens also in conduct books, participating in their construction as well-behaved subjects. In the end, I return to the dichotomy presented in the Tourotte owner-portraits, where the perishability of the embodied subject surfaces as an unsettling disturbance of the notion of limitless consumption and material security.

Although many of my examples will be drawn from luxury manuscripts produced on the Continent, given the fact that most books of hours made for English owners came from the Low Countries and France, particularly Rouen, which became an important center of devotional book production during the years of the British occupation of France, the books I discuss can perhaps be taken as representative of the English trade in luxury books of hours as well.[7] Similarly, although many of my examples are from books of hours produced for the aristocracy, others come from less lavish books of hours marketed to the wealthy, pious, and status-conscious urban middle classes. Despite the routine production of these mass market books of hours, evidence suggests that personalizing touches such as owner-portraits could be added at the last minute at the request of the purchaser.[8] The claims I make about the subjectivity constructed by owner-portraits have to do, then, not just with aristocratic Continental book owners but also with the prosperous English bourgeoisie, for whom books of hours were important possessions.

## Commodified Subjects

To make sense, the dichotomy between the preserved and the perishable self, which I argue is a salient feature of the subjectivity modeled by owner-portraits, needs to be seen within the context of the material and symbolic complexity of books of hours as a cultural discourse. Three issues bear most significantly on the present discussion: the relationship of the luxurious books of hours that contained owner-portraits with the more modest versions that circulated in manuscript form or were produced by early printers as primers for the mass market; the position of books of hours within a wider field of representational practices that employed the media of devotional art to produce and make subjectivities visible; and the blurring of boundaries between religious and lay, public and private that was a central feature of the subjectivities constructed by and through consumption in books of hours.

Although lavishly illuminated books of hours designed for the luxury trade have attracted the attention of scholars, especially art historians, such luxury manuscripts represent only a small portion of the books of hours produced in the late Middle Ages, which were so numerous that they have been described as the best-sellers of the period.[9] In English wills, books of hours are the most frequently mentioned books, and they also formed a substantial part of the output of early printers.[10] Although manuscripts remained relatively expensive and scarce, by the late fourteenth century small devotional books could be bought in England for less than one shilling, thanks to technological and commercial changes, such as the use of paper instead of parchment, that resulted in the cheaper production of manuscripts.[11] Throughout the fifteenth century a boom in consumer demand for devotional books led to the increasing accessibility of manuscript books of hours, and the advent of print made them widely available to even more readers.

Whether in the form of luxurious illuminated manuscripts designed for the luxury trade or inexpensive manuscripts or primers printed for the mass market, books of hours were marketed as devotional aids aimed specifically at a secular readership, the lay equivalent of the monastic breviary. Made up of prayers to be read at set times of the day and featuring a variety of liturgical, biblical, and hagiographical material, a typical book of hours might include a calendar, Gospel sequences, the Hours of the Virgin, the Hours of the Cross, the Hours of the Holy Spirit, penitential psalms, the Office of the Dead, and the Suffrage of the Saints, plus miscellaneous prayers. Drawing on traditional liturgical materials, the book of hours adapted those materials to suit private use and to lead lay readers through a daily devotional program; the book of hours thus followed official public models of worship but reshaped them to conform to individual needs.[12] Although also taken to church services, especially during the sixteenth century, the book of hours was intended primarily for use on a daily basis within the context of the individual's private worship at home.[13] Along with such furnishings as the prie-dieu and the *petit tableau*, books of hours thus formed the centerpiece of a ritual of domestic, household devotion, part of a private culture of worship that focused inward on contemplation and meditation.

As "livres d'eglise, livres de foyer et livres d'instruction elementaire," books of hours were put to multiple uses.[14] Readers may have used books of hours in a variety of ways in public or in private, repeating the whole cycle or saying only a few prayers, perhaps in the morning, as is suggested in *How the Wise Man Taught His Son*. In the fourteenth century, the Menagier de Paris recommended that his wife follow a modified version of the monastic day, and a priest early in the fifteenth century advised a merchant to find a quiet spot in his home where he could say matins and vespers. Queen Isabeau, wife of Charles VII, read her hours at night, as can be deduced from payments in her account books for a "petite paellet d'yvoire pour attacher la chandelle quant la Royne dist ses heures."[15] Henry VI read his book of hours every day, as did Margaret Beaufort, Countess of Richmond.[16] The example of Cicely, duchess of York (1415–95), suggests that some lay people followed strict routines of devotion that closely mimicked monastic practices. Records of the royal household note that Cicely rose at seven and said matins with her chaplain, then heard a Low Mass in her chamber. After breakfast, she went to the chapel to assist at the office of the day and two Low Masses. At dinner she had various pious texts read to her, then spent the afternoon in contemplation and prayer, entering chapel for evensong. During supper she repeated to her companions the readings she had heard earlier in the day at dinner.[17] Cicely's daily devotional round implies that she was attempting to reproduce in the secular world patterns of spirituality associated with the religious life. For Cicely, and probably many other readers, use of the book of hours was an imitative devotional practice that offered access to a realm of official, monastic religiosity. And even for less rigorous users, like the Menagier's wife or the English merchant, the book of hours might have offered a way to integrate a ritualized form of piety into the demands of a busy domestic and business routine. As these examples suggest, books of hours responded to consumer demands for new kinds of spiritual aids, those that catered to a spiritual restlessness that was part of the laicization and privatization of religion in the late Middle Ages.[18]

Books of hours were also used for instruction and were in fact commonly referred to as primers. John Drury's *Parue latinitatis* mentions the instructional use of the book of hours, saying, "Primarium meum iacet in gremio meo qui scio matutinas sancte marie" (my primer lies on my lap as I learn my hours of the Virgin). As Bishop Grandisson's circular of 1357 seems to indicate, with its demand that teachers parse the matins and the hours, books of hours were also used as school texts. In the late fifteenth and sixteenth centuries booksellers often marketed their books of hours specifically for this purpose: in 1489 Gerard Leeu advertised his hours for "usualiter laicis syllabicatae," and an hours printed for F. Byrckman of London in 1514 was designed "pro pueris."[19]

Whether used for devotion or instruction—and admittedly these categories overlapped—books of hours were tied to the system of commodity production and consumption.[20] Bought, sold, bequeathed, and otherwise put into circulation, books of hours were more than devotional aids, their popularity as possessions evidenced by the remarkable numbers still extant today.[21] Like the holy dolls mentioned by Margery Kempe that were dressed up to resemble the Christ child and that women dandled on their laps, books of hours had a cultic function that derived from their status as precious objects.[22] Mere possession of a book of hours appears to have been ritually efficacious, whether or not the book was ever read on the daily, even hourly, basis demanded by its contents. The pristine state of a book of hours from Rouen, circa 1470, for instance, suggests that "the owner may have been proud to take it under her arm or in her hand—perhaps wrapped in a piece of precious velvet—when she went to church, but she certainly did not use it much."[23]

It can be seen that the efficacy of possession was often enhanced by public exhibition. Whether used at home or taken to church bound in a chemisette of cloth, books of hours transferred devotion from the hidden realm of private use to public exhibition.[24] One Italian visitor to England in 1550, for instance, remarked on women's propensity for taking rosaries and books of hours to Mass, where they were conspicuously shown off, sometimes to the point of distracting attention from the acts of worship taking place. As status-enhancing signs of conspicuous consumption, books of hours were often singled out for attack by social satirists, especially those criticizing the pretensions of the urban middle classes.[25] When a Middle English sermon criticized a woman, described as "a grett ientill," who took her book of hours to church to read from but looked up whenever any man entered or left the church, the book's use as a prop in a complicated game of social spectatorship and sexual desire is hard to overlook.[26] Although it is difficult to know for certain, it seems likely that many books of hours carried to church were not necessarily unique luxury manuscripts (the pristine Rouen hours discussed earlier has been described as a mass market book), hence suggesting that even more modest versions could be susceptible to commodity fetishism.[27] The numerous late medieval paintings that show individuals praying before a book of hours in their domestic chambers hint that even when used in private, books of hours were also fetishized to some extent, their possession an essential mark of rituals of devotion.

As signs of status display, books of hours, especially the more lavish versions, were key objects in the rites of social spectacle and self-presentation that historians have identified as a defining feature of middle-class urban culture.[28] The lavish Harley MS 2287, for example, was owned by a London stockfishmonger named Edward Gower.[29] Etienne Chevalier, the owner of the stunning Hours of Etienne Chevalier illuminated by Jean Fouquet, was of bourgeois origins, as was Jean le Meingre, who owned the Boucicaut Hours. Like the vogue for public ceremonials, fashionable dress, large houses, coats of arms, and monograms, books of hours expressed for wealthy urban individuals both pride of ownership and an individuality fashioned for public viewing. Spectatorship, both public and private, was thus at the heart of the social logic of books of hours. As part of the devotional process, the individual gazed at images in the book, including in many cases images of him- or herself, thereby cultivating a strong sense of self-regard. At the same time, the individual hoped to become an object of others' gazes, using the book of hours to attract attention. In this intermingling of self-display and devotion a high degree of self-consciousness about subjectivity was encouraged, especially regarding the subject's construction and its social positioning. Needless to say, this situation was not without irony, given that books of hours were supposed to encourage the user to lose him- or herself in the spiritual experience. This public-private dynamic also has significance for the self-contemplation that occurs with owner-portraits, which I shall discuss shortly.

At the simplest level, having a self-portrait painted into the book was one way of taking possession of it.[30] Like a signature, a nameplate, or scribbled marginalia, the portrait marked the owner's presence in the book and ownership of it. One effect of this act of ownership marking was to confer commodity status on the book, reinforcing its position as an item of consumption and casting it as an object possessed by the owner rather than as a tool, an aid, or a mechanism that could be used to attain spiritual satisfaction. Such marks of ownership may also have had an important psychosocial function, reiterating the self-worth and status of the owner. In the case of the Hours of Etienne Chevalier, for instance, in which the initials E. C. appear in almost every illumination, a kind of compensation for social inferiority might have been at work, given Etienne's nonaristocratic origins.[31]

But when owners had their portraits painted directly into the public imaginary of sacred space, a more complicated act occurred. As the owner was inserted into sacred scenes, witnessing the crucifixion, gazing at the Virgin and child, or being presented to God, sacred space was itself commodified, transformed into a devotional object that could be owned and consumed.[32] Linked in these multiple ways to processes of commodification, the owner-portraits in books of hours, like the books themselves, were positioned from the outset as items of consumption, a phenomenon that had important repercussions for the kinds of subjectivity they modeled.[33]

Finally, owner-portraits in books of hours have to be seen as only one of many other late medieval representational and discursive practices that drew on devotional art to render subjectivities visible. In such media as stained glass windows, panel paintings, and tomb sculptures, owner portraiture was used to create and ratify a sense of the self. Such instances of self-display could be orchestrated with great care and with detailed attention to the kind of image projected, as in the case of the tomb sculpture specified by Isabella Warwick in her will of 1439. Isabella asked that she be depicted "all naked, and no thyng on my hede but myn here cast bakwardys," and that she be surrounded by various saints, including her patron saint Mary Magdalene.[34] One crucial difference between books of hours and these other media of direct self-display has to do with public versus private consumption of the individual subject they put on view. Public portraiture was open to viewing by many spectators, but for the most part the portraits in books of hours were for private consumption, at least so long as the owner was alive and had not yet bequeathed or sold the book to someone else. Unlike tomb sculptures, the portraits in books of hours represented a peculiarly secret kind of self-presentation, a show put on for the privately viewing self who nonetheless had been trained in the arts of public looking by other devotional media.

## Enclosed Bodies

Circulating within this culture of devotion and consumption, the embodied self constructed by these illuminations and then consumed by the self-regarding owner of the book of hours was, perhaps not surprisingly, an explicitly material one, positioned within a private world filled up with material goods that enclosed and safeguarded the individual. The body of the owner in these illuminations is triply armored—by its clothing, by its conventional devotional pose, and by its location within an interior space defined by material plenitude. Within its layers of armor, the body is preserved, protected, and immobilized on the page. Jeffrey Hamburger has argued that in the late Middle Ages "images formed the very constituents of a distinctive spirituality that placed special emphasis on the body and that made the body itself a vehicle of transcendence."[35] Corresponding to a growing interest in the humanity of Christ, corporeal religious images and the experiential or affective devotion they promulgated contributed to a subjectivity based in the body. In the owner-portraits this bodily subjectivity was explored in relation to the viewer's own body, a body represented and constructed in a specific way within the devotional book.[36]

The representation of the viewer's body in books of hours is markedly at odds with the way other subjects of the meditative gaze—such as the bodies of saints and martyrs, the bodies of souls in hell's mouth or emerging from graves in Last Judgment scenes, and of course the naked body of the suffering Christ—were often depicted.[37] These bodies were often located outdoors in exposed spaces, deprived of the sheltering frame of interiors, wall hangings, and the whole panoply of domestic furnishings. They were typically portrayed wearing little or no clothing and being forced into tortured postures, stretched out, often with limbs akimbo, and subjected to various pains—flagellation, decapitation, piercing by arrows, evisceration, and crucifixion—that further penetrated and invaded the body. Thus in various illuminations we see Saint Andrew, his nude body spread-eagled on an X-shaped cross at the foot of a hill; Sebastian tied to a tree, naked but for a loincloth and bleeding from arrow wounds while two archers shoot more arrows into his body (see figure 3); Erasmus lying prone on the ground clothed only in a loincloth while his intestines are wound out through a slit in his abdomen; Catherine stripped to the waist and kneeling between the two broken wheels used to torture her; and Adrian seated on a stump, his bright red intestines spilling over his

Figure 3. The Martyrdom of Saint Sebastian. The Egmont Hours. The Walters Art Gallery, MS W. 719, fol. 134. Belgium, ca. 1440. By permission of the Walters Art Gallery, Baltimore, Md.

loincloth while executioners hack off his legs.[38] In these paintings, rupture and destruction are the themes, projected visually through naked, torn bodies and unsheltering landscapes.

In complete contrast, the bodies of owners are typically accoutered in fashionable and elaborate clothing, serenely arranged in tight devotional poses, and securely housed within a familiar, hospitable, domestic interior. Subjectivity in these images is constituted not only by but *as* an elaborate arrangement of pose, gesture, dress, props, and setting. What these illuminations suggest is that identity is not something that exists outside of these features, but instead is created by them and then, in a proleptic leap, becomes one with them. The embodied subject in such portraits is recognized as of the same order as the goods that surround it. In this way, the subject merges with the object world that encloses and concretizes it, becoming one with it. John Plummer has noted how the artist of the Hours of Catherine of Cleves, circa 1440, has filled his illuminations with everyday goods from bourgeois life, which are transformed into items of luxury through the painting style, especially through the stress on iridescence that emphasizes their glittering surfaces.[39] A similar effect can be found in other books of hours and extends also to portraits of their owners.

Within an arched enclosure in the center of the page, to give one representative example from the Hours of Adolph of Cleves and La Marck, circa 1480, Adolph is shown wearing ornate armor, hands folded and kneeling on a cushion before his prayer book, which lies on a stand draped with a richly embroidered cloth. Behind him is a decorative wall covering, and all around him hang luxurious draperies. The borders around the enclosure are filled with his coats of arms, mottoes, and monograms.[40] It would be difficult to imagine a subject more literally defended and defined by the trappings of his social position, protected by a luxuriously embracing domestic scene that at once valorizes the individual while also safeguarding him.[41] Here the individual subject, immersed in a rich milieu of consumer goods, becomes itself a commodity, another shiny object captured on the page for the viewer's gaze, available for consumption every time the owner looks through the book. Lodged within the material culture of the domestic world, the owner is frozen in place along with his possessions and made to look as luxurious and indestructible as they are.

Some illuminations in books of hours do show patrons more actively engaged than in the preceding example, but they are relatively rare. In the Hours of Catherine of Cleves, for example, a fashionably dressed woman who appears to be Catherine of Cleves is shown outside the door of her home distributing alms to three beggars holding out bowls. And Margaret of York, in another series of illuminations, is represented practicing seven pious acts.[42] Far more common, however, are representations such as those of the patrons in the Beaufort/Beauchamp Hours who appear in an Annunciation scene kneeling before open prayer books and who regard the scene as spectators, not participants.[43] In this, as in many other owner-portraits, the owner is made to adopt a conventional devotional pose. Shown kneeling in prayer, reading a devotional text, or gazing meditatively at a sacred image, the owner is constructed as essentially passive. This body engages in no dangerous activities, indeed, is entirely unmoving. Posed in a posture that reflects the sought-for calm of contemplation, the body of the owner is the model of composed and controlled subjectivity—in stasis, at rest.[44] Like the exemplary embodied subject sketched out by conduct books, this devout body accommodates itself willingly to the strictures of disciplinary control, adopting a harmlessly pious and docile posture.

At the same time, in a move that was perhaps shrewdly aimed at increasing desire to *become* this devout subject, the enclosed body is represented as unharmed as well as harmless. Bodily borders are intact—no open mouths, no limbs akimbo—and bodily integrity is preserved—no exposed flesh, no gaping wounds. Thoroughly disciplined by the devotional pose, the devout self is also protected by it.[45] Hence restraint becomes recoded in these paintings as security. In prayer or meditation, the body is figured as a fortress against danger, unbreachable and indestructible. Rendered inviolate by its compact and contained pose, the owner's body can comfortably contemplate itself, encountering no disturbing images or thoughts of bodily destruction. This promise of protection might have formed an important part of the ideological work of these portraits, inducing a reader to adopt the controlled subjectivity they modeled by seeming to proffer the advantage of self-preservation. An unusual exception to this pattern can be found in a book of hours from Champagne or Rouen made in the late fifteenth century for an owner of modest means; one illumination shows an outdoor scene in which Death with a spear attacks a woman, who is possibly the book's owner.[46] Although this scene has repercussions for the durability of the self modeled by books of hours, it can perhaps also be read as confirming the general strategy of protecting owners by objectifying them within secure domestic settings where they adopt salvific devotional poses.

Self-preservation based on a commodification of the body is further stressed by the positioning of the owner's body within the accumulated goods of the domestic interior. This interior tends to convey an impression of sheltered coziness, indicated in particular by the softly enveloping draperies, rich wall hangings, and other elaborate cloths and tapestries that feature prominently in many owner-portraits. In England, most items of domestic accumulation in noble and wealthy urban households were movable goods such as plate, wall hangings, armor, clothing, furnishings for the household chapel, and other furniture.[47] As Penelope Eames has suggested, such household furnishings could serve as props for a drama of the self: "Rooms were like the stage of a theatre in which certain basic props were permanent, and in which, by the deft arrangement of portable property, the area was transformed into an arena to suit the action which was about to take place."[48] In a late-fifteenth-century book of hours, the bedchamber is made the stage for a display of domestic devotion. The owner is shown kneeling in his chambers saying his morning prayers. The covers on the invitingly rumpled bed, which dominates the room, are turned down and the pillows are creased, vividly suggesting the voluptuous warmth of the bed that he has just left.[49] Other illuminations, such as one in which Gabriel presents a patroness, fill their interiors with vibrant colors and a wealth of detail, surrounding the owner by sumptuous carpets, patterned wall hangings, decorated ceilings, colored glass windows, and rich fabrics (see figure 4).[50] Although pride of ownership is undoubtedly part of what is displayed in the luxurious interiors depicted by these paintings, an additional effect is to locate the owner within a warmly domesticated interior that effectively walls the subject off from outside dangers.[51] Here another form of commodification and consumption, one that provides the material goods to furnish a comfortably padded domestic space, is enlisted in the service of constructing a safely enclosed subject.[52]

As this emphasis on enclosure suggests, self-absorption and inwardness are also often stressed in owner-portraits.[53] In a miniature for the Saturday Mass of the Virgin in Catherine of Cleves's book of hours, for instance, Catherine is painted into the emotionally charged scene of the crucifixion, yet she looks not up at the suffering Christ but down at her own hands folded in prayer. Such representations can be interpreted as graphic instances of interest in an interior subjectivity that encourages the individual to look within in order to find devotional inspiration but also to avoid direct confrontation with disturbing events.[54] This inwardness is vividly illustrated in a painting showing Mary of Burgundy at prayer. In this painting, Mary is shown seated in the foreground reading from her book of hours; her eyes are cast down toward the book in her hands. Directly behind her and dominating the picture is an open window through which can be seen a large chapel where the Virgin and child are seated; off to their left are a group of women, one of whom appears to be Mary of Burgundy.[55] The scene through the window, which seems to represent an image conjured up by Mary during her devotions, strongly attracts the viewer's gaze with its size as well as its richly detailed and dramatic scene; yet Mary's attention is not drawn toward it but remains intently focused on the prayer book in her lap. In a matching illumina-

Figure 4. Gabriel Presenting a Patroness. The Buves Hours. The Walters Art Gallery, MS W. 267, fol. 13v. Northern France or southern Belgium, 1450s. By permission of the Walters Art Gallery, Baltimore, Md.

tion from the same book of hours, another window opens onto the crucifixion scene; although the same pillow can be seen on the ledge in front
of the window, and a book is lying partially opened, the seat occupied by
Mary in the earlier illumination is now empty, its occupant not sharing
any representational space with the violent scene unfolding outside.[56]
These matched paintings suggest a devotion fervently directed inward—
toward the ultimate enclosure of the interiorized self and away from external disturbances.[57]

When we imagine Mary of Burgundy using her book of hours in her
daily devotions and coming across this image of herself looking inward—
into the book and thereby into the self—we are confronted with an inter-
locking series of images of self-scrutiny. Mary reading her book sees a representation of herself reading her book, while behind this representation
of herself is projected the presumed result of her reading—a conjured-up
meditational image of herself, once again, kneeling before the Virgin and
child. The embodied subject constituted by this scenario is walled off from
the outside world by its interiorized gaze. The owner's body, enclosed
within clothing, devotional pose, and domestic interior, is here further protected from contact with the external world by its own inward-directed
gaze. Prohibited even from looking outside, the self becomes absolutely
cut off from exteriority as it is constricted and contained by the private devotional regime that turns it in upon itself.

This tendency to discourage contact with the exterior world is a common theme even in illuminations where owners are not looking inward
but rather gazing raptly at holy figures. In the Boucicaut Hours, for instance, Marshal Boucicaut and his wife are shown praying to the Virgin
and child who float over their heads. Although prayer books are open on
the draped table between their kneeling figures, their heads are tilted
back and their eyes are directed upward toward the vision above them.[58]
They do not gaze outward or even at each other, but rather look toward
the vision. In this instance the eyes are employed less as senses that
allow the individual self to perceive and, by perceiving, to take in and
participate in the outside world than as organs that by looking inward—
in this case toward a conjured-up meditational image—provide access to
the divine.[59] Sight turned inward and used to call up the image of the
holy becomes a tool of devotion; the visions thus generated are taken as
signs that validate the devotional process.

Enclosed, controlled, passive, inert, and contained, the subjects of
owner-portraits become like the foodstuffs, utensils, and household objects surrounding them. Like everyday commodities, they are captured in
all their materiality on the page, a process that is intensified by the paintings' stylistic emphasis on surface rather than depth. Merged with the

world of goods that envelops them, these subjects thus become objects, offering themselves up for the viewer's consumption.

## Spectacular Subjectivity

As objects designed for visual consumption, owner-portraits were caught up in what might be described as a spectacular subjectivity, in which the owner was asked to gaze at him- or herself inhabiting the sacrally charged space of the devotional image.[60] In this way, visualization of sacred scenes involved also self-visualization. In his *Society of the Spectacle*, Guy Debord describes what he takes to be a new phenomenon of existence marking modern conditions of production in which "all of life presents itself as an immense accumulation of *spectacles*. Everything that was directly lived has moved away into a representation."[61] For Debord a salient feature of the spectacle is passivity. The viewer, cut off from experiential reality, which is now accessible only through representations, comes to exist in a state of passive spectatorship, reduced to the position of inert consumer of media images. In Debord's understanding, this passivity is both the means to and the end of a vast project of social coercion, which deliberately deprives the viewing subject of the ability to talk back, produce, or create.[62] The spectacle is thus an instrument of control that works by immobilizing viewers through the production of an overabundance of spectacular goods that saturate and paralyze by providing a simulacrum of satisfaction: "The real consumer," Debord says, "becomes a consumer of illusions."[63]

Although the dynamic of representation described by Debord and identified as a historical phenomenon linked to the development of advanced capitalism can be said to exist at least in part in relation to medieval owner-portraits, Debord's theorization of the spectacle as essentially passive and as offering illusions rather than access to experiential reality needs to be qualified. Popular devotional works such as the illustrated *Meditations on the Life of Christ* or the many illustrated Bibles certainly suggest the centrality of images to the experiential and affective piety of the late Middle Ages. And within late medieval religious practices, visualization was often understood as an aid to devotion.[64] In typical, although unusually detailed fashion, the *Zardino de oration* (Garden of prayer), an Italian handbook written for young girls in 1454, advises the worshiper first to visualize a well-known city as the setting for the Passion (or Last Supper, crucifixion, or whatever other sacred event is to be the topic of the meditation) and then to visualize well-known people as the people involved in the Passion—Jesus, the Virgin, the saints, and so on. The next step is to visualize all the stages of the action, moving from episode to episode through the entire event, meditating on each action.

Whenever the worshiper feels a sensation of piety, she is instructed to stop and savor it as long as it lasts.[65] Michael Baxandall argues that painters of devotional scenes could not compete with the particularity of the kind of imaginative visualizations recommended by such books as the *Zardino* and so had to craft illustrations that meshed with and encouraged them, providing a base on which pious people could draw.[66] The role of the devotional image, Baxandall suggests, was to guide meditation by acting as "rememoratijf or mynding signs" that could incite fuller visualizations and so lead to the most effective kind of meditation.[67]

Such devotional images were by no means consumed by spectators who saw themselves as passive. Medieval viewers, following Augustine's theory of vision as a ray projected onto the object that then passed into the viewer and bonded with the soul, understood themselves to be active agents in the visual experience. This active theory of spectatorship, although challenged at the end of the thirteenth century by Roger Bacon's theory of vision, which argued that the viewer is affected by the object rather than the other way around, dominated popular belief throughout the late Middle Ages.[68] This sense of the viewer's active role in the visual process meshes well with Michel de Certeau's assertion that consumers are active participants in processes of consumption.[69] While consumers in de Certeau's formulation are still dominated by the items of consumption surrounding them, they are dominated less unilaterally, less thoroughly, and more ambiguously than in most other models of mass culture, including Debord's. Although consumption is traditionally understood as the domain of passivity and inertia, de Certeau stresses how consumers can elude power by poaching on and appropriating the items of consumption the dominant culture assumes they will passively ingest. In this way, consumers can take charge of and transform to their own ends the images and goods they receive, although they will always do so, de Certeau claims, under the influence of forces of social control. Hans Belting notes that images in the Middle Ages were understood as part of an intersubjective dialogue that the viewer conducted with the subject in the image. The image thus acquired a communicative and instrumental power as spur to affective devotion and interacted with the viewer.[70] Far from being passive, the viewer often wept before the image, kissed it, and prayed to it. Anecdotes reveal how antagonisms might develop between viewer and image: an Italian shoemaker, for instance, became angry with a painting of Saint John that told him about his wife's unfaithfulness, cursed it, and threatened to abandon it.[71] Such responses were not aberrations but rather were deliberately invited by what Belting has described as "gestures of presentation" within painted images that invited the viewer to participate in them and to respond actively.[72]

Moreover, meditation on images was understood as offering immediate access to the "real" thing. Images were not viewed as abstract illusions but rather as ways of perceiving the religious world and so providing a route to direct sensory experience from which the worshiper might otherwise be shut off. As Belting has said, images articulated "the experience of a newly and personally accessible reality."[73] And that reality was made doubly accessible as individuals entered directly into the world of images when they had themselves inserted into tomb statuary, memorial stained glass, owner-portraits in books of hours, or other representational media. People understood themselves as being part of representational space, and their experience of themselves was to some extent shaped by the awareness that they were always on view.[74]

As devotional images that used vision to induce visions, the owner-portraits found in books of hours were involved in a complexly interwoven dynamics of voyeurism, identification, and reification that shaped the presentation of the devout subject for scopic consumption. Voyeurism takes two forms in owner-portraits. First, the contemplative subject's voyeuristic gaze apprehends the holy figure, who is in most instances the focal point of the painting. At the same time, as the reading subject regards him- or herself within the illumination, the voyeuristic gaze becomes caught looking into a mirror wherein it sees itself. Within late medieval private devotion, the inducement for contemplation is precisely the voyeuristic promise that sacred scenes will be revealed in all their immediacy to the successful worshiper. Hence, being able to see the divine figure in full vividness is the end goal, a goal graphically rendered in Margery Kempe's accounts of her visions. But as the contemplative subject is positioned within sacred space, sharing the visual frame with the holy figure, the reading subject also becomes caught up by the voyeuristic gaze—with a twist that turns it upon itself. In this way the self is asked to look at the self, gazing at it as if it were the same as the sacred image.

Jacques Lacan theorizes voyeurism by positing a split between "the eye and the gaze," suggesting that the eye sees from one point only, while the gaze, located in a place outside pure voyeurism, looks from all sides.[75] It is the gaze's function to catch the viewing subject in the act of voyeurism and so to force an awareness of the desire that motivates the voyeuristic viewing eye.[76] The gaze in this formulation would seem to be located outside the range of the eye, acting as a kind of metaperspective that subsumes the eye's glance. Aligning owner-portraits with these two ways of looking, we can construct a split reading-subject whose gaze is directed at the represented contemplative self, whose eye, in turn, like that of Mary of Burgundy, is directed inward or at the holy vision. The voyeurism of owner-portraits can be unsettling precisely because it calls attention to the split between eye and gaze, reading subject and represented self.

A second scopic operation, that of identification, operates to some degree in opposition to the voyeuristic gaze of the viewing subject, creating not so much alienation and estrangement as immediacy and recognition. As Belting observes, the devotional image was intended to interact mimetically with the viewer, who always "tried to relate himself to the depicted person."[77] Identification in fact marked late medieval spiritual devotions, particularly identification with an exemplary figure. As the popularity of hagiographical writings suggests, exemplars from the past as well as from the present were thought to embody the values of the community and to pass these values on to others through the mechanism of identification. Hence the holy or devout person was seen both as an exemplar of Christ and as a model for individual and communal behaviors.[78]

Within owner-portraits in books of hours identification was two-sided, echoing the split found in voyeuristic looking. First, the reading subject was asked to identify with the exemplary holy figure depicted in the painting, and then the reader was expected to identify with the representation of him- or herself. In the first form of identification, the reading subject is asked to adopt the subject position of the holy figure, becoming that person at least temporarily. The imaginative processes at work here are arrestingly revealed in pictures where the worshiper stands in for a divine figure, such as when Margaret of York takes the Virgin's place and has her vision of the resurrected Christ.[79] In the second form of identification, the reading subject is asked to identify with him- or herself engaged in an exemplary spiritual experience. In this instance, the represented self becomes a model for desirable behavior for the reading self, creating a loop between the real and the represented self.

Both kinds of identification—with the divine figure and with the exemplary self—structure a coherent identity shaped around devotion whereby the reading subject is offered a chance to recognize him- or herself in the officially sanctioned role of devout subject. But both kinds of identification also involve alienation, although to a lesser degree than in the operations of voyeurism. The reading subject is alienated from the divine subject, which is so patently different from the mere mortal. It is also, and more problematically, alienated from itself, that is, from the representational self that has been captured in paint and objectified on the page and with which the reader is asked to identify, but cannot ever fully do so. In the latter instance, the reading subject is forced to see him- or herself as an object, not a subject—as something outside and alien to the self rather than coterminous with it. The subject is thus confronted with its own reification as it is turned into an object before its own eyes. The duality of this process is similar to that posited by the Marxist theory of the commodity fetish, in which humans become objectified and alienated by the processes of production, while commodities take on the signs of human desire.

In this situation, the viewing subject is asked to gaze at him- or herself as simultaneously subject and object, to engage in both identification and voyeurism at the same moment. What this suggests is the importance not just of self-representation, but also of self-contemplation. John Benton argues that the frequent use of the third person in late medieval auto-biographical writings, such as Margery Kempe's reference to herself as "this creatur," does not represent an attempt at objective or disinterested examination of the self, but rather allows the writer "to appear as an actor in his own account."[80] But to appear as an actor in a drama of one's own scripting, or to refer to oneself as "this creatur," does seem to imply a splitting of the self into both subject and object, even if that objectification is by no means disinterested. A similar effect might have resulted from owner-portraits' objectification of the owner. In these pictures we can see the owner as one of the central actors in the ritual performance— a kind of participant-observer who both watches and is involved in the scene. Like the self-conscious social performances that Erving Goffman describes as "the presentation of self in everyday life," owner-portraits enact scenarios of how the owner wishes to be seen—crafting idealized images of the self available for constant scrutiny and replaying.[81]

One effect of this recurrent self-scrutiny might have been to under-score the sense of a stable, coherent, enclosed self projected by the picto-rial codes of the portraits. As the owner repeatedly came across his or her portrait in the course of using the book, the permanence of the self mod-eled by the content and style of the portraits would have been stressed. The message of this continual return to contemplation of the self might have been to suggest that, although the reading subject is vulnerable to change, the represented self encountered in the painting is not. Return-ing over and over again to the same self, depicted in the same safely en-closed space, the viewing subject was offered the chance to experience a sense of permanence, continuity, and immutability. Captured like a still life, the self was preserved for perpetual scrutiny, frozen in a state of con-tinual devotion.

At the same time, the repeated return to the image of the self also had the effect of valorizing the individual subject, testifying to its significance. As Jacques Derrida has argued, iterability is what makes signification possible in the first place: in order to mean anything, a sign has to be able to be repeated in a variety of different contexts.[82] Repetition is thus a nec-essary condition of meaningfulness. By enabling an endless re-viewing of the self, owner-portraits elevated the self out of the realm of the meaning-less into representation, iteration, and hence signification. Thus through repeated self-scrutiny the self was made meaningful to itself.

The spectacular self structured by owner-portraits is, then, spectacular in the sense of being a spectacle, a visual extravaganza that pushes itself into the forefront of regard and demands the attention of the spectator's gaze. In this sense, the spectacular subject found in these illuminations marks a key moment in the construction of the subject. In this particular moment of the somatizing of cultural agendas, the embodied self becomes aware of itself—and its value—as object, as item of consumption, and as meaningful entity. It is asked to view itself as passive, docile, and self-contained but is thereby assured of safety, security, and protection from the vicissitudes of time since it is placed within the serene boundaries of a domesticated and sanctified space. Exalted into the sacred space of the holy image and valorized by processes of reiteration, the self becomes of prime significance, stepping to center stage. All of this is what the first Tourotte family portrait so compellingly projects.

Domesticated, contained, and contented, its movements directed toward the unassailable end of private devotion, the devout subject constructed by owner-portraits was quintessentially disciplined. With its whole being and all its material goods organized around what was meant to be an all-consuming daily routine of interiorized devotion, this embodied self posed little threat to forces of social control. Eschewing the public sphere almost entirely, this devout subject occupied itself with itself, turning inward and controlling itself through its devotional regime. When we recall Debord's insistence that all images endorse the status quo by situating the viewing subject in a position of passive acquiescence and by offering the appearance of satisfaction of desire and of coherence and wholeness, then this devout subject modeled in owner-portraits looks all the more disciplined.[83] Moreover, as Norbert Elias has argued, the officially sponsored civilizing process depends on self-scrutiny. When the self is taught to view itself as it appears to others and to avoid behaviors that could be seen as rude or shameful, a decorum based on detachment and restraint is created, from which docile, well-behaved subjects result.[84] The self-regarding self found in books of hours, taught to scrutinize its devotional practices, seems not at all at odds with these disciplining processes.

## Perishable Selves

Nonetheless, an inescapable consequence of this objectification and scrutinizing of the self is that the subject so constructed becomes in spite of itself vulnerable to loss and destruction. As the self is figured as a valuable commodity, an item of visual consumption, it risks all the damages that can befall material objects under the logic of consumption. This is the state depicted in the second Tourotte family portrait. Here anxieties about perishability are brought to the surface and confronted. Kneeling precariously in an apocalyptic landscape, the Tourottes are exposed to the mutability of time and body. What the two Tourotte portraits do is to separate into distinct representational spaces features that often coexist in other owner-portraits. Although owner-portraits celebrate the safely embodied individual, reveling in its placid, solid, privileged status, they also unwittingly offer up images of contingency, mortality, and loss.[85] Concerned as much with disintegration as with solidity, owner-portraits thus reveal themselves as anxious as well as self-confident constructions of subjectivity. The second Tourotte portrait underscores the deathly animation of the human figures in owner-portraits, suspended as they are in a twilight zone where they appear as half object, half subject—partly present, partly already absent.

The workings of this anxiety about incipient loss and destruction and hence about the tenuous nature of subjectivity, although heavily repressed in most owner-portraits, can be glimpsed in several places. First of all, although the subject depicted in owner-portraits is comfortingly enfolded and sheltered within concentric rings of enclosure (clothing, devotional posture, domestic interior, framed space of the illumination, and the book itself), there is a supplementary symbolism of transgression at work in these enclosures that disturbingly unsettles their presumptive protectiveness. Safeguarded though the individual may seem to be, thresholds are stepped over, windows opened up, margins crossed, and barriers pierced with alarming frequency. In these pictures, boundaries are repeatedly shown to be breachable, as is strikingly illustrated in an illumination from an early-sixteenth-century book of hours that depicts a torn curtain through whose ragged edges can be seen a half-concealed hair shirt and a small Madonna floating in a cloud.[86] Half hidden, half revealed, the Madonna and the hair shirt suggest the commingled aura of absence in presence, of destruction and preservation, that pervades owner-portraits.

Mirrors, windows, doors, frames, and all threshold places—of which there are surprisingly many in owner-portraits—can be understood as liminal objects that offer a precariously in-between view of reality. Stressing not stasis but continual movement from one place or state to another, these liminal forms stand as locations of the confrontation of self with other, self with self, inside with outside. Taking away the security of a permanent position, threshold places are destabilizing and therefore potentially threatening to all things fixed.

In an illumination in a book of hours of circa 1450 from Belgium, in which Saint Catherine presents a patroness to Christ, a window positioned between the kneeling patroness and the enthroned Christ opens onto an urban scene with large buildings and two male figures walking by (see figure 5).[87] Although the illumination seeks to contain the patroness—and the viewer's gaze—within the interior of the room, the window dramatically breaks the boundaries of that enclosed space. The viewer's at-

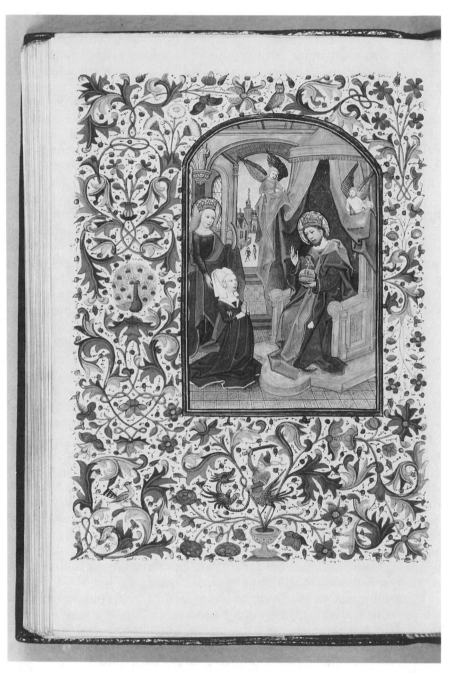

Figure 5. Saint Catherine Presenting a Patroness. Book of Hours. The Walters Art Gallery, MS W. 220, fol. 150v. Belgium, Bruges, ca. 1450. By permission of the Walters Art Gallery, Baltimore, Md.

tention is drawn inexorably outward, away from the patroness, the interior space, and the religious scene at hand. The open window thus doubly destabilizes, first by opening up a gap in the safely enfolding interior space and then by distracting the viewer's gaze away from the devotional activity being performed, refocusing it on the lively and enticing quotidian world beyond. In this instance, the presentation of simultaneous actions—one occurring within the room and the devotional frame and one taking place outside it—has the effect of catching the viewer in a boundary state, trapped between both scenes and unable to disregard either.

One of the most complex of these over-the-threshold breaches of the devotional frame occurs in the *mise-en-abîme* image of Mary of Burgundy reading from her book of hours. In this illumination a seated Mary is shown reading in the left foreground, surrounded by symbols of domestic comfort—a vase of flowers, an embroidered cloth, a small dog on her lap. The center of the painting, however, is dominated by a large, open window through which we can see an architecturally elaborate chapel with vaulted ceiling and numerous arched windows. Inside this chapel, a small scene is being enacted in which the seated Virgin and child receive an entourage of women. What is particularly interesting about this illumination is the way it compels the gaze to move ever further inward, away from Mary in the foreground, to the Virgin and child, and then beyond them to the back of the chapel, and back all the way to the chapel's windows through which we cannot see. Like the popular *vierge ouvrante* statues that opened up to reveal the Christ child hidden inside the Virgin Mary, these threshold images deliberately expose what would otherwise remain hidden, showing interiorized scenes usually not visible. In so doing, these liminal scenes confuse inside and out, there and not there.

In an analysis of van Eyck's famous Arnolfini portrait, Ervin Panofsky described the illusion of limitless penetration found there.[88] In this painting, which in some ways resembles the threshold portrait of Mary of Burgundy, the eye is led back between the standing figures of Giovanni Arnolfini and his wife, past a wealth of domestic items strewn about the room's interior (shoes, a carpet, a hanging lamp, a tiny dog) to a small round mirror hanging on the far wall. Inside this mirror, barely visible, is a mirror image of the scene our eyes have just traversed—showing it to us from the other direction, the backs of the couple and the objects in their room all now seen in reverse. Although we are led onward and inward in this painting, when we step over the threshold of the mirror we are suddenly thrown back to where we came from, caught in a perceptual loop that keeps us uneasily suspended in the liminal moment. Similarly, in the painting of Mary of Burgundy, once our eyes penetrate through the window to the chapel we are also led to look back onto the scene we passed through, since one of the women in the entourage looks suspiciously like Mary of Burgundy herself, thus beckoning our eyes to look back at her to match them up. Trapped once more in a loop, the gaze moves endlessly back and forth between the two scenes unable to know where it should rest.

Both portraits—of the Arnolfinis and of Mary of Burgundy—expose an underlying uneasiness that troubles many other owner-portraits. In these scenes of thresholds and penetrations, the boundaries around the devout subject are broken and the sacred space is opened to the outside world, destabilizing the enclosed subject the painting seeks to construct and trapping the gaze indefinitely between the two scenes. In another, more typical example, from a book of hours commissioned in Utrecht around 1460, the kneeling owner is positioned half in the border and half intruding on the Annunciation scene he is watching. Divided between two different representational spaces, with their differing aesthetic and symbolic norms, the owner is not allowed to rest comfortably in either.[89] What is suggested by these scenes is just how tenuous the stable devotional space portrayed by these illuminations is and how open to breach are the boundaries that define and shape the individual.

Similarly, the voyeuristic gaze of the owner-viewer who reads the book of hours also functions as a destabilizing force, calling into question notions of bodily integrity and singularity, as well as the uniqueness of the self. By gazing at a representation of him- or herself engaged in devotion, the viewer, who is also at the same moment engaged in an analogous act of devotion that involves using the book of hours, is drawn into an Arnolfini-like mirror where reality and representation are inseparable. Which self is the true self—the reading self or the represented one? Which devotional act is the genuine one—that of the reader or that of the depiction? The impact of this blend of dissociation and identification on the notion of a stable, coherent self is not hard to imagine; as one critic has said, "The self-regarding self is rarely at ease."[90]

Finally, to return to questions of commodification, the self that is destabilized by these scenes of spatial transgression and dissociative self-regard is further unsettled by the way that it is constructed in these paintings as an object of consumption. Construed as a commodity available to be used over and over again by the reader, the embodied self in owner-portraits becomes as a consequence vulnerable to perishability. As a consumer object, the self runs the risk precisely of being consumed, depleted, and exhausted. Although the ability of representation to fix the self in a permanent form, capturing it at one specific moment and preserving it indefinitely, would seem to offer a reassuring message about the immutability and permanence of the embodied self, nonetheless these owner-portraits cannot avoid raising the possibility of the decay and destruction of the commodified self.

Since traces are all that it leaves, perishability can be difficult to detect in these portraits. For that reason, a related example might help make more visible the hidden preoccupation with loss and impermanence that I am arguing unsettles owner-portraits. In his analysis of Dutch still-life painting, written in 1953 at the height of his structuralist phase, Barthes attacked what seemed to him to be the obsession these paintings had with consumption, reading them as manifestations of a crassly acquisitive and philistine bourgeois culture. Focusing as they do on the shiny surfaces of a clutter of material objects—foodstuffs, tableware, and other goods—these paintings appeared, from the lingering modernist perspective from within which Barthes wrote, as early moments of commodity fetishism that glorified the materialist world of consumption and so lacked all moral, ethical, or spiritual sense. Catalogs on canvas of capitalist excess, inventories in oil of grasping acquisitiveness, these paintings, Barthes argued, used art in the degraded service of consumption, annexing aesthetics to the grasping work of merchandising.[91]

Extending his theme about consumption, Barthes provocatively claimed that seventeenth-century Dutch group portraits also fell into this same pattern. In these paintings, according to Barthes, the human body became just another commodity painted in homage to the superficial forces of materiality. Transformed into human flora and fauna, like "fleshy blooms," the faces of these burghers were dehumanized and reconfigured as commodities fit for consumption. As a result, the identity of these burghers was fashioned from blood and meat, not spirit or soul, Barthes complained.[92] In Barthes's reading, then, the human body in these paintings was reified and commodified, following the lead of the dominant genre of the still life, and so was submitted to the demands of a mercantile culture.

Although Barthes saw such paintings as enslaved to a brutish order of materiality, consumption, and commodification that celebrated the world of goods and thereby proclaimed a moral vacancy, Dutch still-life paintings can also be read as artworks that reveal anxieties about materiality, as Simon Schama has shown.[93] Precisely because of their obsession with the material world, these paintings are acutely aware of the consequences of materiality. Death, as Schama notes, is always present at the feast for the eye spread out in these paintings. Foods are half eaten; wine glasses are partly empty; things are precariously balanced, about to roll off the table or fall from a plate; dead animals and heaps of fruits are carelessly strewn about.[94] There is an eerie living-death quality about these still-life paintings, which explore, in Schama's words, "the ambiguous relationship between materiality and spirituality, concreteness and insubstantiality."[95]

In their subtle but persistent invocation of decay in the midst of scenes of freshness and of loss in the portrayal of permanence, Dutch still-life paintings strongly resemble owner-portraits in books of hours. In owner-portraits there can be seen a similar intrusion of the ephemeral into scenes of the permanent, the spiritual into the material, and the doomed into the protected. Where this can be most readily observed is in the use of the domestic interior as the setting for an otherworldly encounter. Here spirituality is deliberately brought into a concretized material space that is asked to represent it, ill-equipped though it is to do so. In the miniature of Catherine presenting a patroness to Christ (which I discussed earlier), it is not the patroness but Christ who looks out of place, his throne jutting into what seems to be, if not the owner's room, then at least a fairly ordinary, although sumptuous, chamber.[96] Part of what seems to be suggested in this painting is an intensification of the spiritual event, whose efficacy is increased by its intrusion into the ordinary material world. But the juxtaposition of material and spiritual also calls attention to the ambiguous connection between the two. As Catherine and Christ—who are now beyond the realm of corporeality—appear to the patroness, both their contrast with her and their similarity to her are stressed. They are like her, yet they are not, since they are no longer material entities. Similarly, in the first Tourotte portrait, the Tourottes' ephemeral embodied state is emphasized by the figures of Saints Anthony and Peter, who stand behind and protect them in their encircling arms, acting as mementos of incipient death while appearing in material form in the Tourottes' room. When holy figures enter human space, they bring with them a reminder of the ultimate dissolution of the things of the material world, including the human body. Since a standard illumination found in many books of hours is the deathbed scene, although not usually one predicting the owner's death, the theme of destruction and decay is never far away.[97]

Even in scenes where the owners do not encounter sacred figures, this same suggestion of latent perishability lurking beneath the surface of the object world can be detected. In an illumination depicting the Butler family at Mass, from the mid-fourteenth-century Butler Hours, the family is shown kneeling in the foreground while in front and a bit above them stands the priest with elevated host (see figure 6).[98] Richly dressed in red and blue fur-trimmed robes, the Butlers kneel on carpeted steps; behind them is a screen of alternating blue and red squares, beyond which can be seen a wall covered in a blue and red pattern. Although the human figures in this miniature follow the model of enclosed, commodified, spectacular subjectivity I have been describing, there is an undertone of something less secure. The Butlers might appear to be the intended focal point, yet they in fact fade away, disappearing into near invisibility. And their disappearance is caused by their very materiality. The kneeling Butlers are located in the foreground of the painting where they would seem to be poised to attract the viewer's eye and dominate the painting. But their

Figure 6. The Butler Family at Mass. The Butler Hours. The Walters Art Gallery, MS W. 105, fol. 15. England, ca. 1340. By permission of the Walters Art Gallery, Baltimore, Md.

costuming (in red and blue like the background screen and wall) and positioning (posed in vertical and horizontal lines that match the tall vertical frame of the screen and the horizontal stairs) have the effect of making them extremely difficult to distinguish from the furnishings of the surrounding room. Visually linked as they are with the material world that encompasses them and provides the setting for their devotional act, the Butlers dissolve into it, losing their bodies to the objects that surround them. Intensified by the symbolism of the host held up by the priest who stands before them (a symbolism predicated on the complex intermingling of material and spiritual, of flesh and spirit), this disappearance of the Butlers into the object world seems less mere chance than deliberate theme. Displayed in all their seemingly solid, prosperous, permanent materiality, the Butlers paradoxically are captured at the very moment of loss of self, disintegrating into their material milieu. Caught in a trompe l'oeil moment, they are both there and not there.

In the two contrasting Tourotte portraits, this theme of loss within permanence is explicitly brought to the surface. The second portrait, in which the Tourottes kneel in a barren landscape on either side of a grinning death's head, can be easily read as a deliberate and direct confrontation with the impending destruction of the body. Dressed in exactly the same clothes they are wearing in the first portrait and settled in the same kneeling, hands-folded posture, the Tourottes appear to have just been whisked away from their cozy household and dropped down into this hostile terrain. Within the context of the Tourottes' book of hours, the memento mori effect is enhanced by the positioning of the two owner-portraits on opposite pages so that the eye moves easily from one to the other; in rapid succession the viewer sees the Tourottes fully immersed in domestic life, then brought ominously face to face with death. The loss hiding behind the seeming permanence of their materially defined world, and the world of the reader of the book, is thus made unavoidable.

I have been arguing that consumers of the self-representations found in books of hours were engaged in an ongoing process of self-creation, of which the Tourotte portraits represent two linked aspects conjoining the themes of permanence and perishability. Cultural notions of what it meant to be an embodied subject were concretized in these owner-portraits, portraits that were embedded within the commodified devotional medium of the book of hours and hence were susceptible to a similar process of acquisition, possession, and consumption.[99] Given their status as commodities, it is perhaps not surprising that the central dynamic of the subjectivity modeled in these owner-portraits features an interplay between the themes of permanence and loss, materiality and disembodiment.

Goods such as books of hours are performative; they can inculcate and enact cultural attitudes and beliefs that, given the pervasiveness of dominant cultural forces, often support hegemonic notions. As Rosalind Coward and John Ellis note, the function of ideology "is to fix the individual in place as subject for a certain meaning. This is simultaneously to provide individuals with a subject-ivity, and to subject them to the social structure with its existing contradictory relations and powers."[100] The thematic emphasis of books of hours on permanence and materiality and the attendant creation of an enclosed, docile, self-regarding subject—the most valuable commodity of all—seems to manifest such a hegemonic bias, constructing a malleable subject who could easily be conscripted into dominant cultural forces.

At the same time, goods can act as instruments of change or resistance, functioning as a medium for experimenting with or critiquing social categories and cultural meanings.[101] This might have been the at least latent impact of the hidden images of decay, instability, and transgression found in owner-portraits, images that I have argued shook the stable subject by breaching the boundaries of the enclosed self so comfortably ensconced within its plush object world. By evoking the consequences of materiality—loss and destruction—these illuminations confronted the perishability of the self, a notion that, although consistent with church teachings about the value of spirit versus body and hence readable as entirely within the purview of the dominant culture, nonetheless could have troubling consequences for authority, consequences that are explored in the next chapter.

✛

# CHAPTER 6

# Violated Bodies:
## The Spectacle of Suffering in
## Corpus Christi Pageants

*Here þei xal bete Jesus about þe hed and þe body.*
—N-Town Trial before Annas and Caiaphas

The central body for late medieval England was the *corpus Christi*, deployed across a wide range of cultural practices and represented in the ritual of the Eucharist, a rite that took a simple item of daily consumption and turned it into a powerful symbol of the divine.[1] This transformation of bread into flesh, of commodity into body, found dramatic expression in the large-scale urban performances of the fourteenth through sixteenth centuries known as the Corpus Christi pageants.[2] In and through these pageants conflicting understandings of corporeality and embodiment in relation to the socioeconomic structures of the late medieval town were articulated and enacted by and for participants and spectators.

In an autobiographical letter to his son in 1664, the royalist preacher John Shaw commented on two elderly parishioners, "exceeding blind and ignorant as to religion," who came to him for religious instruction. When Shaw spoke to them about Jesus, one of the men said that he thought he had heard of that man of whom Shaw spoke, having seen a play called Corpus Christi at Kendall where "there was a man on a tree, and blood ran down."[3] What this spectator recalled from the play and took as its definitive feature was not the celebratory moment of the resurrection or the theological message of suffering and redemption, as might be expected, but rather a stark image of bodily suffering and destruction crudely detached from the interpretive frame of religious symbolism. A man, a tree, blood—this is what the man remembers. Although Shaw takes his elderly parishioner's words as a mark of profound spiritual ignorance, the man's recollection nonetheless usefully refocuses attention on what is, in fact, a dominant though often ignored part of the Corpus Christi plays—their extreme violence.

In the late Middle Ages, violence was often on display. In public spectacles of the punishment and execution of criminals as well as in violent sports such as tournaments, bull and bear baiting, and combat games, assaults on human and animal bodies were commonplace. Devotion could also incorporate large doses of violence, as is evidenced by the relish with which Chaucer's Prioress describes the brutal and gory murder of the "litel clergeoun" and the subsequent revenge taken on the Jews who committed the deed. Late medieval art and drama likewise stressed the realistic representation of the physical suffering of saints and martyrs while also lavishly depicting the brutality of those who inflicted that suffering. A frequent ingredient in cultural representations of all kinds, violence and its effects could hardly have been less hidden.

Especially prevalent were depictions of violence against marginalized groups such as Jews and women. The bodies of Jews were often shown being mutilated or tortured, as in the Croxton *Play of the Sacrament*, which features a scene in which the hand of the Jew Jonathas is torn off, or in the fifteenth-century French *Mystery of the Acts of the Apostles*, attributed to the Gréban brothers, especially in the Bourges 1536 production: when Belzeray, Prince of the Jews, lays his hands on the Virgin's coffin, they are torn from his arms.[4] The bodies of women, especially holy women, were also frequently represented as the victims of acts of violation, as for example in Jean Fouquet's illumination of Saint Apollonia in the Hours of Etienne Chevalier, which shows Apollonia having her teeth pulled out as part of her torture, or in the more than a dozen French plays performed between 1448 and 1539 that feature Saint Barbara, who was tortured by having her breasts cut off. Given the wide cultural dissemination of such representations of violence, it is difficult to dispute the view of John Gatton that images of cruelty, suffering, and blood "attracted rather than repelled men and women of the Middle Ages" and that in this context theatrical stagings of violence should be understood as "violent theatre for a violent era."[5]

Despite Gatton's claims, rarely does the violence of late medieval cultural productions receive scholarly attention. Most critics, in fact, have tended to downplay such violence and, in the case of the Corpus Christi plays, erase the horror associated with the many representations of bodily suffering.[6] In his influential book on the Corpus Christi pageants, for example, V. A. Kolve identifies devices in the Passion scenes that deflect attention from and help make tolerable the torture of Christ, especially as part of an aesthetic experience, by alleviating the emotional distress of watching Christ's suffering. Kolve claims that the plays use a number of strategies to distance the perpetrators of violence from the results of their actions, chief among these strategies being the reframing of torment as game or jest. In this way, Kolve argues, the ignorance of the torturers is stressed, making them appear not sadistic but foolish and causing the audience to pity their ignorance rather than focus on their violent acts.[7] Given the modern queasiness about the violence in the plays, a queasiness that Kolve's analysis crystallizes, it is not surprising to learn that slaughter and scenes of torture were deliberately censored in early-twentieth-century stagings of the Corpus Christi cycles, when medieval drama first began to be revived on modern stages.[8]

Rather than looking through the violence in these plays, trying to deny it, explain it away, or mitigate its effects, I propose to confront it as an important aspect of the cultural and ideological work performed by the cycle plays within their urban milieus. Although scenes of suffering inscribed on the flesh in Corpus Christi pageants were part of a drama of redemption in which spectators were asked to leap over physical suffering and destruction to the moment of resurrection and salvation, these acts of violence, I wish to suggest, evaded at least partially that redemptive reading, opening the way for a more resistant critique of various social and economic processes. The drama of suffering staged in such pageants as the Slaughter of the Innocents or the Buffeting, Scourging, and Crucifixion of Christ permits actor and audience to participate vicariously in acts of torture, dismemberment, and death. In so doing, these depictions of violence questioned the notion of orderly social harmony based on an enclosed, self-contained, and inviolable subjectivity of the sort modeled by the devoted bodies found in owner-portraits in books of hours. Moreover, violated bodies as well as violent ones could serve as images of resistance, since only whole, intact bodies were useful to the patterns of production required by the late medieval urban economy. And finally, the dissolution of the body as it is tortured and ultimately destroyed in these plays could become a positive maneuver in the struggle for control over subjectivities, since it offered a way out of norms of subjectivity grounded in whole and healthy corporeality. By slipping away into death, bodies and subjects could take themselves permanently out of circulation, exiting systems of production and consumption with seeming finality.[9] Although it need not inevitably have done so for all observers, the theatrical representation of damaged and disappearing bodies could nonetheless suggest for some spectators under the right circumstances ways of evading power. Especially since within late medieval urban communities power often took for itself the image of the body corporate, damaged bodies might have served as gestures of resistance to themes of social unity.

If for the late Middle Ages the body, and especially the paradigmatic body of Christ, provided a key way of imagining social communities and the position of individuals within them, then it was the whole, perfect, fully functioning, and intact body that was understood to stand as the exemplary model for the community.[10] From the idea of the king's (healthy) body as a symbol of divine and social order to the notion of the urban polity as a mutually beneficial body corporate, the ideal medieval social grouping, at least in the eyes of elites, was structured around an image of healthy corporeality. Demands for bodily integrity as a requirement for entrance into a community could be extended even to the terrain of the individual body, as is made evident in an ordinance from the Coventry Weaver's Guild in 1452–53 that limited apprenticeships to men who possessed all of their limbs. As Peter Travis has pointed out in a discussion of this ordinance, being physically flawed was a violation of ideals of social wholeness attached to the metaphor of the urban body politic and hence constituted grounds for exclusion from the guild system.[11]

What is also implied by this ordinance is a connection between bodily wholeness and the urban economy, particularly the manufacturing work that was the province of the craft guilds that sponsored the Corpus Christi plays.[12] Historians have recently argued that the chief economic division in late medieval urban life was between a merchant elite and manufacturers or artisans.[13] In the view of Heather Swanson, who has perhaps most thoroughly taken up this argument, mercantile power derived expressly from control of the system of exchange in which commercial dominance was assured by carefully dividing labor up into small units of production. The craft guilds were developed to regulate the nonmercantile worker and from this perspective can be seen as repressive institutions that were part of a general movement to control labor by keeping wages down to preplague levels. By putting into place a structure of divide and conquer in which master craftsmen controlled a fragmented labor force, any common cause among manufacturers, especially in terms of their ability to coordinate distribution, which Swanson argues was the real source of urban wealth, was diminished. In this way, the mercantile elite who formed the urban oligarchy in most towns maintained its own economic dominance by thwarting any challenge from consolidated manufacturing-trading interests.[14]

The ideal manufacturing body, which if Swanson is correct is the body the craft guilds were designed to police, had to be intact, unharmed, hale, and hearty; the worker needed "all his ryght lymes" if he were to be productive and hence welcomed into the economic fellowship of a guild. More important, if the body was healthy (and belonged to someone from the laboring classes), then it must of necessity submit itself to work. The Statute of Laborers of 1349, for instance, required that every man and woman of the realm, free or bond and not from the ruling classes, who is "able in body" be put to work. If the able-bodied refused to work, they could expect no charity: the statute also prohibited the giving of alms to healthy beggars who "refuse to labour."[15] In this statute the equivalence between bodily wholeness and productivity is made brutally explicit; only bodily disability can exempt the laboring subject from the demands of an economic order that forces workers to work. Swanson observes that the one issue on which the master craftsmen and the city councilors were in most agreement was control of the labor force, with the guilds serving as the primary agencies for regulating work. On this issue, the interests of merchants and master artisans coalesced.[16]

The Corpus Christi plays' violence against the paradigmatic body of Christ, displayed for all to see on his shattered, crucified form, presented a striking discordance with the urban oligarchic theme of bodily wholeness figured in both social and economic terms.[17] In these pageants, Christ's naked and tortured body is open and vulnerable, the opposite of the safely enclosed and intact bodies of owners in books of hours or of the whole, healthy laborer's body so emphatically insisted upon by the ruling powers of the late medieval town. The central irony of the Corpus Christi plays is that Christ's broken body does not unilaterally and unambiguously support the communal or economic ideals it was intended to serve: Christ's body does not articulate the image of the body corporate that underpinned the mercantile elite's preferred view of the town, but instead undercuts it.[18] Moreover, linked as it is with the violated bodies of women and children in the Slaughter of the Innocents pageants that prefigure the crucifixion scenes, Christ's body in these performances takes up a subject position that testifies to the logic of subjugation underlying late medieval urban economies. Despite the strong recuperative forces at work in the narrative of the resurrection, these representations of violence against the bodies of Christ, women, and children question the ideology of social wholeness and its cultural work, "unlocking the emancipatory critique" that Sarah Beckwith claims is the other side of the cultural story of the crucifixion.[19] In so doing, as I hope to show, these representations open a space for resistance to the work imperative inscribed on healthy, intact bodies.[20]

## Murder and Theft

Earlier liturgical dramas are restrained in their treatment of the Slaughter of the Innocents, focusing on the mothers' laments and avoiding explicit treatment of the children's deaths.[21] In contrast, the Corpus Christi pageants dealing with the Slaughter revel in the cruelty of Herod and his soldiers, graphically depicting the murder of the children and the mothers' ultimately fruitless but determined resistance. The enthusiasm for violence that marked these later dramatizations of the Slaughter episode is vividly conveyed by the Chester banns of 1539–40, which announce that the Goldsmiths and Masons will show "how herode King of Galalye / for that Intent Cryst to distrye / Slew the Inosents most Cruely."[22] The children in the various Slaughter pageants are beheaded, torn, impaled, made to "hop" on the soldiers' sharpened spears, and stabbed; their mothers not only lament, but cry out and fight back. The numerous special effects specified for other dramatic acts of violence, such as the beatings, stonings, scourgings, and stabbings in a 1536 performance at Bourges of Gréban's *Mystery of the Acts of the Apostles,* suggest how the Slaughter scenes might have been played for maximum violent realism.[23] These special effects included trick knives and swords, rocks made of painted sponge, whips fabricated out of dyed cloth that would stripe the actor's skin when he was beaten, false heads for decapitations, and dummies that could stand in for actors in execution scenes. The pageant from the Towneley cycle makes reference to the bodies of the dead children as being "strayd" (strewn) in the streets, suggesting the use of rag or wooden dolls that could readily have been subjected to all the graphic violence called for by the texts of the plays.[24] Perhaps these dolls resembled the wooden ones used in the French *Passion* enacted at Mons in 1501, one of which was constructed so that it could be cut in half.[25] A sixteenth-century pageant of Saint Thomas à Becket at Canterbury lists payment for "a new leder bag for the blode," implying that at least sometimes the dolls might have had sacks of red liquid hidden inside them from which "blood" spurted.[26]

What is particularly interesting about the technologies of suffering in these pageants is how they are used to draw attention to specific cultural tensions. As critics have long noted, the pageants dramatize unchecked power, embodied in Herod as well as in the soldiers whom he sends to kill the children;[27] the pageants critique such power through the broken bodies of the children and the mothers' resistance. At the same time, as Theresa Coletti has recently argued, there is a more complex social narrative being presented than just a critique of nobility and tyranny. As Coletti has pointed out, the Slaughter plays focus on power distributed across generational, status, and gender lines, the major categories of social organization—and social tension—in late medieval towns. In Coletti's view, the Slaughter plays "deploy gender, age, and status categories in dramatic conflicts that are paradigmatic of late medieval social structure itself" but that also "bear a more discordant relationship with the very categories and identities they appear to affirm." This occurs particularly through the female body, which is able to call into question the bases of masculine authority and to destabilize accepted patterns of social control.[28]

Although late medieval urban authority constantly sought ways to legitimize itself and ratify its power—one method being, as Coletti notes, to continually reaffirm the social categories (of gender, status, wealth, and age) on which it was predicated—it could never entirely rule out a transgressive slippage toward questioning the terms of its own authority. When in the Slaughter pageants the murder of the children is equated with theft, for instance, this substitution of crimes can be read as an exposure of how the laboring body becomes transfigured as a commodity to be bought, sold, or possessed as part of the operation of systems of capitalist production. Thus the bodies of the mothers and their children perform the contrapuntal or transgressive ideological work of these pageants, scrutinizing masculine control over subjected bodies while also raising questions about the place of the worker's body within the economic order established by an urban mercantile elite.

Critics have called attention to the way that the Slaughter plays critique feudal tyranny, but they have not noticed how masculine power is figured in these pageants in terms that are less feudal than mercantile-urban, particularly in terms of the authority to regulate work and to control the flow of commodities. Although Herod is usually taken as an icon of unrepentant feudal or royal power, in fact both the violent language and the violent actions of Herod and his men are thoroughly grounded in a commercialized urban milieu.[29] The N-Town Slaughter of the Innocents introduces Herod characteristically ranting—here in alliterative verse that draws attention to and underscores his tirade—about the pain he intends to inflict on the children. "Popetys and pap-hawkys I xal puttyn in peyne" (20/11) he proclaims, urging his knights to strike the children "Tyl rybbys be to-rent with a reed ray!" (20/33). After carrying out the killing, the two knights then report back to Herod, boasting about their murderous deeds: "Lord, we han spad / As e bad: / Barnis ben blad / And lyne in dych!" (20/113–16). Herod's language in the Towneley Herod the Great pageant is similarly steeped in a rhetoric of violence.[30] When he summons his soldiers in order to instruct them to kill the children, he exhorts them: "Spare no kyns bloode, / Lett all ryn on flood" (10/452–53). Herod's violent language is echoed by his men, one of whom in the Chester version vows: "These congeons in there clowtes I will kill / and stowtly with strokes them destroye" (10/209–10), while the other promises "right all downe shall I dinge / these laddes everychone" (10/235–36).[31] Similarly, in the Digby Killing of the Children play, Herod's messenger Watkin vows that he will "choppe . . . on a blokke" any male child he encounters (220).

These words have the effect of locating responsibility for the violence within the speaking agents who perform it, making it clear who owns the killings. This issue of ownership, raised again when the mothers accuse the murderers of theft, has important repercussions for these pageants' construction of the laboring body as a commodity. More important, these utterances frame the violence within the circle of power established by Herod and his men, focusing attention on the prerogatives of rule that can with impunity authorize such acts. Although the killing takes place beyond Herod's view and in his absence, talk about it preoccupies Herod and his men: he rants and threatens murder in their presence; they boast about their killings in his. As the Chester pageant's opening speech by Herod—in which he urges princes, prelates, and barons to beware of him (10/1–3)—makes apparent, the locus of this display of violence is a masculine circle of power, which in the opening scenes of the Towneley Herod the Great pageant is defined as absolute possession of all things and absolute regulation of all bodies. As Herod proclaims in this pageant: "For I haue all in wold: / In me stanys lyfe and dede" (16/133–34).[32]

But violence is understood in the Slaughter pageants not just as an aspect of feudal rule but also as an underpinning of the urban economy. In a treatment that can be read as both parody and exposure of the normative system of wage labor, violence is seen as a form of work that must be fitting and must earn a just wage. In the Chester version, for example, one of the soldiers complains that killing children is too lowly a job for him: "A villanye yt weare, iwys, / for my fellowe and mee / to sley a shitten-arsed shrowe" (10/155–57). Once Herod assures them that they will kill thousands, not a mere one or two, the soldiers go off to do his bidding, reassured that the labor they are being asked to perform is suitable for their social standing. As Coletti observes, these plays seem preoccupied with male status and age hierarchies, which in the case of Herod and his men are threatened by the socially inferior youths they set out to kill.[33] When Herod's men are sent out to kill the children, their "work" becomes linked to concerns about social standing, with an equivalence set up between status and employment.

Likewise, the pageants emphasize just payment for the labor that is performed. The soldiers serve Herod with violence, and in turn he repays them with material goods, as well as symbolic capital such as honor and prestige. What is set up is thus a system in which violence is one coin offered in the circulation of power. The Towneley pageant develops the symbolics of exchange with particular thoroughness, explicitly using the language of commercial transactions to describe the violence. Here Herod says: "If this crowne may bere, / That boy [Jesus] shall by for all" (16/163–64). In payment for their counsel to kill all male children, Herod promises to reward his advisers with "Markys, rentys, and powndys, / Greatt castels and groundys" (16/387–88). After his soldiers kill the children, Herod recompenses them with women to wed, as well as other material goods, including castles and towers (16/647–50). From the perspective of this paradigm of violent rule, the effects of violence—the children's dead bodies and the bereft mothers—are the necessary signs of the effective functioning of the system, required in order to ratify lines of authority and subservience. To show that male power is in fact in charge, its violent handiwork must be made visible. In the Chester version, this system breaks down when one of the slain children turns out to be

Herod's own son. In despair, Herod damns himself and his soul is taken away by a demon.

The preoccupation with masculine power and its undergirding systems of exchange based on violent labor construes control of bodies as similar to control of commodities. This is made especially evident in the mothers' characterization of their children's murder as a form of theft. In the Towneley pageant, one mother laments: "My comforth and my kyn, / My son thus al to-torne!" (16/499–500), suggesting in the word "comforth" the child's significance to her as an agent of economic well-being. This reaction might seem little more than a conventional understanding of male offspring as important resources for their parents, but when murder is redefined as theft the implicit economic issue is brought to the surface where it can be scrutinized. In the Towneley pageant one mother cries out against the murder of her child by reviling the soldier as a "Fals thefe" (16/490). Another mother protests in the same pageant, "Thefe, thou shedys my chyldys blood!" (l6/543). In the Chester and York pageants, the mothers similarly characterize the murderers as thieves. "Owte on ow theves, I crye, / e slee my semely sone," cries a mother in the York play (19/194–95).

Although this locution might simply be a generally derogatory epithet, it also seems to have a more pointedly specific function that ties the murders to processes of commodification. There is also a gender valence to this locution as well. One reason for the mothers' description of murder as theft might have had to do with the fact that robbery was treated more harshly in late medieval England than was rape or murder. Medieval juries put a relatively high value on property and a low value on life, if we can take as evidence the fact that juries were much more lenient in punishing crimes against persons than against property.[34] In light of this privileging of property over life, the mothers' complaints that they are being robbed can be seen as a clever tactical move to arouse sympathy for their plight and to underscore the seriousness of the crime against them. It also, however, suggests a deliberate exposure of a commodity system in which ownership of bodies means ownership of production and profits. Marxist theories understand the capitalist mode of production as removing labor from its symbolic contexts by refiguring production not as an activity but as a *quantity* that could be measured in money. Wage labor recreates work as a special form of bodily activity—one which is seen as uniquely *productive* whereas other bodily activities, are now viewed as unproductive—that can be measured in wages. Work itself thus becomes commodified and is turned into a product for which payment can be exacted; at the same time, work is set off from other bodily activities, which are figured as unproductive since they cannot be directly translated into commodity terms. In the process the individual's relation to the body changes as well, with the body now understood as a tool, or piece of property, that the worker owns and that can be bought and sold on the marketplace. In this way capitalism turns the body into a commodity, making labor a product in its own right.[35]

The economic implications of the children's deaths might well have had special resonance for the original spectators of the plays, given that in urban environments there was heightened risk of parents losing their children: there was greater infant mortality in towns, and when children survived, they were often separated from their parents at an early age to be raised in other households as servants or apprentices.[36] In this context, the treatment of murder as theft, of loss of son as loss of productive labor and hence loss of valuable property, would have taken on an obvious economic meaning, linked as it was to real issues of livelihood. At the same time, the "theft" of the children could also evoke complex emotions attached to the parental separation from offspring that was a prevalent part of late medieval urban life, whether that separation came in the form of child mortality or as apprenticeship or entry into service.[37]

A second feature of the economic order inscribed in the Slaughter scenes comes in the pageants' staging of an explicitly gender-based battle between the soldiers and the mothers, a battle waged by the women with the traditional implements of the household—the distaff and ladle.[38] This "business of distaffs and pot-ladles" has been seen by more than one critic as "unsatisfactory," since it is often thought to be "unseemly to make their sorrow take the form of grotesque and comic violence."[39] But the use of distaffs and ladles to stage the mothers' resistance to the murder/theft of their children has a strong ideological effect within the contested economies of the Slaughter pageants. The Digby version, which develops the mothers' resistance most fully, includes a scene that dramatizes their assault on Watkin, Herod's buffoonish messenger. In this scene, the women beat Watkin with their distaffs until he is rescued by Herod's knights. Although this inversionary image of housewives beating an unmanly man is taken straight from the stock repertoire of comic misrule, it also acts as a confrontation of two forms of labor: women's work and men's work.[40] Here the implements of women's business, the distaffs, are used to attack a man engaged in the masculine work of killing in the name of power. The use of tools of opposing trades—distaffs and ladles versus swords and pikes—highlights the exploitative economic logic underlying the Slaughter scenes. Recent studies emphasizing the critical role that women played in urban economies, particularly in terms of their control of inherited properties and businesses, help explain why the Slaughter pageants construe women, as Coletti points out, as threats to male status and power.[41] In these pageants, women use the economic resources at hand to fight back, attempting to intervene, however unsuccessfully, in the theft of their children. The mutilated and lifeless bodies of the children become signs of the failure of women's work to stand up to men's work. At the same time, the bodies of the slaughtered children—wearing the marks of the ruthless operation of power and strewn about the performance space—draw attention to fissures in the urban corporate body, as well.[42]

Recuperative strategies were of course available to help deflect attention from the children's deaths as well as from the social and economic consequences, strategies that might have found implicit favor with the urban elites whose social, economic, and political policies the Slaughter plays at least partially critiqued. John Mirk's *Festial*, for instance, an early-fifteenth-century collection of sermons for use by parish priests, points to the slaughtered children as examples of loving one's enemies. Mirk says of the children, "For thay dydden lagh on hom that slowen hem, and playde wyth hor hondes when thay seen hor bryght swerdes schyne."[43] While stressing their innocence, Mirk also emphasizes the childlike lack of revenge or hatred that in his view informed the children's response to the soldiers—a response, it should be noted, that is not an explicit part of the Corpus Christi dramatizations of this event. The pageants themselves attempt to recuperate and diminish the disruptive effects of the violence by invoking a religious interpretation that defines the slaughtered children as martyrs who go straight to heaven (as the liturgy for Candlemas, February 2, indicates). Hence the violence against them is coded as part of a divine plan for salvation. Nevertheless, the sight of the children's mutilated bodies, however obviously fake, strewn about the stage might have lingered uneasily in spectators' minds, as difficult to forget as the ineffectual efforts of the mothers or the sadistic violence of the soldiers. Taken together, this representation of the violent soldiers working in the service of a masculine power construed in commercialized terms, the mothers fighting back with women's tools of production, and the economically valueless bodies of the dead children sets the stage for the appearance of Christ's broken body and its more subversive ideological work.

## The Broken Body of Christ

The Slaughter looks forward to the Passion, not just in terms of the image of the sacrificial lamb, but also in its attitudes toward bodily economics, as the patterns developed in the Slaughter scenes are intensified and played out in the dramas dealing with Christ's sufferings. Although in the twelfth century the image of Christ on the cross was usually taken to represent divine power, with the cross functioning as a kind of earthly throne, by the fourteenth century the crucified Christ had become an image not of power but of suffering, manifested particularly through the medium of his bleeding and wounded body. This historical shift in meaning is played out in the different treatments of Christ's suffering found in liturgical and cycle dramas of the Passion. Few liturgical dramas feature the crucifixion, and when they do, as in the thirteenth-century Benedickt-beuern play, the crucifixion is, in Kolve's words, "grave and decorous."[44] In contrast, the Chester banns of 1539–40 reveal how much the emphasis has changed in the cycle plays' treatment of Christ's sufferings, declaring that the pageant put on by the Fletchers, Bowyers, Coopers, and Stringers will dramatize "the Tormentors / that bobbyde god with gret horrors."[45] This "bobbing" of Jesus with all its attendant "horrors," presented as an assault on the body, is the focal point of the pageants dealing with the Scourging, Buffeting, and Crucifixion of Christ.

In the Corpus Christi plays, the body of Christ, like the bodies of the slaughtered children, is made to show its bloody wounds and welts, to bear iconic testimony to the torturers' blows.[46] Reflecting the late medieval addition of graphic and sensationalistic details of cruelty not reported in the Gospels—such as stories in which Christ's body is burned with torches and hot irons; stretched beneath a table and beaten by drunken tormentors; and dragged through foul pits or thrown into a cesspool in acts of ritual degradation and violence—the cycle plays stress the technologies of torment.[47] The physical marks of these technologies of torment left on Christ's body were made visible through the use of costumes like the "vj skynnys of whit ledder" listed in the Smiths' expenditures at Coventry in 1451, tight-fitting skins that could have been painted to simulate torn, bruised, and beaten flesh.[48] Similarly, stage treatment of the flogging might have involved a beating with red-dyed birch branches, which would leave stripes of "blood" on the actor playing Christ.

My interest in these scenes of suffering has to do with how they continue the critiques of the body and productivity initiated by the Slaughter of the Innocents pageants. As Christ's body is tortured in the service of Christian ideology's themes of subservience, obedience, and suffering, it also paradoxically becomes a sign of resistance. As has been well documented, there was an intimate involvement of the body in late medieval spirituality. The divine revealed itself in and through the body in the Mass, in relics, in martyrdoms, and in miracles. Holiness also was lodged in the body, and bodily effluvia such as tears and blood were signs of saintly privilege. At the same time, medieval Christianity also distrusted the body—its carnality, its sexuality, its weakness—and manifested a persistent ascetic strain. Although the suffering body was often given a positive religious valorization, other bodies were repudiated, especially the bodies of women, of homosexuals, and of Jews, which could be taken as suitable targets of violence but could also, by their very repudiation, be places from which critiques of official attitudes could be launched.[49]

In the pageants about Christ's sufferings, both the dramatic focus and the ideological emphasis are on the violation and humiliation of his body. Christ is beaten with bare hands as well as with whips. He is knocked down, spat upon, stripped naked, and nailed to the cross, all with considerable relish on the part of the perpetrators.[50] In the N-Town Trial before Pilate, the Jews "pulle of Jesus clothis and betyn hym with whyppys," saying "Jesus, þi bonys we xal not breke, / But we xal make þe to skyppe" (30/237–38). They then beat him "tyl he is all blody," as the stage directions demand. In the York plays the soldiers similarly batter Jesus, vowing that "He may banne þe tyme he was borne" (33/340). They strip off his clothes, bind him, and hit him with "bittir brasshis" (33/351), flaying him until he is "dressed" in red blood ("Alle rede with oure rowtes we aray hym / And rente hym," 33/355–56). Continuing their torment, they "hertely hitte on his hippes / And haunch" (33/367–68), proclaiming "þus with choppes þis churll sall we chastye" (33/377). The soldiers stop only when they are afraid that their violence has become so excessive it might kill him ("for and he dye for this dede vndone ere we all," 33/385).

Despite their fears, excess is a persistent feature of the assaults on Christ's body, which culminate in a sadistic frenzy that makes unavoidable a confrontation with power's effects on the body. In the Towneley Buffeting Jesus is so badly beaten that, as Froward says, "In fayth, syr, we had almost / Knokyd hym on slepe" (21/610–11). The Chester pageant of the Trial has the four Jews buffet Christ and spit in his face ("Spytt we in fere / and buffett him alls," 16/76–77). When Pilate orders Jesus to be scourged, one of the Jews says to Jesus: "On thy bodye bare / strockes shalt thou beare" (lines 309–10). The York Crucifixion pageant begins with a long, drawn-out description of the soldiers nailing Jesus to the cross, emphasizing such sadistic details as the pounding of nails into "bones and senous" (35/103), as well as the setting of the cross heavily into the hole "so all his bones / Are asoundre nowe on sides seere" (lines 223–24). Violent as these acts sound when encountered written on the page, they might well have been intensified in performance, where physical abuses not explicitly mentioned in the script could be stressed through improvisation by the actors. In one modern staging, for example, a reviewer remarked on "the brutal realism of the . . . Buffeting, with soldiers urinating on Christ."[51]

To a striking degree the violence against Christ is personalized, staged as the actions of individual agents, not as an anonymous exercise in abstract power, an emphasis that again calls attention to the operations of power embodied in real individuals.[52] In Herod, Pilate, Caiaphas, and Annas, as well as in the various Jews and soldiers who carry out these men's orders, evil is personal.[53] The York pageant of *Christ before Pilate 2: The Judgment*, opens with Pilate's threat that "I myself sall hym hurte full sore" (33/24). Pilate is quickly seconded by the *Preco*, who expresses his willingness to obey Pilate's orders in torturing Jesus, saying: "I am fayne / My lorde for to lede hym or lowte hym. / Vncleth hym, clappe hym and clowte hym / If ʒe bid me" (33/140–43). The scourging scene that follows takes place in explicit accordance with Pilate's direct orders: "Sir knyghtis þat ar comly, take þis caystiff in keping, / Skelpe hym with scourges and with skathes hym scorne. / Wraste and wrynge hym to, for wo to he be wepyng" (33/336–38). In the Towneley *Buffeting*, Caiaphas angrily says: "Bot I gif hym a blaw / My hart will brist" (21/276–77). After Jesus speaks briefly, Caiaphas continues with his desire for violence: "I shall hym styk / Euen with my awne hend / . . . Let me put hym to deth" (21/382–87), adding "It wold do me som good / To se knyghtys knok his hoode / With knokys two or thre" (21/453–55).

The treatment of Christ's body in these scenes resembles the treatment of the children's bodies in that, like theirs, Christ's body is subjected to personalized masculine assaults that penetrate and invade it.[54] In the Corpus Christi plays, Christ's body is pierced, probed, and violated. As his body is laid open in this way, the character of Jesus is made to take up a subject position more frequently occupied by women or Jews, whose bodies were the objects of ritual mutilation in the various representations I discussed at the beginning of this chapter. In the Towneley *Buffeting*, this subject position is made more explicit through Jesus' silence, which continues in the face of threats by Annas and Caiaphas. Like women and other marginalized figures, Christ here is denied a chance to speak and so is refused subjectivity, being treated instead as an inert object of the masculine attacks. This marginalization is further stressed by repeated references to Christ as "boy" or "child" or "ladde" in these scenes, intensifying his helplessness as well as his powerlessness. Paradoxically, however, this linking of Christ's body with other marginalized and subjected bodies has the unintended effect of highlighting the potential social threat posed by his body once it has been broken and torn. Like women's bodies, Christ's violated body—no longer pure and intact but now sullied and open—becomes a possible source of pollution and danger, and, like the violence to which it is prey, it becomes difficult to control or contain. As Mary Douglas has argued, invasions of the body disturb the social and economic order, rupturing the maintenance of pure and distinct categories, and opening the way for disorder, a condition to which Christ's broken body becomes susceptible, as well.[54]

The immense difficulties involved in containing either the violence itself or the effects of the violated body are revealed in the way the torture scenes are refigured as game or play. As Kolve has pointed out, the violence against Christ is framed within the context of other violent and competitive games, such as cockfighting, ninepins, tournaments, and hot cockles.[56] In the Towneley Buffeting, Caiaphas names Jesus "Kyng Copyn" in their "game" (21/239–41), and the *Primus Tortor* begins his torture of Jesus by saying: "We shall teche hym, I wote, / A new play of Yoyll" (21/497–98). Both the York and Towneley pageants make a game out of the buffeting, similar to the children's slapping game called hot cockles. York's Annas says that the "game" has begun (29/205), and the knights taunt Jesus with a drinking game (29/369) and plan how they will play "popse" with him (29/355). In the Towneley Crucifixion pageant, Jesus is described as playing in a tournament, with the cross as his horse. Playful competitiveness is also a part of many of these pageants, as in the Towneley Scourging, in which the Torturers vie to see who can hit Jesus hardest, urging each other on, saying: "Do rug hym! / Do dyng hym!" (22/192–93). Evidence suggests that at least some medieval spectators made a similar connection between torture and play; John Bromyard, for instance, in a fifteenth-century sermon links the buffeting and scourging of Christ with the game of blindman's buff.[57]

Although Kolve reads the use of game and play in the cycles as a distancing device that delegitimizes the torturers, thereby deflecting attention from the violence and keeping it under control, treating torture as game can have precisely the opposite effect. Rather than downplaying the work of pain and distancing the audience from it, configuring torment as play can emphasize the sadistic pleasure of the torturers while also inviting the audience to join in vicariously, since after all it is just a sport.[58] The pageants in fact take pains to draw the spectators into this pattern of sadistic pleasure that refashions torture as amusing pastime. In his speech to the audience in the Towneley Crucifixion, for instance, Jesus draws explicit attention to his bodily suffering and makes it clear that the audience is responsible for what he has endured. He says:

> I pray you pepyll that passe me by,
> That lede youre lyfe so lykandly,
> Heyfe vp youre hartys on hight!
> Behold if euer ye sagh body
> Buffet and bett thus blody.
> (23/233–37)

He goes on to add: "Blo and blody thus am I bett, / Swongen with swepys and all to-swett, / Mankynde, for thi mysdede" (23/525–27), making it hard for the audience not to feel in some degree culpable. In the York pageant, the audience is invited to share responsibility for the crucifixion when the soldier leading Christ to Calvary says to the spectators:

"But helpe me holly alle þat are here / þis kaitiffe care to encrees" (34/14–15). Like devotional images in books of hours, cycle plays asked from the spectator an imaginative projection into the representation such that the acts of spectatorship and participation were blurred. Watching a cycle play, like reading a book of hours, was a participatory act that deliberately drew the viewing subject into the scene being presented and thus made it difficult to maintain distance from the events being depicted or enacted.

There is little solid evidence pointing to how audiences might have reacted. Although Kolve sees only one reading of the plays' intended effect—"These dramatists presented the death of Christ as a thing of consummate horror and shame, clearly intending that the violence and laughter on stage should be answered by silence and awe in the audience"— more than one reaction to the spectacle of Christ's suffering might well have been possible.[59] Passion scenes, according to the *Tretise of Miraclis Pleyinge*, apparently did move some spectators "to compassion and devocion, wepinge bitere teris."[60] Similarly, Margery Kempe tells us that in a vision she saw "owr Lordys body wyth hys precyows blood þat it drow a-awey al þe hyde & al þe skyn of hys blissyd body. . . . And so had sche a newe sorwe þat sche wept & cryid ryth sor."[61] The ritual reenactment of Christ's bodily suffering in these pageants might thus have offered a way of understanding and channeling individual suffering, providing a public space for the expression of private pains that might otherwise have had no outlet.[62]

At the same time, since official church teachings saw Christ's pain as endowed with the power to purify, cleanse, and save, these dramas could also have acted as forms of sacramental penance that erased sin through bodily suffering and mortification. Certainly this would have been consistent with the cult of mortification that advanced bodily torture in the name of heaven, seeing pain and suffering as the means to a spiritual end.[63] In line with this understanding of bodily torture as salvific, it is worth recalling that within the symbol system of Christianity, blood was seen as ritually powerful and so was viewed as a "clean" bodily emission, unlike excrement or spit. To bleed was thus to participate in ritual purification.[64] (Medieval medical theory likewise believed that the shedding of blood did not defile or damage people but rather cleansed or purged them.)[65] From this perspective Christ's broken and bleeding body would seem a completely sanitized image, safe and without threatening implications. Through this reading, Christ's mutilated body would be easily contained within dominant social and economic structures that sought to subdue and control the body.

Certainly there is an ascetic impulse at work in the *imago pietatis* of these scenes that asks the spectator to view bodily torture as a way, albeit an extreme one, of subduing the body, especially the sexual body, in order to release the spirit.[66] But the violence in the Corpus Christi plays exceeds the logic of asceticism. Although the noise, violence, and rowdiness of the torturers have been interpreted as dramatizing the silent suffering of Jesus, pointing up his asceticism in contrast with their almost libidinous pleasure in torment, that reading relies perhaps too heavily on a unilateral valorization of the ascetic impulse.[67] Instead, the very exuberance with which violence operates in these pageants escapes a reading that would see the torture of Christ as a set of abhorrent acts that must be condemned. The plays seem rather to encourage spectators to enjoy the attacks on Christ's body as moments of undisguised sadistic delight in the inflicting of bodily pain. In these scenes, which develop the torture of Christ into a long and grotesque drama focusing on whips, wounds, and bloodshed, a highly charged erotics is revealed as the nearly naked, brutalized body of Christ is scourged by other men's hands.[68] In the process, violence refuses to be limited to safe cultural zones.

Moreover, blood is open to more complex and conflicting social interpretations than a salvific reading would imply. Particularly when gender difference is factored in, blood, as in menstrual blood, becomes a more ambivalent cultural sign, associated less with purity than with degradation, another of the "lower" bodily functions described by Bakhtin as markers of the grotesque body.[69] In this context the feminization of Christ's body as a result of his tortures takes on increased importance. Not only is Christ's body eroticized as it is penetrated but it is also refigured as feminine, with Christ's wounds becoming vagina-like images of desire and danger, representing at once the sacred body of the Savior and the menacing body of woman.[70] At the same time, the "pure" blood flowing from his torn flesh, fetishized in late medieval art and devotional writings, simultaneously becomes a sign of impurity, shame, and danger. As Christ is associated with woman, wound is coded as vagina, and blood as unclean bodily discharge; in the process, the suffering holy figure is rendered symbolically volatile, its cultural meanings pointing the way not only to redemption but also to transgression.[71]

As Elaine Scarry has argued, torture makes visible structures and processes that are usually kept hidden, private, and incommunicable. In so doing, torture represents a spectacle of power, but one that is based on the reality that the power so displayed is contestable and the regime it reflects is unstable.[72] In light of this, I would like to consider another possible response to these scenes of torture, dismemberment, and death, a response that would read the damaged body as a way of questioning the illusion of civic harmony based on the idea of an enclosed inviolate body corporate and would see the damaged body as a lesson in resistance to the imperatives of the urban economic order.

## Learning Not to Labor

Work—regulated, disciplined, and carefully scrutinized—was the organizing principle behind late medieval urban life.[73] As early as the twelfth century, professional workers such as craftsmen and merchants had sought religious and cultural justification for their labor, beginning a process that historians have described as a valorization of the ideology of work.[74] Within late medieval towns, work was a condition of admission to the community via the craft guilds and promised access to wealth, status, and political influence, although it did not necessarily come through on that promise. Through work carried out under the supervision of the guilds that Charles Phythian-Adams has described as "the basic reference-group" of urban society,[75] individual males took up their positions within the urban social system. By participating in the manufacturing activities allocated to the various crafts, these men were also located within the urban economy, the results of their labor distributed by the merchant elites who dominated late medieval towns. Not surprisingly, idleness was discouraged, and a variety of regulations attempted to prevent nonlaboring individuals from gaining a foothold in the urban community.[76]

The Corpus Christi plays were themselves deeply immersed in the labor economy of the urban communities that produced them, functioning as an important means of status display for the guilds, as sources of income for the town, and as mechanisms of economic rule that aided in regulating labor, manufacture, and trade. The plays also bore a strong relationship to lived experiences of labor, which they in key ways reproduced and critiqued within their performance space. This was especially true in the case of York, a city for which there is detailed information about the intersection of the town's social and economic life and the performance of the cycle plays. As recent scholarship has shown, the York plays supported the illusion of corporate solidarity that served the interests of York's mercantile oligarchy while also solidifying the artificial division of labor set up through the craft system.[77] In 1399, for example, the York plays are described as being performed not just "en honour & reuerence nostre seignour Iesu Crist" but also for the "honour & profitt de mesme la Citee."[78] As this suggests, the performance of the cycles could be idealized as a form of "work" done in honor of God and city.[79] The plays were also understood to perform spiritual work as well, spurring spectators to contrition and salvation.[80]

Sarah Beckwith has recently explored the work of work in the York cycle. Reading the plays in light of the economic forces that structured York, Beckwith argues that the York plays and especially the Crucifixion pageant articulated an "artisanal ideology" that emphasized making or manufacture and that this artisanal ideology effectively undercut the illusion of the corporate community that mercantile elites sought to create through the plays. Rather than projecting corporate holism, Beckwith asserts, the crucifixion is understood in terms of the "divisions enforced on the artisan body" by merchants and so demonstrates both "the kinds of political regulation necessitated by the body as a central mechanism of imaginary social order" and how that political regulation could be contested.[81]

In this context, the nonwork implied by a broken body, such as the bodies of the slain children or of Christ's after being tortured, shatters the myth of mutually productive labor that underpinned the urban economy as controlled by merchants. In capitalist societies, representing the body is always potentially subversive because to acknowledge the body is also to acknowledge the exploitative labor practices centering on the body that make capitalism possible. Capitalism thus must encourage various cultural strategies to cope with the "problem" of the body, including subduing it through violence.[82] As Michel Foucault has argued, the instruments of violence—which is, of course, the ultimate discipline—further the subjection of the body, making it submissive to a capitalist economic order that requires both "a productive body and a subjected body."[83] In the premodern period, according to Foucault, public torture made the condemned body the focal point of the display of power and also provided "an opportunity of affirming the dissymmetry of forces" that also emphasized the lack of power of those subjected to punishment.[84] Although forms of public violence such as torture call attention to the absolute hold that the powerful have on the bodies of the weak, public violence also ratifies the absolute right that the powerful have to possess and wield their might. In this view, public violence acts to protect divine, social, and political power, playing a central role in the construction and maintenance of authority, particularly by drawing on the idea of God's right to inflict violence and his license to punish—a divine prerogative that extended to ruling elites as well.[85] Like the "salutory violence" endured by Christ that stressed his passive obedience to divine will, public violence could function as a useful tool for preservation of the structures of authority.

In a similar argument about the social utility of violence, René Girard has emphasized the nearly universal cultural need for a surrogate victim who can effectively channel and contain violence that would otherwise be inflicted on the society itself. "The function of sacrifice," Girard claims, "is to quell violence within the community and to prevent conflicts from erupting."[86] A ritual sacrifice such as the crucifixion enacted in the Corpus Christi plays would in Girard's reading have the functionalist effect of venting cultural tensions and thereby safeguarding the society. Through acts of generative violence, which substitute a single victim for the whole community, the community is preserved intact and potential discordances are mitigated. For Girard, then, Christ's broken body would be a sign of communal solidarity, demonstrating that social tensions had been effectively released.

But violence could have a less functional and more disruptive effect than Girard allows, especially given that preservation of the community and its status quo might not be in the interests of all individuals, particularly those excluded from reward systems. Although violence might often serve power, or in Girard's terms the community, it could also be used against power. As James Given notes, in late medieval England violence was most often "a tool resorted to by the poor and the weak" who had few other routes to power or social justice.[87] As such, it offered ways of challenging the structures of rule and the distribution of wealth. If real violence could contest power, then so perhaps could theatrical violence, finding a way of short-circuiting dominant social and economic systems. Thus, although Herod, Pilate, and the powerful tormentors in the Corpus Christi plays represent unchecked masculine power using violence in its service and so would seem to be proof of a Foucauldian reading of violence as ratifying power, these perpetrators of violence also undermine their own power by consistently calling attention to how self-destructive it is. Moreover, since these powerfully violent men are coded by the plays as evil—even monstrous—their use of violence, and by extension any ruler's use of it, can hardly be seen as authorized. Instead, characters like the raging Herod, figured as slaughterer of innocent children, function in effect as critiques of violence used in the service of power.

At the same time as it questioned power's right to violence, theatrical violence also put the dismembered body on display and so opened the door to rejection of notions of corporeal wholeness, with all the social and economic implications of that rejection. In this way, the mutilated body—directly tied, as the children's bodies remind us, to economic systems in which healthy, lower-status, and submissive bodies are taken as agents of production—could become not just a sign of victimization but also an inspiration for resistance. Although images of bodily torture and death are usually read not as deviance and rupture but as conformist and officially sanctioned means of access to the divine,[88] they could not be confined to a restricted field of cultural meanings. Instead, these suffering and disappearing bodies could operate adversarially as well as normatively. Like the sick body, the wounded body could be deployed as a sign of anti-instrumentality—a tool that refuses to, indeed cannot, work. For this reason, the sacrificial mutilation in these pageants, performed in the service of absolute masculine power, spills over any attempt to contain it to the one unambiguous meaning of purification and redemption. Instead, the broken body also stands as a sign of refusal, particularly refusal of the world of work of the urban craft guilds who sponsored the plays that showcased these damaged bodies.

The transgressive potential of representations of broken bodies would have been enhanced not only by the mercantile-manufacturing split that Swanson has identified as the defining feature of late medieval towns and that might have encouraged thoughts of rebellion on the part of manufacturers, but also by the performance context, including the very notion of "playing." Endorsed by an alliance of civic and ecclesiastical authorities, the Corpus Christ plays, like all mimetic activity in the late Middle Ages, were nonetheless suspected of being by their very nature a source of disturbance to established structures of social and economic order.[89] Certainly the close connection between drama and other forms of violent play popular in the late Middle Ages—such as combat games like Robin Hood or bull and bear baiting—goes a long way toward underscoring the threat of violence and disruption that came to be connected with any public performance. The casual way in which spectators could move from watching a dramatic performance to watching public violence is strikingly revealed in the Coventry City Annals of 1511, which describe King Henry's visit to the city and the three pageants played for him, one with "the 9 orders of Angels," another with "divers beautifull Damsells," and a third "a goodly stage Play." The annals continue on to explain that immediately after these three pageants there "were certaine persons peached of Heresy where of some bare ffaggotts before the Procession on the Markett day the Principall of them were one Mrs Rowley & Ioan Ward, who afterwards was burned for the truth."[90] Here pageantry and punishment, drama and death, represent two fluidly connected types of public performances.

Disruptive and unruly conduct was often associated with the Corpus Christi plays. Clifford Flanigan has called attention to the plays' "festival, almost saturnalian, atmosphere," with their "prodigious eating and drinking" and other forms of disorderly conduct that civic and ecclesiastical authorities tried to curtail.[91] In 1426 the Franciscan preacher William Melton complained about those who came to the York cycle plays "not only to the play . . . but also greatly to feastings, drunkenness, clamours, gossipings, and other wantonness."[92] Since there was often a meeting of interests between friars and civic government, Melton's words can perhaps be taken as an expression of a common concern of authorities.

Corpus Christi performances, as historical records indicate, often went beyond mere disorderliness.[93] At Chester, in the Corpus Christi procession of 1358, for example, master weavers attacked their journeymen. The *A/Y Memorandum Book* from York records a complaint in 1419 about a disturbance at a Corpus Christi procession in which several carpenters and cordwainers used staves and axes to break torches being carried in the procession. And at Coventry there was mention in 1495 of "dyuers riottes & offences & gret discordes don & commytted vppon lammasse day."[94] The point that should be made here is that for these craftsmen, engaging in violence and disruption, what might look to urban authorities like an inappropriate use of their bodies, might be for them, however inchoately, a form of rebellion against strictures governing their laboring bodies. The connection Foucault makes between docility and utility suggests how at such moments the disorderly body could be figured as the nonproductive body, its lack of docility a mark of its incommensurability with the demands of labor.[95]

Various attempts were made to control or avert disturbances arising from performances, as the following examples, all from Chester, show. The Chester Assembly files of 1531–32 record the mayor's request that all people attending plays be "pecible" and avoid "eny assault affrey or other disturbans," including use of "vnlaufull wepons." In 1596, the city council passed an ordinance forbidding bull baiting and plays within the city. In a crackdown against some of the excesses of performances, but also apparently showing a personal grudge against a particular craft, Mayor Henry Hardware in 1599–1600 caused the midsummer giant belonging to the shoemakers ("whoe he much opposed") to be broken, the bull ring at High Cross to be taken up, and the dragon, the naked boys, and the butchers' devil to be banned from midsummer shows. And in 1615, performance of plays at night in the Common Hall was banned to prevent servants and apprentices from going to inns and plays where they would waste their masters' money and to forestall the disorder was that apt to occur at nighttime entertainments.[96]

Given this proclivity for disorder, the acts of represented violence within the plays might have been particularly potent.[97] If, as the records claim, the York Masons' Fergus play was so full of slapstick that it provoked not just laughter but also quarrels and fights among spectators, then what effect might the taunts and sadistic violence of the killers of the children or the torturers of Jesus have had?[98] If nothing else, the sheer dramatic energy of these violent characters makes it hard to dismiss them. And if we recall that the soldier leading Christ to Calvary in the York pageant asks the spectators to join in and participate in the brutality being heaped on Christ's body, then the impact of this violence on the audience would seem even stronger. We can get a glimpse of the possible reaction of performers from an exemplum in a Good Friday Sermon that describes a passion play in which Christ was stretched out, crucified, beaten, and mocked mercilessly; whoever among the performers tormented him the most was reckoned the best actor. When after the performance the players considered playing the game again and asked who should be Christ, the others replied that the man who had just played Christ should play him again, since he had done such a good job. When asked to replay the role, this man replied that he had played Christ and was tortured and crucified; therefore, if he has to play again he wants to be not Christ but a tormentor or demon.[99]

Although spectators might have identified with the tormentors within these pageants, given the various textual and dramatic overtures that encouraged them to do so, I am interested less in the dynamics of that identification than in what impact the broken bodies of the children and Christ had on spectators.[100] These violated bodies, I wish to suggest, offered a deviant reading of the sacrificial drama in which the image of the injured body became a locus for antilabor sentiment. In the scenes of the Slaughter of the Innocents and of Christ's sufferings, attention is called to the way the body becomes a commodity. Thus the mothers describe the murderers as thieves and equate the deaths of their children with loss of property. Similarly, Christ's body is denatured and turned into an object by the tortures to which it was subjected. In some pageants, Jesus is expressly treated like chattel. The Towneley Buffeting, for instance, opens with the two torturers driving Jesus like an ox to Caiaphas and Annas, calling out to him, "Do io furth, io!" (21/1). After beating him, the Torturers and Froward then lead Jesus off like a beast ("We shall lede the a trott," 21/621), with Froward driving him from behind ("Then nedys me do nott / Bot com after and dryfe," 21/623–24). Prodded and goaded in this way, Jesus' body recalls his status as the sacrificial lamb but also suggests the way that punishment results in the body's dehumanization and commodification. As his body is tortured, it exposes the objectifying and commodifying systems lying beneath the social and economic order. In this context it is worth noting that other bodies outside of the productive economy, such as imprisoned bodies, were treated in much the same way: imprisonment in medieval England usually involved such bodily hardships as solitary confinement, torture, and being forced to drink polluted water and eat rotten food.[101]

At this point, I wish to turn to a related aspect of the representation of violence against Christ's body, which also intersects with questions about the materiality of the body and its commodification—that is, relics. Perhaps the most obvious way in which the body's materiality was made explicit for late medieval individuals was through the trade in relics. Relics—bits and pieces of holy bodies and objects—represented the direct transformation of the body into a commodity. Used as devotional aids to further contemplation and taken as embodiments of the saints themselves, relics divided the body into an assortment of pieces that could be bought and sold, a process not unlike that effected through the division of labor in the craft guilds.[102] Since this process occurred only when the body was destroyed and broken apart, commodification of the body was linked to its dismemberment and dissolution.[103] Coinciding with the late medieval spurt of interest in Christ's suffering and with a drama that enacted scenes of pain and punishment, relics of the Passion also increased in number from the fourteenth century on.[104] As this suggests, relics were explicitly linked with the instruments of bodily torture, transforming suffering into a system of exchange that—like the Corpus Christi plays—sold pain and torture to an eager public.

Like the holy bodies that were dismembered and commodified through the trade in relics, the broken bodies of Christ and the children were similarly caught up in the sale and consumption of bodily suffering. In these performances, the body was produced, reproduced, and consumed as a commodity, increasingly alienated from the self and fetishized as an object. Plays like the Croxton *Play of the Sacrament* stage the re-membering of the dismembered body—as Jonathas's severed hand is reattached—and the reincorporation of the perished body—as Christ appears out of the oven, re-embodied from the tortured wafer. In such scenes, a dramatic recuperation of the battered body into the social whole takes place as both broken body and riven society are reintegrated and made whole.

But similar reintegrations are lacking in the scenes of the Slaughter of the Innocents and the Crucifixion; these damaged bodies are not made whole again, are not brought back to life, and are not restored to the social whole. Instead, these bodies, disarticulated on stage, dissolve out of being and disappear.[105] They stay broken and lost, taken out of the productive order. Emphasizing the breakdown of the autonomous body and an attendant loss of self, the body in these pageants is no longer figured as self-contained and controlled, but instead is fragmented and shattered. The enclosed, contained, self-sufficient body found in books of hours disappears. In its place appears a shattered body that cannot participate in the economic order and hence threatens to rupture the system.[106] This breached body perhaps inevitably troubles the system within which it is inscribed; the breakdown of the body thus figures the breakdown of the social and economic order, which is itself modeled on the body.

From the perspective of urban authorities, such a breakdown was of course undesirable since it risked the destruction of the dominant order. But from the perspective of the powerless it was perhaps just the opposite: liberatory. Freeing the body from economic constraints that forced it to become an agent of production, representations of broken bodies might have offered a model of resistance to the regime of work. Sponsored by the craft guilds under the aegis of urban elites who sought to enhance their own position and power and, as Phythian-Adams has said, "to preserve the social order on which their influence rested,"[107] the Corpus

Christi plays were cultural performances that at some imaginary level exposed contradictions between work and nonwork, between production and profit, in the late medieval urban community. Not only were such moments of contradiction present in these plays, as seen in the equivocal character of the plays' representation of Christ's broken body and the slain bodies of the children, but such contradictions were responsible for and infused the ambiguous form of the cycle plays themselves.

Although violence is often the most coercive discipline of the body, its logic can also be reversed. The beaten or broken body, chastised by violence into submission, can nonetheless become resistant, impervious to future punishment and so free to defy authoritative systems. As Foucault notes, the condemned person at public executions, who had nothing left to fear, was at that moment licensed to say what he wished, cheered on by the crowd.[108] By virtue of the analogous tortures inflicted on their bodies, the murdered children and the crucified Christ of Corpus Christi plays were similarly licensed to speak, however obliquely, against the status quo.

According to Foucault, the disappearance of public executions marked not just the decline of the spectacle, but also "a slackening hold on the body."[109] The modern period, in his reading, thus saw the gradual removal of the theatrical representation of pain from the field of punishment, and the tortured body was no longer put on public display. In late medieval England, however, the hold on the body was still strong, and theatrical representations of pain were potent cultural resources. Although violence against the body could serve the interests of power, modeling a way of bringing bodies into line, it could also work to the opposite end, that of resisting power. Such, it seems to me, is what might have happened with the broken bodies of children and Jesus in the Corpus Christi plays, where the body's subservience to systems of commodification and production was made apparent and by being exposed was opened to resistance. Thus these theatrical scenes of suffering could do contrapuntal ideological work, even while in the service of a dominant religious message and a civic power-structure.

# Afterword
+
## Domination, Resistance, and the Consumer

*You're so sure that's rain. How do you know it's not sulfuric acid from factories across the river? How do you know it's not fallout from a war in China?*

—Don DeLillo, *White Noise*

How do you know?" is of course the question that haunts all historical and cultural critique, reminding us that historiographical knowledge is a mediated affair, one in which present desires intersect with past representations of at best dimly glimpsed events. To look for moments of resistance within late medieval culture, as I have done, thus inevitably reveals as much about the searcher as it does about the practices found and scrutinized. That said, the processes of control and resistance that I have been arguing can be seen in late medieval England must be acknowledged as inseparable, part of the polyvalency of all cultural forces. No matter how thorough or unilateral official culture's program of control, it was also open to internal contradictions and inconsistencies that made it vulnerable to revisionist appropriations. Despite their tactics of persuasion, disciplinary models often came up short, if only because the representational forms they inhabited were themselves ungovernable. The rules of discourse, as we know them today, are rarely compliant with the intentionality of authors, no matter how determined they might be. Although late medieval disciplining discourses were powerful, enlisting as they did the weight of cultural consensus in their aid, they could not impose their regimes with complete coherence or consistency, unless subjects were willing to go along with them.

At the same time, theatrical performances, although positioned to expose the hand of power and to stage resistances to it, were also complicitous with its operations. Like other forms of popular culture, the theater cannot be seen simply as a place of repressive social control on the part of elite groups or as a site of rebellious self-expression by the oppressed. Instead, it falls somewhere in between, as contested territory that sometimes resists and sometimes capitulates to authority, depending upon the varied interpretations of spectators within specific and changing cultural contexts. How cultural representations are used by spectators, readers, and other consumers is thus a key question.

Studies of modern mass culture—the field where spectator response has been most thoroughly theorized—have tended to foreground the oppositional potential of audience responses, emphasizing how individuals can resist the dominant ideology encoded in mass market texts.[1] Cultural critics like John Fiske, Dick Hebdige, Tania Modleski, and Janice Radway, for example, have construed the spectator as relatively "strong" in the face of cultural pressures, empowered to shape cultural material to his or her own needs, an activity these critics often view as subversive or antistructural. Such, for example, is the position Fiske takes in his analysis of Madonna fans, interpreting teenage girls' appropriation of this pop culture icon as in effect a liberating and creative activity that helps them resist the various social pressures brought to bear on modern adolescents. Similarly, the work of Modleski and Radway on fantasies for women foregrounds the way in which individual female readers refashion romances and soap operas to satisfy their own desires.[2]

Studies positing a resisting spectator are in many ways appealing, especially given the nearly irresistible desire on the part of the cultural critic to discover resistance, but they run the risk of underestimating the strength of cultural determinism. Individuals may in fact possess the ability to deflect the dominant force of a text, but their power of resistance dims considerably in comparison with the weight of cultural conditioning. In an analysis of what she calls "cinematic digressions," Barbara Klinger has cautioned against this tendency to privilege oppositional responses. Cinematic digressions, the outbursts heard in any movie house— the teenager who recites lines from *The Terminator* while watching *The Golden Child*, or the spectator who comments aloud on the past roles or personal lives of an actor in a film, or the man who sings along with every song in *Sweet Dreams*—are often considered to be disruptive and hence resistant responses. But while digressive responses might seem to mark a lack of textual control (the film has failed to model the appropriate response for its viewers and so has been unable to turn them into "ideal" spectators) or to demonstrate the resisting power of the spectator, Klinger sees them instead as encouraged by "social and intertextual agencies within mass culture" that structure response in a way that, rather than being subversive, ultimately supports the dominant ideology.[3]

What these mass culture critics suggest is that coercion can look like resistance and resistance can look like coercion. If anything is certain, and few things are, it is that control and resistance are dialectically bound together in a tightly drawn knot. In late medieval England, both official culture's project of control and the theater's involvement in the staging of deviant subjectivities were complex ideological processes in which the consumption of the product was indeterminate and open to conflicting understandings, with the effects on individuals being more plural than singular. The embodied subjects who were the consumers of the disciplining discourses I have been examining need not have acquiesced to the lessons taught by those discourses and performances—or may have recognized only their authority, not their desirability. At the same time, there is no assurance that the oppositional tactics that I have argued can be found in various theatrical performances were ever actualized in people's lived experiences; they might have remained at best merely hypotheses about what might have been. But even as hypotheses such performances might have opened up a space for the contemplation of alternatives, offering ways of at least *imagining* ways to evade power and to reshape the boundaries of embodied and commodified subjectivity beyond the scope of the licensed world of performance.

# Notes

✣

## Introduction. Bodily Transactions: Performance, Identity, and Commodification

1. Terry Eagleton, *Against the Grain: Essays, 1975–1985* (London: Verso, 1986), 145.

2. The predicament of postmodern identities has been described by Arthur Kroker and Marilouise Kroker, "Theses on the Disappearing Body in the Hyper-Modern Condition," in *Body Invaders: Panic Sex in America*, ed. Arthur Kroker and Marilouise Kroker (New York: St. Martin's Press, 1987), 20–34.

3. For a critique of the persistent tendency to read medieval subjectivity as unproblematic, a tendency that is especially pronounced in the writings of scholars of early modern England, see David Aers, "A Whisper in the Ear of Early Modernists; or, Reflections on Literary Critics Writing the 'History of the Subject,'" in *Culture and History, 1350–1600: Essays on English Communities, Identities, and Writing*, ed. David Aers (Detroit, Mich.: Wayne State University Press, 1992), 177–202.

4. For a succinct summary of these developments, see Steven Ozment, *The Age of Reform, 1250–1550: An Intellectual and Religious History of Late Medieval and Reformation Europe* (New Haven: Yale University Press, 1980), esp. 5–8.

5. The *locus classicus* for this notion is Foucault's *History of Sexuality*, trans. Robert Hurley, vol. 1 (New York: Pantheon, 1978). For an analysis of Foucault's ideas about desire and its suppression through discipline, see Bryan S. Turner, *The Body and Society: Explorations in Social Theory* (Oxford: Blackwell, 1984), 157–76.

6. For a range of recent investigations into the social construction of medieval bodies, see the essays in *Framing Medieval Bodies*, ed. Sarah Kay and Miri Rubin (Manchester: Manchester University Press, 1994).

7. John Metham, *Physiognomy*, in *The Works of John Metham*, ed. Hardin Craig, Early English Text Society (hereafter EETS) os 132 (London: Kegan Paul, Trench, Trübner, 1915), 145.

8. For an overview of the political use of body metaphors in the Middle Ages, see Ernst H. Kantorowicz, *The King's Two Bodies: A Study in Mediaeval Political Theology* (Princeton: Princeton University Press, 1957), and Jacques Le Goff, "Head or Heart? The Political Use of Body Metaphors in the Middle Ages," in *Zone: Fragments for a History of the Human Body*, ed. Michel Feher, with Ramona Nadaff and Nadia Tazi, 3 vols. (New York: Urzone, 1989), 3:12–27. For a cultural anthropological approach to the concept of body as a way of understanding the social, see Mary Douglas, *Natural Symbols: Explorations in Cosmology* (New York: Pantheon, 1970), 65–81.

9. These ideas can be found spread across much of Bourdieu's work. See in particular *Outline of a Theory of Practice*, trans. Richard Nice (Cambridge: Cambridge University Press, 1977), 81–90, and *The Logic of Practice*, trans. Richard Nice (Stanford, Calif.: Stanford University Press, 1990), 52–71. The quotation is from *Logic of Practice*, 56.

10. See the discussion of the impact of consumption on the body in Mike Featherstone,

"The Body in Consumer Culture," *Theory, Culture and Society* 1, no. 2 (1982): 18–33. I would disagree, however, with Featherstone's assumption that "consumer culture" began only with the modern era. See also Anthony Giddens, *Modernity and Self-Identity: Self and Society in the Late Modern Age* (Stanford, Calif.: Stanford University Press, 1991); like many humanist critics, Giddens sees the commodification of the self as a process to be deplored: in modern culture, Giddens complains, "the project of the self becomes translated into one of the possession of desired goods and the pursuit of artificially framed styles of life" (198).

11. Patricia Fumerton's *Cultural Aesthetics: Renaissance Literature and the Practice of Social Ornament* (Chicago: University of Chicago Press, 1991) provides a useful investigation of how commodities were used in constructing early modern identities.

12. For a discussion of consumption from the perspective of symbolic anthropology, see Mary Douglas and Baron Isherwood, *The World of Goods* (New York: Basic Books, 1979). Douglas and Isherwood describe consumption as "the very arena in which culture is fought over and ordered into shape" (57). Recent studies of early modern commodity culture in England include Colin Campbell, *The Romantic Ethic and the Spirit of Modern Consumerism* (Oxford: Blackwell, 1987); Neil McKendrick, John Brewer, and J. H. Plumb, *The Birth of a Consumer Society: The Commercialization of Eighteenth-Century England* (London: Europa, 1982); and Joan Thirsk, *Economic Policy and Projects: The Development of Consumer Society in Early Modern England* (Oxford: Clarendon, 1978). For studies of late medieval consumption, see Fernand Braudel, *Capitalism and Material Life, 1400–1800*, trans. Miriam Kochan (New York: Harper and Row, 1973), and Chandra Mukerji, *From Graven Images: Patterns of Modern Materialism* (New York: Columbia University Press, 1983).

13. Christopher Dyer, "Were There Any Capitalists in Fifteenth-Century England?" in *Enterprise and Individuals in Fifteenth-Century England*, ed. Jennifer Kermode (Wolfeboro Falls, N.H.: Sutton, 1991), 1–24. For a fuller description of these developments, see R. H. Britnell, *The Commercialisation of English Society, 1000–1500* (Cambridge: Cambridge University Press, 1993), esp. 156–77.

14. For a useful discussion of de Certeau's theories of consumption, see Mark Poster, "The Question of Agency: Michel de Certeau and the History of Consumerism," *Diacritics* 22, no. 2 (1992): 94–107.

15. Michel de Certeau, *The Practice of Everyday Life*, trans. Steven F. Randall (Berkeley: University of California Press, 1984); the quotation is from xii. Like Bourdieu, de Certeau is aware of the way that practices tend to disappear in object-oriented analyses, especially since he sees practice as essentially a nondiscursive domain, a domain that analysis tries (often unsuccessfully) to submit to discourse. Practice, de Certeau insists, always has to be seen as ambiguous—as both beyond discourse and produced by it.

16. Judith Butler, *Gender Trouble: Feminism and the Subversion of Identity* (New York: Routledge, 1990), 32.

17. See Gail McMurray Gibson, *The Theater of Devotion: East Anglian Drama and Society in the Late Middle Ages* (Chicago: University of Chicago Press, 1989), 68.

18. Erving Goffman, *The Presentation of Self in Everyday Life* (New York: Doubleday, 1959). For a comprehensive survey of conceptualizations of "identity" within the social sciences, including a discussion of Goffman's contributions, see Philip Gleason, "Identifying Identity: A Semantic History," *Journal of American History* 69 (1983): 910–31.

19. See James C. Scott, *Domination and the Arts of Resistance: Hidden Transcripts* (New Haven: Yale University Press, 1991), for a discussion of the enactment of dissident stances, which he terms "hidden transcripts." Judith Butler has similarly described how a subordinated group can perform within a system that excludes or marginalizes it, forcing a reexamination of hegemony and of spectators' own positions within the social order; see her *Bodies That Matter* (New York: Routledge, 1993), esp. 109–18.

20. As has become increasingly clear, no form of popular culture can be seen as either a place of repressive social control on the part of elite groups or of rebellious self-expression by the oppressed. Instead, popular culture has to be conceptualized as contested territory that sometimes resists and sometimes capitulates to hegemony; see the discussion in Gareth Stedman Jones, "Class Expression versus Social Control? A Critique of Recent Trends in the Social History of 'Leisure,'" in *Languages of Class: Studies in English Working Class History, 1832–1982* (Cambridge: Cambridge University Press, 1983), 76–89.

21. Bourdieu, *Logic of Practice*, 37.

## Chapter 1. Fashioned Subjectivity and the Regulation of Difference

1. James A. Clifford, *The Predicament of Culture: Twentieth-Century Ethnography, Literature, and Art* (Cambridge: Harvard University Press, 1988), 289.

2. Ibid., 278.

3. My sense of the difficulties of reading the signifying system of fashion stands in contrast to structural analyses such as those of Roland Barthes and Marshall Sahlins, which assume that clothing is an unambiguously legible code; see Roland Barthes, *Système de la mode* (Paris: Editions du Seuil, 1967), and Marshall Sahlins, "The American Clothing System," in *Culture and Practical Reason* (Chicago: University of Chicago Press, 1976), 179–204.

4. Most analyses of fashion, assuming that clothing becomes semiotically significant only in the twentieth century, focus on clothing within late capitalism. For a sampling of such studies, see Jennifer Craik, *The Face of Fashion: Cultural Studies in Fashion* (London: Routledge, 1994); Gail Faurschou, "Fashion and the Cultural Logic of Postmodernity," in *Body Invaders: Panic Sex in America*, ed. Arthur Kroker and Marilouise Kroker (New York: St. Martin's Press, 1987), 78–93; and Elizabeth Wilson, *Adorned in Dreams: Fashion and Modernity* (London: Virago, 1985).

5. For a discussion of these changes, see François Boucher, *A History of Costume in the West* (London: Thames and Hudson, 1967); James Laver, *Costume and Fashion: A Concise History* (London: Thames and Hudson, 1982); and Stella Mary Newton, *Fashion in the Age of the Black Prince: A Study of the Years 1340–1365* (Woodbridge, Suffolk: Boydell, 1980). Since I am less interested in the fashions themselves than in discourses about them, my description broadly sketches the chief changes in fashion after 1340.

6. See R. H. Britnell, *The Commercialisation of English Society, 1000–1500* (Cambridge: Cambridge University Press, 1993), 168–69, and Christopher Dyer, *Standards of Living in the Later Middle Ages: Social Change in England, c. 1200–1520* (Cambridge: Cambridge University Press, 1989). Britnell claims that between 1350 and 1500 demand shifted away from locally produced fabrics of low quality to imports from well-known centers of clothmaking (169). Dyer argues that even English peasants had the spending power to buy the more costly new fashions (177). In the late fifteenth century, approximate annual income from land for the various ranks might have been as follows: duke, £4,000; marquis, £3,000; baron, £500; knight banneret, £200; knight of the shire, £40–£100; and yeoman, £5; during the same period, day wages for manual labor ranged from 5d. to 10d.; see *The Agrarian History of England and Wales, vol. 3, 1348–1500*, ed. Edward Miller (Cambridge: Cambridge University Press, 1991), 526–27 and 471.

7. *The Brut*, ed. Friedrich W. D. Brie, 2 vols., EETS os 131, 136 (London: Kegan Paul, Trench, Trübner, 1906–8), 2:296–97. The passage refers to the 1340s.

8. For a useful discussion of commodity fetishism and subjectivity, see Jack Amariglio and Antonio Callari, "Marxian Value Theory and the Problem of the Subject: The Role of Commodity Fetishism," in *Fetishism as Cultural Discourse*, ed. Emily Apter and William Pietz (Ithaca: Cornell University Press, 1993), 186–216. Amariglio and Callari attempt a revisionist reading of Marx to show that, contrary to what is often claimed, Marxism does not

ignore subjectivity but rather assumes that "social agency is a necessary and constituent aspect of the depiction of the economic practices of market capitalism" (216).

9. Marjorie Garber, *Vested Interests: Cross-Dressing and Cultural Anxiety* (New York: Routledge, 1992), 142.

10. See Victor Turner, *The Anthropology of Performance* (New York: PAJ, 1987), 74.

11. For a fuller discussion of sumptuary laws as discursive events or social practices, see my "Narrating the Social Order: Medieval Clothing Laws," *CLIO* 21 (1992): 265–83.

12. This claim can be found throughout Bourdieu's writings, but for a succinct discussion, see his "Structures, *Habitus*, Practices," in *The Logic of Practice*, trans. Richard Nice (Stanford, Calif.: Stanford University Press, 1990), 52–65. Bourdieu describes the *habitus* as "structured structures predisposed to function as structuring structures, that is, as principles which generate and organize practices and representations that can be objectively adapted to their outcomes without presupposing a conscious aiming at ends or an expressed mastery of the operations necessary in order to attain them" (53).

13. Michel Foucault, *The History of Sexuality*, trans. Robert Hurley (New York: Pantheon, 1978), 1:101.

14. Robert Mannyng, *Handlyng Synne*, ed. Idelle Sullens (Binghamton, N.Y.: Medieval and Renaissance Texts and Studies, 1983), lines 3219–24.

15. *Wimbledon's Sermon "Redde Rationem Villicationis tue": A Middle English Sermon of the Fourteenth Century*, ed. Ione Kemp Knight (Pittsburgh, Pa.: Duquesne University Press, 1967), lines 523–26.

16. MS Harl. 4894, fol. 176b; quoted in G. R. Owst, *Literature and Pulpit in Medieval England* (Cambridge: Cambridge University Press, 1933), 404–5.

17. For a discussion of the tendency to link clothes with morals, see John Scattergood, "Fashion and Morality in the Late Middle Ages," in *England in the Fifteenth Century*, ed. Daniel Williams (Woodbridge, Suffolk: Boydell, 1987), 255–72.

18. 3 Edward IV; *Statutes of the Realm* (1810–28; reprint, London: Dawsons, 1963), 1:380. Subsequent mentions of the statutes refer to this edition. Despite the fact that the new fashions eroticized the male body (through tight trousers, short jackets, codpieces, and penis-shaped shoes called *poulaines*) more than the female, discursive attacks usually targeted women's dress. For a survey of preachers' complaints about female dress, see Owst, *Literature and Pulpit*, 390–404; for songs and poems attacking women's clothing, see *Satirical Songs and Poems on Costume*, ed. Frederick W. Fairholt (London: Percy Society, 1849).

19. Mannyng, *Handlyng Synne*, lines 7613–14.

20. *Jacob's Well*, ed. Arthur Brandeis, EETS os 115 (London: Kegan Paul, Trench, Trübner, 1900), 159.

21. *Middle English Sermons*, ed. Woodburn O. Ross, EETS os 209 (London: Oxford University Press, 1940), 234–35.

22. MS Harl. 2398, fol. 9; quoted in Owst, *Literature and Pulpit*, 401; my translation.

23. *Middle English Dictionary*, ed. Hans Kurath (Ann Arbor: University of Michigan Press, 1952), s.v. "disgise."

24. *The Receyt of the Ladie Kateryne*, ed. Gordon Kipling, EETS os 296 (Oxford: Oxford University Press, 1990), 52–68.

25. For a discussion of the role of dress in establishing inner and outer, real and constructed selves, see Dyan Elliott, "Dress as Mediator between Inner and Outer Self: The Pious Matron of the High and Later Middle Ages," *Mediaeval Studies* 53 (1991): 279–308.

26. See the meanings listed under "countrefet" in *Middle English Dictionary*.

27. For a fuller discussion of why female cross-dressing was more permissible than male cross-dressing, see Vern L. Bullough and Bonnie Bullough, *Cross Dressing, Sex, and Gender* (Philadelphia: University of Pennsylvania Press, 1993). Medieval perceptions of the female as inferior were responsible for the assumption that a woman who wore men's clothes was

behaving in a rational way, by attempting to adopt a male role, whereas a man who dressed like a woman would be perceived as acting irrationally (51).

28. Thomas Aquinas, *Summa theologica*, vol. 44, ed. and trans. Thomas Gilby (New York: McGraw-Hill, 1972), 238–39. Aquinas argues in the same passage that most cross-dressing is wrong because it leads to lasciviousness.

29. Henry Knighton, *Chronicon*, ed. Joseph R. Lumby, 2 vols. (London: Eyre and Spottis-woode, 1889–95), 2:67; referring to the tournament of 1347, Knighton describes a group of women ("dominarum cohors") who showed up looking like male actors ("quasi comes interludii, in diverso et mirabili apparatu virili") (57).

30. *Eulogium historiarum sive temporis*, ed. Frank S. Haydon, 3 vols. (London: Longman, 1863), 3:230–31. The writer criticizes men's tunics that are fashioned in a feminine rather than masculine mode ("quaedam sunt longa usque ad talum, non in parte anteriori, ut decet viris, aperta, sed modo mulierum usque brachia in costis distenta") (230), then complains that men so dressed look more like performers of various kinds than like barons, soldiers, or knights ("citherones et nebulones quam barones, histriones quam milites, mimi quam armigeri") (231). For iconographic tendencies to equate new fashions with the (disreputable) dress of entertainers, see Ruth Mellinkoff, *Outcasts: Signs of Otherness in Northern European Art of the Late Middle Ages*, 2 vols. (Berkeley: University of California Press, 1993), 1:12–13, and 2: figs. 1.16–18.

31. Thomas Hoccleve, *The Regement of Princes*, in *Hoccleve's Works*, ed. Frederick J. Furnivall, vol. 3, EETS es 72 (London: Kegan Paul, Trench, Trübner, 1897), 1–197; the quotation is from lines 463–76 and 482–83.

32. Ibid., lines 436–37.

33. Ibid., lines 444–45.

34. See Mellinkoff, *Outcasts*, 2: figs. 1.22–25.

35. The most comprehensive study of English sumptuary laws is still Frances E. Baldwin, *Sumptuary Legislation and Personal Regulation in England* (Baltimore: Johns Hopkins University Press, 1926). Useful perspective is cast on the English laws by studies of European sumptuary legislation; see Diane Owen Hughes, "Distinguishing Signs: Ear-Rings, Jews and Franciscan Rhetoric in the Italian Renaissance City," *Past and Present* 112 (1986): 3–59; Ulrike Lehmann-Langholz, *Kleiderkritik in Mittelalterlicher Dichtung* (Frankfurt am Main: Peter Lang, 1985); and Michael Stolleis, *Pecunia nervus rerum: Zur Staatsfinanzierung der frühen Neuzeit* (Frankfurt am Main: Klostermann, 1983). Regulation of dress goes back at least to republican Rome, but began in medieval Europe in the thirteenth century, reaching its peak in the late medieval and early modern periods.

36. 37 Edward III; *Statutes of the Realm*, 1:380–82.

37. 3 Edward IV; *Statutes of the Realm*, 2:399.

38. A proclamation of 1577 refers to the difficulty of ascertaining the value of a person's estate for the purposes of telling whether or not the law is being violated. The problem was dealt with by using the individual's assessment rate in the subsidy books; anyone charged with violating a sumptuary law could challenge that assessment, but would then be liable for a higher subsidy rate; see the *Book of Proclamations* (Brit. Mus., G. 6463), fol. 168; quoted in Wilfrid Hooper, "The Tudor Sumptuary Laws," *English Historical Review* 30 (1915): 444.

39. 37 Edward III; *Statutes of the Realm*, 1:381.

40. 3 Edward IV; *Statutes of the Realm*, 2:400.

41. MS Worc. Cath. Libr. F.10, fol. 49b; quoted in Owst, *Literature and Pulpit*, 410.

42. These differences of rank within the group were often a source of friction. In a dispute of 1396 between the masters of the London Saddlers and the yeomen of the same trade, the yeomen demanded that they be allowed to wear livery and meet as a fraternity, a demand that the masters refused; see David Wallace, "Chaucer and the Absent City," in

*Chaucer's England: Literature in Historical Context*, ed. Barbara A. Hanawalt (Minneapolis: University of Minnesota Press, 1992), 76–77.

43. See T. F. Reddaway, *The Early History of the Goldsmiths' Company, 1327–1509* (London: Arnold, 1975), 236–37.

44. *Coventry Corporation Leet Book*; quoted in *Secular Lyrics of the Fourteenth and Fifteenth Centuries*, ed. Rossell Hope Robbins (Oxford: Clarendon, 1952), 115.

45. *City of York House Book*; quoted in *Secular Lyrics*, ed. Robbins, 117.

46. See Sheila Lindenbaum, "The Smithfield Tournament of 1390," *Journal of Medieval and Renaissance Studies* 20 (1990): 4.

47. William Caxton, *Vocabulary in French and English: A Facsimile of Caxton's Edition, c. 1480*, with an introduction by J. C. T. Oates and L. C. Harmer (Cambridge: Cambridge University Press, 1964).

48. Discussed in Rodney Hilton, *Class Conflict and the Crisis of Feudalism: Essays in Medieval Social History*, rev. 2d ed. (London: Verso, 1990), 128.

49. *Testamenta Eboracensia*, Surtees Society 30 (London: George Andrews, 1855), 41 and 106, respectively.

50. See Britnell, *Commercialisation*, 164–69 and 218–27. E. F. Jacob, *The Fifteenth Century, 1399–1485* (Oxford: Clarendon, 1961), 384, estimates average wages for the period from 1351 to 1540 at 5½d. per day for carpenters, 6d. for masons, and 4d. for agricultural laborers.

51. Anthony Fitzherbert, *The Book of Husbandry*, ed. W. W. Skeat (London: Trübner, 1882), 102.

52. See Beverly Lemire, "Consumerism in Preindustrial and Early Industrial England: The Trade in Secondhand Clothes," *Journal of British Studies* 27 (1988): 1–24; Lemire speculates that the trade in secondhand clothes had existed "for generations or even centuries before it came to the notice of contemporary writers and correspondents" (3).

53. Cited in Hilton, *Class Conflict*, 125.

54. See Barbara A. Hanawalt, *Crime in East Anglia in the Fourteenth Century: Norfolk Gaol Delivery Rolls, 1307–1316* ([Norwich]: Norfolk Record Society, 1976), 82.

55. 22 Edward IV; *Statutes of the Realm*, 2:468.

56. Hoccleve, *Regement of Princes*, line 450.

57. *The Book of the Knight of La Tour-Landry*, ed. Thomas Wright, EETS os 33 (London: Trübner, 1868), 65–69; the quotation is from 67.

58. 3 Edward IV; *Statutes of the Realm*, 2:399; italics indicate expansion of abbreviations.

59. For a discussion of sumptuary laws from an economic perspective, see N. B. Harte, "State Control of Dress and Social Change in Pre-Industrial England," in *Trade, Government and Economy in Pre-Industrial England: Essays Presented to F. J. Fisher*, ed. D. C. Coleman and A. H. John (London: Weidenfeld and Nicolson, 1976), 132–65.

60. *Middle English Dictionary*, s.v. "inordinat(e)."

61. Hoccleve, *Regement of Princes*, line 440.

62. The sumptuary law of 1554 included a provision imposing a fine of one hundred pounds on masters who retained in their service servants whom they knew had violated the act. See 1 and 2 Philip and Mary; *Statutes of the Realm*, 4:239.

63. *Book of the Knight of La Tour-Landry*, ed. Wright, 29–31.

64. Mannyng, *Handlyng Synne*, lines 3355, 3358, and 3389–90, respectively.

65. Cf. Morton Bloomfield's definition of pride as "the sin of exaggerated individualism," a rebellion against God and hence against "a disciplined and corporate society," in *The Seven Deadly Sins* (East Lansing: Michigan State College Press, 1952), 74–75.

66. John Bromyard, "In vesibus ex transverso scissis"; discussed in Owst, *Literature and Pulpit*, 81–82.

67. Quoted in Owst, *Literature and Pulpit*, 95–96.

68. *Jacob's Well*, ed. Brandeis, 80, lines 27–34.

69. *Book of the Knight of La Tour-Landry*, ed. Wright, 62.

70. A story from *Handlyng Synne* takes up the same theme, relating "How a lady was pyned yn helle." We learn that this lady's sin was that she loved "feyr tyffyng / On here hed ouer al þyng." After she died, her squire fell sick and thought she came to him in a vision and took him to a field where he watched as four devils put a burning wheel on her head and she was burned to the ground. The squire asks why she suffers this torment, and she replies that she has earned it because "Y dyghte myn hed ful moche wyþ pryde / For to be preysed ouer alle ladys," hence seeking to assert social difference and make herself stand out from other women; see Mannyng, *Handlyng Synne*, lines 3242–3332.

71. BL MS Additional 41321, fols. 101b–2; quoted in Owst, *Literature and Pulpit*, 369. Owst notes that the reference to bag sleeves dates the passage to somewhere between 1380 and 1440.

72. Clothing laws show little desire to legislate the dress of the poor. Instead, their interest in the lower groups seems purely rhetorical. When the lower social strata are cursorily included in the laws, their inclusion is largely part of a need to create a complete social hierarchy covering all social groups.

73. See, for example, Jean A. Hamilton and James W. Hamilton, "Dress as a Reflection and Sustainer of Social Reality: A Cross-Cultural Perspective," *Clothing and Textiles Research Journal* 7 (1989): 16–22.

74. Elizabeth was particularly assiduous in enforcing sumptuary laws. In 1559, a Privy Council letter proposed that two watchers be appointed for every parish, with a list of all persons assessed at twenty pounds per year or two hundred pounds in goods in order to ensure that the prohibition against silk trimmings was obeyed. The suggestion gave rise to a countrywide system of surveillance. In London, watchmen were appointed at each of the city gates to monitor the apparel of everyone entering the city; see Hooper, "Tudor Sumptuary Laws," 437 and 443.

75. The 1363 statute was backed by threat of confiscation of the offending item; the 1463 statute included fines and required the oversight of justices of the peace and mayors; the 1510 statute arranged for the splitting of the fine with the informer; the 1515 statute charged ushers of the King's and Queen's Chambers with seizing the offending piece of clothing; see the discussion in Harte, "State Control of Dress," 144.

76. Cited in Hooper, "Tudor Sumptuary Laws," 438.

77. City Corporation Records, Repertorium 15, fols. 414b and 416b; quoted in Hooper, "Tudor Sumptuary Laws," 440–41. Another offender had the stuffing and lining of his offending hose cut and pulled out, and was led home through the streets wearing them.

78. Garber, *Vested Interests*, 161, says that the decoding of vestimentary codes is an erotics, "one of the most powerful we know."

79. This point has been made by Jacques Derrida; see in particular his "Structure, Sign, and Play in the Discourse of the Human Sciences," in *The Structuralist Controversy*, ed. Richard Macksey and Eugenio Donato (Baltimore: Johns Hopkins University Press, 1972), 247–72.

80. Sally F. Moore, *Law as Process: An Anthropological Approach* (London: Routledge and Kegan Paul, 1978), 39.

## Chapter 2. Counterfeit in Their Array: Cross-Dressing in Robin Hood Performances

1. For the full text of this ballad, see "Robin Hood and the Bishop," in Francis J. Child, *The English and Scottish Popular Ballads*, 5 vols. (Boston: Houghton, Mifflin, 1883), 3:191–93.

2. See "Robin Hood and Guy of Gisborne," in Child, *Ballads*, 3:89–94.

3. Peter Stallybrass, "'Drunk with the Cup of Liberty': Robin Hood, the Carnivalesque, and the Rhetoric of Violence in Early Modern England," in *The Violence of Representation: Literature and the History of Violence*, ed. Nancy Armstrong and Leonard Tennenhouse (London: Routledge, 1989), 45–76.

4. See John Bellamy, *Robin Hood: An Historical Enquiry* (Bloomington: Indiana University Press, 1985); Richard B. Dobson and John Taylor, *Rymes of Robyn Hood: An Introduction to the English Outlaw* (London: Heinemann, 1976); Eric J. Hobsbawm, *Bandits* (London: Weidenfeld and Nicolson, 1969); James C. Holt, *Robin Hood* (London: Thames and Hudson, 1983); Stephen Knight, *Robin Hood: A Complete Study of the English Outlaw* (Cambridge, Mass.: Blackwell, 1994); and Maurice Keen, *Outlaws of Medieval England*, 2d ed. (London: Routledge, 1977). The *Past and Present* essays from the 1950s are reprinted in *Peasants, Knights, and Heretics: Studies in Medieval English Social History*, ed. Rodney Hilton (Cambridge: Cambridge University Press, 1976); more recent investigations are summarized in Paul R. Coss, "Aspects of Cultural Diffusion in Medieval England: The Early Romances, Local Society and Robin Hood," *Past and Present* 108 (1985): 35–79.

5. Kathleen A. Biddick, "The Historiographic Unconscious and the Return of Robin Hood," in *The Salt of Common Life: Individuality and Choice in the Medieval Town, Countryside, and Church* (festschrift for Ambrose Raftis), ed. Edwin B. DeWindt (Kalamazoo, Mich.: Medieval Institute Press, 1996). I am grateful to Professor Biddick for generously sharing the prepublication proofs of her essay with me.

6. For a sampling of this work, see Marjorie Garber, *Vested Interests: Cross-Dressing and Cultural Anxiety* (New York: Routledge, 1992); Jonathan Goldberg, *Sodometries: Renaissance Texts, Modern Sexualities* (Stanford, Calif.: Stanford University Press, 1992); Stephen Greenblatt, "Fiction and Friction," in *Shakespearean Negotiations: The Circulation of Social Energy in Renaissance England* (Berkeley: University of California Press, 1988), 66–93; and Valerie Traub, "Desire and the Difference It Makes," in *The Matter of Difference: Materialist Feminist Criticism of Shakespeare*, ed. Valerie Wayne (New York: Harvester Wheatsheaf, 1991), 81–114.

7. See, for example, Meg Twycross, "'Tranvestism' in the Mystery Plays," *Medieval English Theatre* 5 (1983): 123–80, and Richard Rastall, "Female Roles in All Male Casts," *Medieval English Theatre* 7 (1985): 25–50.

8. Interestingly, cross-dressing continues to be featured in twentieth-century films about Robin Hood: in *The Adventures of Robin Hood* (1938) Robin Hood and his men force the captured sheriff of Nottingham and his men to exchange clothes with them; in *Robin Hood: Prince of Thieves* (1991), Maid Marian cross-dresses.

9. I take my cue in part from Jean E. Howard's forceful reading of female cross-dressing on the Renaissance stage in "Crossdressing, the Theatre, and Gender Struggle in Early Modern England," *Shakespeare Quarterly* 39 (1988): 418–40; Howard argues that "struggle, resistance, and subversive masquerade are terms as important as recuperation and containment" in analyzing such cross-dressing (419).

10. Garber, *Vested Interests*, 17. See also speculations about the possibility of a "third sex" or "third term." Greenblatt, for example, reads the boy actress as a third sex, a vestigial link between male and female that is necessary in order to maintain the distinction between the two. Garber criticizes Greenblatt for his tendency to renaturalize binary definitions by confining the possibility of becoming the "third sex" either to exclusively males or exclusively females; Garber prefers to see the figure of the cross-dresser as not just the necessary vestigial link, but also as the state of flux that both allows and disrupts binaries and thus provides the "ground of culture itself" (16). See also Stephen Orgel's critique of Greenblatt's claims in "Nobody's Perfect; or, Why Did the English Stage Take Men for Women?" *South Atlantic Quarterly* 88 (1989): 7–30.

11. For this anthropological reading of the transvestite, see Mary Douglas, "The Two

Bodies," in her *Natural Symbols: Explorations in Cosmology* (London: Barrie and Jenkins, 1971), 93–112, and Karen Hastrup, "The Sexual Boundary: Transvestism and Homosexuality," *Journal of the Anthropological Society of Oxford* 5, no. 3 (1974): 137–47.

12. Stephen Knight, "Bold Robin Hood: The Structures of a Tradition," *Southern Review: Literary and Interdisciplinary Essays* 20 (1987): 157, also makes this point in an essay that focuses on the antiauthoritarianism of Robin Hood.

13. See Child, *Ballads*, 3:90. Almost all of the midsummer plays mentioned in parish records involve Robin Hood in some role; see Alexandra F. Johnston, "What If No Texts Survived? External Evidence for Early English Drama," in *Contexts for Early English Drama*, ed. Marianne G. Briscoe and John C. Coldewey (Bloomington: Indiana University Press, 1989), 7. The manuscript of the surviving fragment is now in Trinity College Library, Cambridge, and was published in facsimile in 1908 by the Malone Society, along with a hypothetical expansion of the play; see *Malone Society Collections* 2 (London: Malone Society, 1908), 117–36. The fullest treatment of the early Robin Hood performances is by David Wiles, *The Early Plays of Robin Hood* (Woodbridge, Suffolk: Brewer, 1981), but see also Knight, *Robin Hood*, 98–115.

14. For a discussion of the N-Town playbook, see Douglas Sugano, "'This game wel pleyd in good a-ray': The N-Town Playbooks and East Anglian Games," *Comparative Drama* 28 (1994): 221–34. For the Croscombe Robin Hood plays, see *Church-Wardens' Accounts of Croscombe . . . 1349 to 1560*, ed. Bishop Edmund Hobhouse (London: Somerset Record Society, 1890), 1–44. Wiles, *Early Plays*, 8, argues that the terms Summer Lord or King of the May were interchangeable and that Robin Hood and the summer lord were "one and the same." E. K. Chambers, *The Mediaeval Stage* (Oxford: Oxford University Press, 1903), 1:177, has asserted that stage plays were a common feature of summer festivities and that many of these plays were often "drawn from the ballads of the Robin Hood cycle." Glynne Wickham, *Early English Stages, 1300–1600*, 3 vols. (London: Routledge and Kegan Paul, 1981), 3:19, claims that the May Game, the King Game, and the Plough Play were all variants of the so-called Mummers' Play featuring Robin Hood, Saint George, the Green Man, or the Wildman as its protagonist. The first known Robin Hood game was in 1427 at Exeter; see *Records of Early English Drama: Devon*, ed. John M. Wasson (Toronto: University of Toronto Press, 1986), 89.

15. Henry Machyn, *The Diary of Henry Machyn, Citizen and Merchant-Taylor of London, 1550–63*, Camden Society os 42 (London, 1848), 201.

16. See Chambers, *Mediaeval Stage*, 1:174 n. 4.

17. The first comprehensive and still indispensable collection of Robin Hood legends was made by Joseph Ritson, *Robin Hood: A Collection of All the Ancient Poems, Songs and Ballads, Now Extant, Relative to That Celebrated Outlaw*, 2 vols. (London, 1795). Dobson and Taylor, *Rymes of Robyn Hood*, 7, claim that many ballads derive from the early performances.

18. This is the date of the *Gest* preferred by Knight, *Robin Hood*, 46–48, who offers a cogent argument against Child's much earlier dating of the ballad.

19. Michael J. Preston, "The Robin Hood Folk Plays of South-Central England," in *The Drama of the Middle Ages: Comparative and Critical Essays*, ed. Clifford Davidson, C. J. Gianakaris, and John H. Stroupe (New York: AMS Press, 1982), 343–45.

20. Chambers, *Mediaeval Stage*, 1:177, says of the plays performed in May and at midsummer, "So far as they were secular, the subjects of them were naturally drawn . . . from the ballads of the Robin Hood cycle."

21. Knight, *Robin Hood*, 49.

22. See Dobson and Taylor, *Rymes of Robyn Hood*, 7; Dobson and Taylor do not include "Robin Hood and the Bishop" in this group, but its cross-dressing is too striking to be ignored here.

23. See Dobson and Taylor, *Rymes of Robyn Hood*, 15.

24. For this characterization of woodland districts, see David Underdown, *Revel, Riot and Rebellion: Popular Politics and Culture in England, 1603–1660* (Oxford: Clarendon, 1985), 103. For a general study of the cultural functions of the forest, see Robert Pogue Harrison, *Forests: The Shadow of Civilization* (Chicago: University of Chicago Press, 1992).

25. For a discussion of the forest's significance for early modern insurrections, see Richard Wilson, "'Like the Old Robin Hood': *As You Like It* and the Enclosure Riots," *Shakespeare Quarterly* 43 (1992): 1–19. Andrew Ayton claims that by the 1260s the name Robin Hood was recognized as a nickname for fugitives from the law and by the fifteenth century was widely associated with collective criminal activity in the greenwood; see his "Military Service and the Development of the Robin Hood Legend in the Fourteenth Century," *Nottingham Medieval Studies* 36 (1992): 143.

26. Wiles, *Early Plays*, 4, points out, however, that Robin Hood plays and games center on the Severn Valley, the Thames Valley, and the Southwest, especially near old market towns, not the towns of the north central midlands referred to in the early ballads.

27. Most readings of the early Robin Hood downplay his criminality, stressing instead his role as an agent of rough justice; see, for example, Hobsbawm, *Bandits*, 42–43, who views Robin Hood as a social bandit who upholds the collective values of the poor against the rich, of peasant society against capitalism. Whether Robin Hood should be seen as a criminal or an agent of rough justice depends in large part on the observer's social and economic allegiances. For a comparison of the Robin Hood of the ballads with actual fourteenth-century outlaws, see Barbara A. Hanawalt, "Ballads and Bandits: Fourteenth-Century Outlaws and the Robin Hood Poems," in *Chaucer's England: Literature in Historical Context*, ed. Barbara A. Hanawalt (Minneapolis: University of Minnesota Press, 1992), 154–75.

28. Child, *Ballads*, 3:94–101.

29. The quotation is from "Robin Hood and Guy of Gisborne," in Child, *Ballads*, 3:93, stanza 44.

30. Male rioters often adopted female dress not just to conceal their identities, but also to use the symbolics of the "unruly woman" to their advantage, as has been demonstrated by Natalie Zemon Davis, "'Women on Top': Symbolic Sexual Inversion and Political Disorder in Early Modern Europe," in *The Reversible World: Symbolic Inversion in Art and Society*, ed. Barbara A. Babcock (Ithaca: Cornell University Press, 1978), 147–90.

31. For the text of this ballad, see Child, *Ballads*, 3:115–20.

32. Robin Hood's subversion of urban values is tacitly supported by historians who link him with yeoman interests. Ayton, "Military Service," 127, for instance, connects the development of the Robin Hood legends to the start of the Hundred Years' War and the rise of the yeoman class. Dobson and Taylor, *Rymes of Robyn Hood*, 34, similarly view Robin Hood as "a yeoman hero for a yeoman audience," neither gentry nor peasant but somewhere in between. It should be pointed out, however, that the term "yeoman" is fraught with confusion in late medieval England; see Coss, "Aspects of Cultural Diffusion," 74.

33. For a particularly striking instance of Robin Hood's use of cross-dressing to challenge the social order, see "Robin Hood and the Beggar," in Child, *Ballads*, 3:155–58, in which Robin Hood exchanges clothes with a beggar and thus disguised enters Nottingham and summons his men to free three yeomen held by the sheriff. As in the case of the clothing exchange with the old woman, garbing himself in the clothes of the socially marginal enhances Robin Hood's subversive powers.

34. Early Robin Hood ballads often link Robin Hood with highway robbery, a common late medieval crime; see Keen, *Outlaws*, 193.

35. See Dobson and Taylor, *Rymes of Robyn Hood*, 25–29, for a discussion of highway robbery in the late Middle Ages. Hanawalt, "Ballads and Bandits," 165, points out that real

bandits tended to steal lower-valued, ordinary goods; in contrast, Robin Hood's thefts appear quite glamorous.

36. For the text of the ballad, see Child, *Ballads*, 3:108–14. For a somewhat different reading of the resistant economic forces at work in this ballad, see Knight, *Robin Hood*, 54–56, and Richard Tardif, "The 'Mistery' of Robin Hood: A New Social Context for the Texts," in *Words and Worlds: Studies in the Social Role of Verbal Culture*, ed. Stephen Knight and S. N. Mukherjee (Sydney: Sydney Association for Studies in Society and Culture, 1983), 140. Knight sees Robin Hood's mercantile subversion as mimicking lordly generosity, while Tardif views it as expressing artisan wage discontents.

37. Knight, "Bold Robin Hood," 160, argues that this ballad displays a market-oriented version of the rich-poor dynamics, altering the terms in favor of the consumer.

38. This subversiveness seems also to be echoed in the early modern proverb about selling "Robin Hood's pennyworths," which refers to selling commodities priced at robbers' rates, far below their market value; see Dobson and Taylor, *Rymes of Robyn Hood*, 291.

39. For connections between the Robin Hood legends and the beginnings of an English military that increasingly depended on bowmen, see Ayton, "Military Service," 135–37.

40. Cf. prohibitions against the wearing of disguises during Christmas holiday mummings, like the proclamation from the mayor and sheriff of Bristol to the effect that "no maner of personne, of whate degree or condicion that they be of, at no tyme this Christmas goo a mommyng with cloce visaged, nor go aftir curfew rong at St. Nicholas, withoute lighte in theire handes"; see Robert Ricart, *The Maire of Bristowe is Kalendar*, ed. Lucy Toulmin Smith, Camden Society ser. 2, no. 5 (Westminster, 1872), 85. This proclamation expresses the ruling classes' fear that the concealing of identity, whether under cover of a mask or darkness, leads to social disruption.

41. The quotation is from "A Gest of Robyn Hode," in Child, *Ballads*, 3:77, stanza 422.

42. Ayton's linking of fourteenth-century legends of Robin Hood with out-of-work soldiers suggests one acceptable use for the fit-for-battle construction of the male body in the legends; see "Military Service," 139–41.

43. Maid Marian is a later addition to the Robin Hood stories and performances, first mentioned in 1500, who seems to have become linked with Robin Hood through the May festivities and morris dances; the early ballads and performances all figure the outlaw band as an exclusively masculinist society; see Dobson and Taylor, *Rymes of Robyn Hood*, 41–42. Evidence suggests that the Marian in the morris dance at Kingston upon Thames might have been played by a woman; in 1509 Marian is paid "for hir labor" and in 1507 a "rylys [Rillys] Kempe" is mentioned who presumably played Marian; see Sally-Beth MacLean, "King Games and Robin Hood: Play and Profit at Kingston upon Thames," *Research Opportunities in Renaissance Drama* 29 (1986–87): 93 n. 20. But also see Twycross, "Transvestism," 128, for a caveat about assuming that a female pronoun or name in account books refers to the actor rather than the character.

44. Hanawalt, "Ballads and Bandits," 158, notes that ordinary gangs usually included blood relations.

45. This connection of Robin Hood's band with royal and magnate households is made by Hanawalt, "Ballads and Bandits," 161.

46. Child, *Ballads*, 3:131, stanza 12.

47. Dressing across gender and status lines is a regular aspect of such festive rituals of inversion as carnivals, allowing for "wild men," "wild women," boy bishops, and peasant kings.

48. For the Kingston statistics, see MacLean, "King Games," 86.

49. For the Reading figures, see Wiles, *Early Plays*, 13.

50. Philip Stubbes, "The Lords of Mis-rule," in *The Anatomie of Abuses* (London: Richard Jones, 1583).

51. In fact, a statute of Henry VIII had made the distributing of liveries illegal; see *Tudor Royal Proclamations*, ed. Paul L. Hughes and James F. Larkin, 3 vols. (New Haven: Yale University Press, 1964–69), 1:124.

52. Livery badges were a form of clientage worn by a lord's dependents; they served as immediately recognizable cognizances. Badges could be used to increase the size of a household through retainers symbolically and usually materially joined to a lord's service, so that by 1390, the year of the first attempts to regulate it by law, badge wearing was a major feature of society; see the discussion of badges in David Starkey, "The Age of the Household: Politics, Society and the Arts, c. 1350–c.1550," in *The Later Middle Ages*, ed. Stephen Medcalf (New York: Holmes and Meier, 1981), 264–67.

53. By the late thirteenth century, the name Robin Hood was already associated with outlawry, and by the fifteenth century, with collective criminal activity in the greenwood; see Ayton, "Military Service," 143.

54. See W. O. Hassall, "Plays at Clerkenwell," *Modern Language Review* 33 (1938): 564–70.

55. Quoted in Charles Phythian-Adams, *Desolation of a City: Coventry and the Urban Crisis of the Late Middle Ages* (Cambridge: Cambridge University Press, 1979), 114–15.

56. The information in this paragraph comes from MacLean, "King Games," 87–89. For another discussion of Robin Hood games as civic fundraisers, see James D. Stokes, "Robin Hood and the Churchwardens in Yeovil," *Medieval and Renaissance Drama in England* 3 (1986): 1–26.

57. See *Collections for a History of Staffordshire* ns 10, no. 1 (1907): 80–82.

58. Cited in Stallybrass, "'Drunk,'" 47.

59. This incident is quoted in Jane Garry, "The Literary History of the English Morris Dance," *Folklore* 94 (1983): 225.

60. See Wiles, *Early Plays*, 55. In 1443 the mayor and citizens of Norwich elected John Gladman mock king and followed him through the streets in a procession that was interpreted as a challenge to Henry VI's authority; see *Selected Records of the City of Norwich*, ed. W. Hudson and U. J. C. Tingay (Norwich, 1906), 1:340.

61. See Holt, *Robin Hood*, 149–51.

62. See Rudolf M. Dekker and Lotte C. van de Pol, *The Tradition of Female Transvestism in Early Modern Europe* (New York: St. Martin's Press, 1989), 7. Dekker and van de Pol claim that many cross-dressing women inhabited marginal social spaces even before they began cross-dressing: many were foreign-born and far from home and family; many came from the lower classes; many were also orphans or had left their families after a conflict; most had already worked at female forms of labor—as servants, seamstresses, knitters, or street peddlers—before trying their hand at male labor; most were unmarried; and most were between the ages of sixteen and twenty-five (11–13).

63. Judith Butler, *Bodies That Matter* (New York: Routledge, 1993), 109–18.

64. Johnston, "What If?" 7.

65. Dekker and van de Pol, *Female Transvestism*, 6. Dekker and van de Pol argue that female cross-dressing in northern Europe was widespread but remained underground; it was never institutionalized as it was in some non-European societies, as in the figure of the "berdache" among some Native American tribes, for example (40–41).

66. See R. Valerie Lucas, "*Hic Mulier*: The Female Transvestite in Early Modern England," *Renaissance and Reformation* 24 (1988): 65.

67. *The Anonimalle Chronicle, 1333 to 1381*, ed. V. H. Galbraith (Manchester: Manchester University Press, 1927), 40–41; a modern English translation is provided in Holt, *Robin Hood*, 158.

68. *Rotuli Parliamentorum*, 6 vols. (London, 1783), 2:332; translated in Ayton, "Military Service," 139. Ayton describes the Black Prince's response as the view of "a military commander who recognised the importance of maintaining reserves of suitable manpower" (138).

69. For the text of Grindal's proclamation, see *Records of Early English Drama: York*, ed. Alexandra F. Johnston and Margaret Rogerson, 2 vols. (Toronto: University of Toronto Press, 1979), 1:258.

70. For the first quote, see Stallybrass, "'Drunk,'" 58; for the banns, see *Records of Early English Drama: Chester*, ed. Lawrence M. Clopper (Toronto: University of Toronto Press, 1979).

71. See Stallybrass, "'Drunk,'" 62–69, for a discussion of the various strategies of appropriation of Robin Hood in the early modern period; Stallybrass argues that Robin Hood is "an ideological sign, intersected by 'differently oriented social interests,'" whose meaning is constantly "produced and reproduced within the hegemonic process" (63).

72. Knight, "Bold Robin Hood," 157–58, says, "Making Robin Hood a distressed gentleman [was] a crucial step in stripping the tradition of its innately radical force."

73. Child, *Ballads*, 3:39–89.

74. See MacLean, "King Games," 87.

75. Edward Hall, *Hall's Chronicle* (1547; London: Johnson, 1809), 520.

76. See Stallybrass, "'Drunk,'" 68.

77. Hall, *Hall's Chronicle*, 582.

78. The quotation is from "A Gest of Robin Hood," in Child, *Ballads*, 3:72, stanza 324.

79. In saying this I am following Foucault's description of an "archaeology of change" that would focus on *transformation* in analyzing discursive formations rather than on *change*, which is, in Foucault's words, "a general container for all events and the abstract principle of their succession"; see Foucault, *The Archaeology of Knowledge*, trans. A. M. Sheridan Smith (New York: Harper and Row, 1976), 172. For an overview of modern appropriations of the outlaw, see Knight, *Robin Hood*, chap. 6.

80. For the suggestion that cross-dressing displays the gap between clothes and body, see Annette Kuhn, "Sexual Disguise and Cinema," in *The Power of the Image: Essays on Representation and Sexuality* (London: Routledge and Kegan Paul, 1985), 49.

81. Judith Butler, *Gender Trouble: Feminism and the Subversion of Identity* (New York: Routledge, 1990), 31.

82. See Knight, *Robin Hood*, 93.

83. Cf. a description of morris dancers from 1646 that mentions "Country fellows . . . and with them a Mayd Marian, and two fooles, who fell a dansing and capering"; see Anthony Wood, *The Life and Times of Anthony Wood, Antiquary, 1632–1695 . . . by Andrew Clark* (Oxford: Clarendon Press, 1891), 1:299.

84. That the theater was a space outside the rules of dress is illustrated by the fact that English sumptuary laws explicitly exempted performers from their regulations; see 1 Henry VIII (1509), *Statutes of the Realm*, 3:9, which excludes "Mynstrelles Players in enterludes" from the act. This is in contrast to the situation in Spain, for example, where Charles V in 1534 specifically extended prohibitions against excessive clothing to include actors; see Emilio Cotarelo y Mori, *Bibliografía de las controversias sobre la licitud del teatro en España* (Madrid: Revista de Archivos, Bibliotecas y Museos, 1904), 619; cited in Ursula K. Heise, "Transvestism and the Stage Controversy in Spain and England, 1580–1680," *Theatre Journal* 44 (1992): 358. Compare Mary Ann Doane's description of masquerade as "an acknowledgment that it is femininity itself which is constructed as a mask—the decorative layer then conceals a non-identity"; Doane, "Film and the Masquerade: Theorising the Female Spectator," *Screen* 23 (1982): 81.

## Chapter 3. Conduct Books and Good Governance

1. Marcel Mauss, "Techniques of the Body," *Economy and Society* 2 (1973): 73.

2. Pierre Bourdieu, *Outline of a Theory of Practice*, trans. Richard Nice (Cambridge: Cambridge University Press, 1977), 94.

3. Mary Douglas, *Natural Symbols: Explorations in Cosmology* (1970; New York: Pantheon, 1982), 65.

4. Pierre Bourdieu, *The Logic of Practice*, trans. Richard Nice (Stanford, Calif.: Stanford University Press, 1990), 17–20.

5. Bourdieu, *Logic of Practice*, 56, writes, "The *habitus*—embodied history, internalized as second nature and so forgotten as history—is the active presence of the whole past of which it is the product."

6. Norbert Elias, *The History of Manners* (1939), vol. 1 of *The Civilizing Process*, trans. Edmund Jephcott (New York: Pantheon, 1978).

7. See Gail Kern Paster, *The Body Embarrassed: Drama and the Disciplines of Shame in Early Modern England* (Ithaca: Cornell University Press, 1993), and Peter Stallybrass, "Patriarchal Territories: The Body Enclosed," in *Rewriting the Renaissance: The Discourses of Sexual Difference in Early Modern Europe*, ed. Margaret W. Ferguson, Maureen Quilligan, and Nancy J. Vickers (Chicago: University of Chicago Press, 1986), 123–42, for analyses of Renaissance culture that extend Elias's ideas to the question of gendered identities.

8. See Michel Foucault, *Discipline and Punish: The Birth of the Prison*, trans. Alan Sheridan (New York: Vintage, 1979).

9. Mikhail Bakhtin, *Rabelais and His World*, trans. Helene Iswolsky (Bloomington: Indiana University Press, 1984), 154.

10. For a typical example of the tendency of Renaissance scholars to read medieval notions of selfhood as rigid, fixed, and unchangeable, see Thomas Greene, "The Flexibility of the Self in Renaissance Literature," in *The Disciplines of Criticism*, ed. Peter Demetz, Thomas Greene, and Lowry Nelson Jr. (New Haven: Yale University Press, 1968), 241–64. Greene argues that the "new" flexibility of self in the Renaissance, embodied by writers like Petrarch, was a direct challenge to medieval habits of thought and to the "relative inflexibility of medieval character" (245).

11. See C. Stephen Jaeger, *The Origins of Courtliness: Civilizing Trends and the Formation of Courtly Ideals, 939–1210* (Philadelphia: University of Pennsylvania Press, 1985). Jaeger sees courtesy as an ideal first developed and promulgated by ecclesiastical courts as models of behavior for courtly life that were later adopted by the lay nobility. According to Jaeger, the "architects of chivalry" were clerics "functioning in their capacity as educators," and one of their motives, as Peter of Blois charged, was their own ambition (213).

12. See Jonathan Nicholls, *The Matter of Courtesy: Medieval Courtesy Books and the Gawain-Poet* (Woodbridge, Suffolk: Brewer, 1985), for a discussion of similarities between monastic customaries and secular courtesy books, especially in terms of rules for eating, sleeping, and the regulation of other kinds of bodily behavior.

13. Conduct books in English arrived a bit later; see John E. Mason, *Gentlefolk in the Making: Studies in the History of English Courtesy Literature and Related Topics from 1531 to 1774* (Philadelphia: University of Pennsylvania Press, 1935), esp. 4–22. See also Diane Bornstein, *Mirrors of Courtesy* (Hamden, Conn.: Archon Books, 1975); Fred B. Millett, "English Courtesy Literature before 1557," *Bulletin of the Departments of History and Political and Economic Science in Queen's University, Kingston, Ontario* 30 (1919): 1–16; and H. Rosamond Parsons, "Anglo-Norman Books of Courtesy and Nurture," *PMLA* 44 (1929): 383–455.

14. Edwin Ramage, *Urbanitas: Ancient Sophistication and Refinement* (Norman: University of Oklahoma Press, 1973), notes that *facetus*, a term meaning "affable or polite man," appears quite early in Latin literature and was later popularized by medieval conduct literature (22–23). See also Sister Mary Theresa Brentano, *The Relationship of the Latin Facetus Literature to the Medieval Courtesy Poems* (Lawrence: University of Kansas, 1935).

15. For the contours of these developments, see Carol Meale, "Patrons, Buyers, and Owners," in *Book Production and Publishing in Britain, 1375–1475*, ed. Jeremy Griffiths

and Derek Pearsall (Cambridge: Cambridge University Press, 1989), 201–38. For a different interpretation of the rise of conduct books, see Paul Zumthor, "From Hi(story) to Poem; or, the Paths of Pun," *New Literary History* 10 (1979), esp. 234–35; in this essay Zumthor follows Elias and Bakhtin in viewing rules of etiquette as representing an unnatural distancing from natural bodily needs and such things as sex, blood, and excrement.

16. On prices of books, see H. E. Bell, "The Price of Books in Medieval England," *Library*, 4th ser., 17 (1936): 312–32. For a discussion of late medieval English book buyers, see Meale, "Patrons, Buyers and Owners." On the impact of paper, see R. J. Lyall, "Materials: The Paper Revolution," in *Book Production and Publishing*, ed. Griffiths and Pearsall, 11–29.

17. Curt F. Bühler, *The Fifteenth-Century Book: The Scribes, the Printers, the Decorators* (Philadelphia: University of Pennyslvania Press, 1960), 33, says, "The trade in books throughout the Middle Ages was largely a second-hand business; only with the invention of printing did a new-book market become commonplace."

18. Nicholls, *Matter of Courtesy*, 71.

19. *Babees Book* (MS Harl. 5086), in *Manners and Meals in Olden Time*, ed. Frederick J. Furnivall, EETS os 32 (London: Trübner, 1868), 9, lines 216–17.

20. See the Ashmole manuscript of *Stans puer ad mensam*, in *A Booke of Precedence*, ed. Frederick J. Furnivall, EETS es 8 (London: Trübner, 1869), 56–64.

21. *The Book of Vices and Virtues*, ed. W. Nelson Francis, EETS os 217 (London: Oxford University Press, 1942), 75–89; middle goods are discussed on 77. Cf. Hugh Rhodes's *Boke of Nurture* (ca. 1530), in *Manners and Meals in Olden Time*, ed. Furnivall, 61–114, which explains in its preface that parents should instruct their children and servants in good behavior because, among other things, "it multiplyeth goods" (63).

22. *Book of Vices and Virtues*, ed. Francis, 75, line 1.

23. Ibid., 77, lines 17–32.

24. Bourdieu, *Outline of a Theory of Practice*, 89.

25. This view is found in various places in Foucault's writings, but for a succinct statement of how subordination is imposed through self-control of the body, see his *Discipline and Punish*, 137.

26. The poems have been edited by Furnivall in *A Booke of Precedence*, 44–55; all subsequent line references are to this edition. The poems also appear together, although not side by side, in Lambeth MS 853 and in Cambridge, Trinity College MS R.3.19. For a recent edition of the five extant manuscripts of *How the Good Wife Taught Her Daughter*, which date from ca. 1350 to ca. 1490, see Tauno Mustanoja, *The Good Wife Taught Her Daughter*, Annales Academiae Scientiarum Fennicae, Ser. B., 61 (Helsinki, 1948).

27. Lyall, "Materials," 12–13, notes that contents and audience often determined whether a fifteenth-century book was produced in paper or parchment; paper books were more acceptable among merchants and tradespeople. For a reading of *How the Good Wife Taught Her Daughter* as serving to inculcate young women into bourgeois culture, see Felicity Riddy, "Mother Knows Best: Reading Social Change in a Courtesy Text," *Speculum* 71 (1996): 66–86.

28. See Mustanoja, *Good Wife*, 83.

29. Mustanoja, *Good Wife*, 126, believes in fact that the author of the *Good Wife* was a male cleric.

30. Not all conduct literature for men assumes that the masculine body comes predisciplined—especially not the lower-class male body. In John Russell's *Boke of Nurture*, for example, there is extensive advice for servants on controlling outward bodily behavior, including prohibitions against scratching, nosepicking, spitting, coughing, belching, and farting; see the *Boke of Nurture*, in *Manners and Meals in Olden Time*, ed. Furnivall, esp. 134–37, lines 270–312.

31. For a similar argument about the tendency of late medieval bourgeois culture to focus on good conduct understood as proper use of material goods, see Kathleen M. Ashley, "The Bourgeois Piety of Martha in the *Passion* of Jean Michel," *Modern Language Quarterly* 14 (1984): 227–40.

32. This fear of sociability is intensified in the Lambeth version, where the son is advised to avoid civic office, serving at inquests, standing as a witness, or otherwise getting entangled in problems deriving from the gap between personal desire and the desires of others, since in these situations "þou moste þi neiȝboris displese & dere, / Or ellis þou muste þi silf forswere"; see *How the Wise Man Tauȝt His Son*, in *Manners and Meals in Olden Time*, ed. Furnivall, 49, lines 44–45.

33. One way *How the Good Wife Taught Her Daughter* can be understood is as a necessary secondary text for the construction of masculine identity, a text that goes hand in hand with and finishes the project begun in *How the Wise Man Taught His Son*. In this way, the Good Wife's advice fashions the well-behaved female subject as, in Barbara Correll's words, an "essential inessential for the constitution of cultural manhood"; see Correll, "The Politics of Civility in Renaissance Texts: Grobiana in Grobianus," *Exemplaria* 2 (1990): 631.

34. Michel Foucault, *The History of Sexuality*, trans. Robert Hurley (New York: Pantheon, 1978), 1:141.

35. See P. J. P. Goldberg, *Women, Work, and Life Cycle in a Medieval Economy: Women in York and Yorkshire, c. 1300–1520* (Oxford: Oxford University Press, 1992).

36. For the equating of women with other chattel, see V. G. Kiernan, "Private Property in History," in *Family and Inheritance: Rural Society in Western Europe, 1200–1800*, ed. Jack Goody, Joan Thirsk, and E. P. Thomson (Cambridge: Cambridge University Press, 1976), esp. 367. See also Gayle Rubin's reappropriation of traditional anthropological views of women as objects of exchange in a male economy in "The Traffic in Women: Notes on the 'Political Economy' of Sex," in *Toward an Anthropology of Women*, ed. Rayna R. Reiter (New York: Monthly Review Press, 1975), 157–210.

37. See Mary Douglas, *Purity and Danger: An Analysis of Concepts of Pollution and Taboo* (Harmondsworth: Penguin, 1970), esp. 13–14.

38. The regulation of speech is a consistent feature of late medieval conduct books. The conduct poem *Whate-ever Thow Sey, Avyse Thee Welle*, for example, consists entirely of advice about minding what you say, including refraining from boasting, telling secrets, speaking in haste, and malicious speech. The poem exhorts the reader to watch "What tow spekyst, & of what wyȝt, / Whare, to wham, whye, and whenne"; see *Manners and Meals in Olden Time*, ed. Furnivall, 358. See Brentano, *Relationship*, 96–98, for a discussion of courtesy books dealing with conversation, especially those giving advice against mocking, speaking angrily, finding fault, laughing at others, swearing, lying, boasting, flattering, gossiping, or rebuking.

39. See *The Goode Wif Thaught Hir Doughter* (MS Henry Huntington Library HM 128), printed in Mustanoja, *Good Wife*, 171–72. The lines run: "ȝif any of hem do amys, curse hem nought, ne blowe, / But take a smerte rodde and bete hem all by rowe" (lines 187–88).

40. Caroline Walker Bynum, "The Female Body and Religious Practice in the Later Middle Ages," in *Fragments for a History of the Human Body*, ed. Michel Feher, with Ramona Naddaff and Nadia Tazi (New York: Zone Books, 1989), 1:212 n. 98.

41. Bakhtin, *Rabelais*, 26.

42. For court cases involving slander, see A. H. Thomas, ed., *Calendar of Plea and Memoranda Rolls of the City of London, 1413–1427* (Cambridge: Cambridge University Press, 1943), esp. 134–36. The early modern connection between closing of women's mouths and their enclosure within the household as mechanisms of social control of the disorderly female is described in Stallybrass, "Patriarchal Territories," 126–27.

43. Such advice, found also in late medieval drama, has been linked by Kathleen M.

Ashley with the needs of female bourgeois culture; see her "Medieval Courtesy Literature and Dramatic Mirrors of Conduct," in *The Ideology of Conduct: Essays on Literature and the History of Sexuality*, ed. Nancy Armstrong and Leonard Tennenhouse (New York: Methuen, 1987), 25–38. Ashley notes how in the later Middle Ages issues of reputation become much more pronounced in both drama and conduct books for bourgeois women (36).

44. See Martha C. Howell, "Citizenship and Gender: Women's Political Status in Northern Medieval Cities," in *Women and Power in the Middle Ages*, ed. Mary Erler and Maryanne Kowaleski (Athens: University of Georgia Press, 1988), 37–60.

45. Bourdieu, *Logic of Practice*, 71.

46. See the useful discussion of women's labor within the family economy in Martha C. Howell, "Women, the Family Economy, and the Structures of Market Production in Cities of Northern Europe during the Late Middle Ages," in *Women and Work in Preindustrial Europe*, ed. Barbara A. Hanawalt (Bloomington: Indiana University Press, 1986), 198–222. Howell's study of women and work in Leiden and Cologne concludes that women had high labor status so long as production remained inside the household where they could be seen as an extension of men (215).

47. On this point, see Michael Curtin, "A Question of Manners: Status and Gender in Etiquette and Courtesy," *Journal of Modern History* 57 (1985): 395–423, who argues that one of the transformations of the courtesy genre by the Victorians was the development of a code of sociability for women; sociability had been earlier seen as a threat to female virtue, but was now seen as desirable for women and became a way of "organizing and directing [female] ambition" (423).

48. For sex-ratio figures for 1377 for York, see P. J. P. Goldberg, "Female Labour, Service and Marriage in the Late Medieval Urban North," *Northern History* 22 (1986): 19. Charles Phythian-Adams, *Desolation of a City: Coventry and the Urban Crisis of the Late Middle Ages* (Cambridge: Cambridge University Press, 1979), 92, found a ratio of 72 women for every 100 men in Coventry in 1523. The ratio might have been more balanced in London; see Sylvia L. Thrupp, *The Merchant Class of Medieval London* (Chicago: University of Chicago Press, 1948), 191–206.

49. *The Goode Wif Thaught Hir Doughter* (Huntington), line 17, in Mustanoja, *Good Wife*, 159.

50. Erving Goffman, *The Presentation of Self in Everyday Life* (New York: Doubleday, 1959), 35.

51. Ibid., 85. Although Bourdieu mounts a compelling critique of the objectivism of the social sciences, especially structuralism, which to some extent would include Goffman, his claims about the *habitus* often mesh well with Goffman's understanding of social performances; see, for example, Bourdieu's discussion of how the *habitus* can produce responses based on its "formula" (*Logic of Practice*, 290 n. 2).

52. Goffman, *Presentation*, 36.

53. Ibid., 75.

54. Erving Goffman, "The Nature of Deference and Demeanor," *American Anthropologist* 58 (1956): 473.

55. Ibid., 474.

56. Ibid., 480.

57. See Bourdieu, *Logic of Practice*, 291 n. 3.

58. Cf. Douglas's assertion in *Natural Symbols*, 12, that the greater the social need for conformity to norms, the greater the demand for physical control.

59. Paul Willis, *Learning to Labour: How Working Class Lads Get Working Class Jobs* (Farnborough, England: Saxon House, 1977).

60. *Stans puer ad mensam* (Ashmole), *Booke of Precedence*, lines 7–8 and 17–23, respectively.

61. The classic discussion of late medieval social mobility is F. R. H. Du Boulay, *An Age of Ambition: English Society in the Late Middle Ages* (NewYork: Viking, 1970). For a description of the importance of display for mercantile groups, see Thrupp, *Merchant Class*, 143–54.

62. Bourdieu, *Outline of a Theory of Practice*, 94–95.

63. William Caxton, *Book of Curtesye*, ed. Frederick J. Furnivall, EETS es 3 (London: Trübner, 1868), esp. 45.

64. Hugh of Saint Victor, *De institutione novitiorum*, cited in Aldo Scaglione, *Knights at Court* (Berkeley: University of California Press, 1991), 56.

65. John Metham, *Physiognomy*, in *The Works of John Metham*, ed. Hardin Craig (London: Kegan Paul, Trench, Trübner, 1916), 140–41.

66. Caxton, *Book of Curtesye*, 45, lines 451–53.

67. See the comments on the subversive power of unruly bodies in Natalie Zemon Davis, "Women on Top: Symbolic Sexual Inversion and Political Disorder in Early Modern Europe," in *The Reversible World: Symbolic Inversion in Art and Society*, ed. Barbara A. Babcock (Ithaca: Cornell University Press, 1978), 154–55. Davis focuses on the disruptive power of the unruly woman, but as my next chapter reveals, I construe the unruly male body as also in possession of this transgressive force.

## Chapter 4. Mischievous Governance:
## The Unruly Bodies of Morality Plays

1. Philip Stubbes, *The Anatomy of Abuses* (London: Richard Jones, 1583), esp. L.viii–xii. For a discussion of sixteenth-century antitheatricality, see Jonas Barish, *The Antitheatrical Prejudice* (Berkeley: University of California Press, 1981), 80–131.

2. *A Tretise of Miraclis Pleyinge*, ed. Clifford L. Davidson (Kalamazoo, Mich.: Medieval Institute Publications, 1993). All line numbers refer to this edition. For a discussion of the date and authorship of the two parts of the *Tretise*, see Davidson's introduction, 1–52.

3. For recent interpretations that do not view the *Tretise* as entirely antitheatrical, see Lawrence M. Clopper, "*Miracula* and *The Tretise of Miraclis Pleyinge*," *Speculum* 65 (1990): 878–905, and Glending Olson, "Plays as Play: A Medieval Ethical Theory of Performance and the Intellectual Context of the *Miraclis Pleyinge*," *Viator* 26 (1995): 195–221. Arguing that "miracula" refers to various lay entertainments rather than to biblical drama, Clopper claims that the *Tretise* is an attack not on religious drama but on other kinds of festivity (895–97). Olson argues that the attack on the "pleyinge" of miracles "reveals an attitude . . . that is much more severe than the dominant tradition but not fundamentally different from it" (206); nevertheless it allows space for appropriate forms of play. For a view of the *Tretise* as entirely antitheatrical, see Barish, *Anthitheatrical Prejudice*, 67–79.

4. Olson, "Plays as Play," 195.

5. *The English Works of Wyclif*, ed. F. D. Matthew, 2d rev. ed., EETS os 74 (London: Kegan Paul, Trench, Trübner, 1902), 206–7. Discussing this passage, Olson, "Plays as Play," 212, points out that the attack on inappropriate entertainments is couched, as it is in the *Tretise* as well, in terms of restraining servants from insulting superiors.

6. *Dives and Pauper*, ed. Priscilla Heath Barnum, 2 vols., EETS os 275 (London: Oxford University Press, 1976), 1:292–98.

7. Marianne G. Briscoe makes a similar point in "Some Clerical Notions of Dramatic Decorum in Late Medieval England," *Comparative Drama* 19 (1985): 1–13, emphasizing that clerical antitheatricality usually does not attack drama per se, but rather focuses on specific abuses of it.

8. This refutation is especially concerned with the clergy, censoring priests who play in or watch interludes; see *Tretise*, 245–51, 272–78.

9. Olson, "Plays as Play," 213.

10. *Records of Early English Drama: York*, ed. Alexandra F. Johnston and Margaret Rogerson (Toronto: University of Toronto Press, 1979), 42–44.

11. For a discussion of carnival as a mode of cultural analysis, see Peter Stallybrass and Allon White, *The Politics and Poetics of Transgression* (London: Methuen, 1986), esp. 6.

12. The functionalist model, based on Emile Durkheim's reconciliatory view of festivity as promoting social cohesion by acting as a cultural "safety valve" that allows alienated social groups to be ritually reincorporated into the structures of the larger social body, underlies the study of the Corpus Christi plays in Mervyn James, "Ritual, Drama and Social Body in the Late Medieval English Town," *Past and Present* 98 (1983): 3–29. The surveillance model can be found in Stephen Greenblatt's "Invisible Bullets: Renaissance Authority and Its Subversions, *Henry IV* and *Henry V*," in *Political Shakespeare*, ed. Jonathan Dollimore and Alan Sinfield (London: Methuen, 1985), esp. 43; Greenblatt argues that subversion is produced by power and serves its interests, in part because power is not monolithic but consists of diverse functions, some of which may contradict each other. In Bakhtinian readings carnival is more thoroughly transgressive, a vehicle of plebeian social protest; see Emmanuel Le Roy Ladurie, *Carnival in Romans*, trans. Mary Feeney (New York: Braziller, 1979), who describes how carnivalesque inversionary symbolism spilled over into a "people's uprising" of urban craftsmen and laborers joined by peasants from local villages. For a reaction against the interpretation of carnival as rebellion, see Terry Eagleton, *Walter Benjamin; or, Towards a Revolutionary Criticism* (London: Verso, 1981), 148, who argues that carnival is a licensed affair, a permissible rupture, and hence ineffectual as revolution.

13. See Mikhail Bakhtin, *Rabelais and His World*, trans. Helene Iswolsky (Bloomington: Indiana University Press, 1984), esp. 25–29.

14. The definitive discussion of medieval moralities is Robert A. Potter, *The English Morality Play: Origins, History and Influence of a Dramatic Tradition* (London: Routledge and Kegan Paul, 1975).

15. See, for example, Sister Mary Philippa Coogan, *An Interpretation of the Moral Play, Mankind* (Washington, D.C.: Catholic University of America Press, 1947), 93–95, who argues that the vice characters serve to intensify the moral themes. Potter, *English Morality Play*, 57, claims that "the traditional morality play is not a battle between virtues and vices, but a didactic ritual drama about the forgiveness of sins."

16. Max Harris, "Flesh and Spirits: The Battle between Virtues and Vices in Medieval Drama Reassessed," *Medium Aevum* 57 (1988): 56–65, reads the vices as playing a dual role as exteriorized manifestations of human frailty and diabolical evil who stage the battle between Christ and Satan over mankind. W. A. Pantin, *The English Church in the Fourteenth Century* (Cambridge: Cambridge University Press, 1955), 192, describes the growing emphasis on penance in post-thirteenth-century religious literature.

17. Richard Whitford, *The Boke of Pacience*, facsimile ed., ed. James Hogg (Salzburg: Universität Salzburg, 1979; reprint, New York: Edwin Mellen Press, 1991), 73.

18. Ibid., 71.

19. See Joerg Fichte, "The Presentation of Sin as Verbal Action in the Moral Interludes," *Anglia* 103 (1985): 30, for a discussion of this dilemma.

20. All line references are to *Mankind*, in *The Macro Plays*, ed. Mark Eccles, EETS os 262 (Oxford: Oxford University Press, 1969), 153–84.

21. As William Tydeman has observed: "The players in *Mankynde* are all too clearly flesh-and-blood. They offer tangible evidence of their corporeal presence as they shove us aside to reach the stage, bellow in our ear to beware of Titivillus, attend to their most urgent bodily needs within a few yards of us"; see his *English Medieval Theatre, 1400–1500* (London: Routledge and Kegan Paul, 1986), 52.

22. For a thorough discussion of this theme, see Kathleen M. Ashley, "Titivillus and the Battle of Words in *Mankind*," *Annuale Mediaevale* 16 (1975): 128–50.

23. Michael T. Peterson, "Fragmina Verborum: The Vices' Use of Language in the Macro Plays," *Florilegium* 9 (1987): 155–67, argues that the vices in these moralities are characterized by their "sardonic eloquence" and "nonsensical volubility" (155–56). Since language is the medium of conflict in the play, according to Peterson, Mankind is presented with two competing discourses from which to choose; the play ultimately ends up in a plurality of discourses that scramble the discourse of spirituality and undermine God's position as the ultimate guarantor of meaning (163). See also Paula Neuss, "Active and Idle Language: Dramatic Images in *Mankind*," in *Medieval Drama*, ed. Neville Denny (London, 1973), 40–67.

24. See *Jacob's Well*, ed. Arthur Brandeis, EETS os 115 (London: Kegan Paul, Trench, Trübner, 1900), 260–64.

25. *Mankind* is in fact steeped in the language of instruction and advice; see W. A. Davenport, "Peter Idley and the Devil in *Mankind*," *English Studies* 64 (1983): 106–12. Davenport links *Mankind* to the mid-fifteenth-century *Instructions to His Son*, arguing that the characters of Mankind, Mercy, Mischief, and Titivillus all appear in embryonic form in Idley's treatment of the sin of sloth, a treatment that is itself based on *Handlyng Synne*.

26. See Theresa Coletti's discussion of slander and backbiting in the N-Town "Joseph's Trouble with Mary" in "Purity and Danger: The Paradox of Mary's Body and the En-gendering of the Infancy Narrative in the English Mystery Cycles," in *Feminist Approaches to the Body in Medieval Literature*, ed. Linda Lomperis and Sarah Stanbury (Philadelphia: University of Pennsylvania Press, 1993), 79–80.

27. The regulation of speech was also a concern of civic officials. See, for example, the ordinance from York in 1578, "that no person enfranchised in the said art or brother of the same presume to rebuke revile or geue anie slaunderous or veleynouse words to the said maister"; cited in *Records of Early English Drama: York*, ed. Johnston and Rogerson, 1:387.

28. For a discussion of late medieval attitudes toward labor relevant to *Mankind*, see Lawrence M. Clopper, "Need Men and Women Labor? Langland's Wanderer and the Labor Ordinances," in *Chaucer's England: Literature in Historical Context*, ed. Barbara A. Hanawalt (Minneapolis: University of Minnesota Press, 1992), 110–29. *Mankind* shares many of Langland's attitudes toward work and piety.

29. For a discussion of the representation of peasants in illuminations aimed at the dominant classes, see Michael Camille, "Labouring for the Lord: The Ploughman and the Social Order in the Luttrell Psalter," *Art History* 10 (1987): 423–54. For the alternate medieval image of the peasant as gross and indecent, see Ruth Mellinkoff, *Outcasts: Signs of Otherness in Northern European Art of the Late Middle Ages*, 2 vols. (Berkeley: University of California Press, 1993), 1:138–39 and 2: figs. X.32–33.

30. For a succinct discussion of late medieval economic developments and their impact on attitudes toward work and charity, see Brian Tierney, *Medieval Poor Law: A Sketch of Canonical Theory and Its Application in England* (Berkeley: University of California Press, 1959), 111–13. The continued migration from agricultural to urban employment in the generations after the Black Death is relevant here as well; see S. A. C. Penn and Christopher Dyer, "Wages and Earnings in Late Medieval England: Evidence from the Enforcement of the Labour Laws," *Economic History Review*, 2d ser., 43 (1990): 362.

31. See Gail McMurray Gibson, *The Theater of Devotion: East Anglian Drama and Society in the Late Middle Ages* (Chicago: University of Chicago Press, 1989), 159–61, and Steven May, "A Medieval Stage Property: The Spade," *Medieval English Theatre* 4 (1982): 88.

32. See the discussion in Clifford L. Davidson, *Visualizing the Moral Life: Medieval Iconography and the Macro Morality Plays* (New York: AMS Press, 1989), esp. 25.

33. The words are Hardin Craig's in his *English Religious Drama in the Middle Ages* (Oxford: Clarendon, 1955), 350. See also David Bevington, *From Mankind to Marlowe*

(Cambridge: Harvard University Press, 1962), 15–18, and Tydeman, *English Medieval Theatre*, part 2, chap. 1. Bevington later modified his position, in response to the line "I wyll into þe 3erde" (561), by moving the booth stage inside the inn; see Bevington, "Popular and Courtly Traditions on the Early Tudor Stage," in *Medieval Drama*, ed. Neville Denny (London: Arnold, 1973), 97–98. Alexandra F. Johnston, "The Audience of the English Moral Play," in *Le Théâtre et la cité dans l'europe médiévale*, ed. Jean-Claude Aubailly and Edelgard E. DuBruck (Stuttgart: Heinz Akademischer Verlag, 1988), 293, claims that because Mankind is a farmer, it is clear that the play was written "for a company to tour in the countryside."

34. See Lawrence M. Clopper, "*Mankind* and Its Audience," *Comparative Drama* 8 (1974–75): 349–54, who suggests that the play was performed indoors for a private audience, and Richard Southern, *The Staging of Plays before Shakespeare* (London: Faber, 1973), 21–43, who concludes that it was acted by a traveling troupe in a great hall.

35. Tom Pettitt, "*Mankind*: An English Fastnachtspiel?" in *Festive Drama*, ed. Meg Twycross (Cambridge: Brewer, 1996), 190–202. In an earlier essay, Pettitt sketched out a similar argument; see his "Tudor Interludes and the Winter Revels," *Medieval English Theatre* 6 (1984): 16–27. Ashley, "Titivillus and the Battle of Words, has also noted many associations with the pre-Lenten and Lenten season in the play. Sandra Billington, "'Suffer Fools Gladly': The Fool in Medieval England and the Play *Mankind*," in *The Fool and the Trickster*, ed. Paul V. A. Williams (Cambridge: Brewer, 1979), 36–54, has pointed out resemblances between *Mankind* and the French *sotties* that were performed at Shrovetide.

36. For the cultural significance of the household, see David Starkey, "The Age of the Household: Politics, Society, and the Arts, c. 1350–c. 1550," in *The Later Middle Ages*, ed. Stephen Medcalf (New York: Holmes and Meier, 1981), 225–90.

37. Gibson, *Theater of Devotion*, 110–12 and 117–21.

38. Richard B. Dobson and John Taylor, *Rymes of Robyn Hood: An Introduction to the English Outlaw* (London: Heinemann, 1976), 34–36; Paul R. Coss, "Aspects of Cultural Diffusion in Medieval England: The Early Romances, Local Society and Robin Hood," *Past and Present* 108 (1985): 74 n. 145.

39. This argument has been made by Potter, *English Morality Play*, 48.

40. All quotations are from *The Interlude of Youth*, in *Two Tudor Interludes*, ed. Ian Lancashire (Manchester: Manchester University Press, 1980), 99–152.

41. On youth and misrule, see Natalie Zemon Davis, "The Reasons of Misrule: Youth Groups in Sixteenth-Century France," *Past and Present* 50 (1971): 41–75, esp. 50.

42. See P. J. P. Goldberg, "Marriage, Migration, Servanthood and Life-Cycle in Yorkshire Towns of the Later Middle Ages: Some York Cause Paper Evidence," *Continuity and Change* 1 (1986): 149–53; Barbara A. Hanawalt, "Coming of Age: Apprenticeship in Medieval London," paper delivered at the 22d International Congress on Medieval Studies, Kalamazoo, Mich., 1987; David Harris Sacks, *Trade, Society and Politics in Bristol, 1500–1640*, 2 vols. (New York: Garland, 1985), 2:657–69 and 2:687–91; and Heather Swanson, *Medieval Artisans: An Urban Class in Late Medieval England* (Oxford: Blackwell, 1989), 115–16. Hanawalt notes that servanthood and apprenticeship practices meant that most urban youth were socialized outside their parents' homes. Swanson observes that city ordinances attempted to prevent these youth from forming associations of their own (115).

43. For a relevant discussion of the "problem" of "masterless men" and apprentice riots in late Tudor and early Stuart England, see Roger B. Manning, *Village Revolts: Social Protest and Popular Disturbances in England, 1509–1640* (Oxford: Clarendon, 1988), esp. 159–70 and 191–94. Manning notes that popular disturbances were often ascribed to apprentices, especially on Shrove Tuesday, which was their special holiday (192).

44. Pettitt, "*Mankind*," 197–98. For a discussion of the parallels between *Youth* and the mummers' plays, see Richard Axton, "Folk Play in Tudor Interludes," in *English Drama:*

*Forms and Development,* ed. Marie Axton and Raymond Williams (Cambridge: Cambridge University Press, 1977), 8–9.

45. Lancashire, ed., *Two Tudor Interludes,* 27.

46. Ibid., 53.

47. See Potter, *English Morality Play,* 231–32.

48. The Huntington Library owns the only known English prose version, which is available in a facsimile edition by Harry M. Ayres and Adriaan J. Barnouw, *Mary of Nimmegen* (Cambridge: Harvard University Press, 1932), and in a scholarly edition by Margaret M. Raftery, *Mary of Nemmegen* (Leiden: Brill, 1991). All quotations in my discussion are drawn from Raftery's edition. For the dating of the two versions, see Ayres and Barnouw, *Mary of Nimmegen,* 3–5. For information on Jan van Doesborch, see Robert Proctor, *Jan van Doesborgh, Printer at Antwerp* (London: Bibliographical Society, 1894).

49. See Raftery, *Mary of Nemmegen,* 15 n. 54.

50. Numerous books were produced in the Low Countries for the English market; see Edmund Colledge, "South Netherlands Books of Hours Made for England," *Scriptorium* 32 (1978): 55–57. Gibson, *Theater of Devotion,* 22–23, notes the close cultural links between East Anglia and the Low Countries, including Lollard and Protestant sympathies. Raftery, *Mary of Nemmegen,* 24, claims that Van Doesborch's book "bears signs of having been prepared in a relatively careful and time-consuming fashion," suggesting he anticipated selling enough copies to recoup his time and effort.

51. On the *Elckerlijc-Everyman* connection, see Elsa Strietman, "The Low Countries," in *The Theatre of Medieval Europe,* ed. Eckehard Simon (Cambridge: Harvard University Press, 1991), 246–47. *Eerste Bliscap* and the *N-Town* play have been discussed by Peter Meredith and Lynnette Muir, "The Trial in Heaven in the *Eerste Bliscap* and Other European Plays," *Dutch Crossings* 22 (1984): 84–92. For an important discussion of the links between the merchants who sponsored civic festivities and the drama of the Low Countries, see Alexandra F. Johnston, "Traders and Playmakers: English Guildsmen and the Low Countries," in *England and the Low Countries in the Late Middle Ages,* ed. Caroline Barron and Nigel Saul (New York: St. Martin's Press, 1995), 99–114.

52. For an analysis of the female body's powers and dangers from an anthropological perspective, see Peggy Reeves Sanday, *Female Power and Male Dominance: On the Origins of Sexual Inequality* (Cambridge: Cambridge University Press, 1981), esp. 91–92.

53. Like *Youth,* *Mariken van Nieumeghen* has a political topicality, making clear that Mariken's aunt has backed the wrong political candidate; see Leopold Peeters, "Mariken van Nieumeghen: Bourgondische politiek en dominicaanse vroomheid," in *Ic ga daer ic hebbe te doene,* ed. Jacobus J. T. M. Tersteeg and Pieter E. L. Verkuyl (Groningen: Wolters-Noordhoff, 1984), 167–78.

54. The play's hostility to female homosocial relations, shown in Mary's failed relationship with her aunt, is striking and recalls the attitudes of *How the Good Wife Taught Her Daughter,* where the daughter is cautioned against forming female friendships. The suggestion of both texts is that the female can safely be allowed to operate only within the narrow confines of the household, where she is under the control of a male guardian.

55. See *Jacob's Well,* ed. Brandeis, 147–48, for an example of the common understanding of the tavern as the devil's church, where the Seven Deadly Sins are taught. Like Mary Magdalene in the Digby *Mary Magdalene,* Mary's sin of *luxuria* (enjoying the pleasures the devil offers her) is linked to the pleasures of food and drink within the tavern; see Theresa Coletti, "The Design of the Digby Play of *Mary Magdalene,*" *Studies in Philology* 76 (1979): 318–19.

56. For ecclesiastical attitudes toward prostitution, see James A. Brundage, "Prostitution in the Medieval Canon Law," in *Sisters and Workers in the Middle Ages,* ed. Judith M. Bennett et al. (Chicago: University of Chicago Press, 1990), 86–87.

57. Elsa Strietman notes that the cult of Mary Magdalene was associated with the Dominicans and was well known in the southern Low Countries, where the Dutch play originated; see "The Face of Janus: Debatable Issues in *Mariken van Nieumeghen*," *Comparative Drama* 27 (1993): 64.

58. David E. Underdown has identified the late medieval and early modern period as being especially preoccupied with concerns about female assertiveness and revolt, perceived as threats to the family and by extension to the patriarchal social order; see his "The Taming of the Scold: The Enforcement of Patriarchal Authority in Early Modern England," in *Order and Disorder in Early Modern England*, ed. Anthony Fletcher and John Stevenson (Cambridge: Cambridge University Press, 1985), esp. 116–18.

59. See James A. Brundage, *Law, Sex, and Christian Society in Medieval Europe* (Chicago: University of Chicago Press, 1987), 544–45. In Lichfield in 1466, for example, according to Brundage, 90 percent of the people brought to court were charged with either adultery or fornication (544).

60. See Raftery, *Mary of Nemmegen*, 6–7.

61. The nunnery she enters is dedicated to Mary Magdalene and houses other fallen women. On the cultural symbolism of Mary Magdalene and her significance for the Middle Ages, see Susan Haskins, *Mary Magdalen: Myth and Metaphor* (New York: Harcourt, 1993).

62. Although Mary is never accused of being a witch, witchcraft haunts the story. Christina Larner, *Enemies of God: The Witch-hunt in Scotland* (Baltimore: Johns Hopkins University Press, 1981), 20, argues that witchcraft was a state-encouraged, nationalist ideology in which the enemies of society were defined as the enemies of God. Witch-hunts, Larner claims, provided a form of social control of unruly women, which hitherto had been the responsibility of fathers and husbands.

63. The emphasis on enclosure of the female body stressed by the ending of the play recalls the late medieval fascination with the enclosed body of the Virgin Mary; see Marina Warner, *Alone of All Her Sex: The Myth and Cult of the Virgin Mary* (New York: Knopf, 1976), esp. 34–49.

64. See the discussion of how prisons create delinquency in Michel Foucault, *Discipline and Punish: The Birth of the Prison*, trans. Alan Sheridan (New York: Vintage Books, 1979), 278–79 and 285.

65. See the discussion of this process in Judith Butler, *Bodies That Matter* (New York: Routledge, 1993), esp. 109–18.

66. See Carol Clover, "Her Body, Himself: Gender in the Slasher Film," *Representations* 20 (1987): 187–228.

67. The words are Sister Mary Coogan's in *Interpretation of the Morality Play, Mankind*, 108.

## Chapter 5. Devoted Bodies:
## Books of Hours and the Self-Consuming Subject

1. The Tourotte Hours, Walters Art Gallery, Baltimore, Md., MS W. 222, fols. 1v–2, 51v, and 96.

2. The two emended illuminations portray Madame Tourotte. In the first she is shown being presented to the Virgin by Saint Clare; in the second, Saint Barbara presents her to Saint Anne, the Virgin, and the child Jesus; see the Tourotte Hours, fols. 51v and 96.

3. Ownership was also asserted through the inscription of names in books of hours, especially in more modest ones lacking illuminations, and through modifications made to suit different owners, especially in vernacular prayers. See, for example, the Madresfield Hours, which was in continuous use from around 1330 through the second half of the sixteenth century and was changed to suit subsequent owners; discussed by Janet Backhouse,

*The Madresfield Hours: A Fourteenth Century Manuscript in the Library of Earl Beauchamp* (London: Roxburghe Club, 1975).

4. The Sforza Hours (British Library, Additional MS 629997), fol. 61r; see Mark Evans, *The Sforza Hours* (London: British Library, 1992), 15.

5. For a discussion of the commodification of worship in the late Middle Ages, including the founding of private and communal chantries, the veneration of images, and the use of devotional aids like books of hours, see Richard A. Goldthwaite, *Wealth and the Demand for Art in Italy, 1300–1600* (Baltimore: Johns Hopkins University Press, 1993), esp. 105–28; and William R. Jones, "Art and Christian Piety: Iconoclasm in Medieval Europe," in *The Image and the Word*, ed. Joseph Gutmann (Missoula, Mont.: Scholars Press, 1977), 87.

6. See Barthes's analysis of what he takes as the commodity fetishism of Dutch still-life painting in his "Le Monde-objet," in *Essais critiques* (Paris: Editions du Seuil, 1964), 19–28. Available in English translation by Richard Howard in *Calligram: Essays in New Art History from France*, ed. Norman Bryson (Cambridge: Cambridge University Press, 1988), 107–15. My thoughts on owner-portraits in books of hours have been guided by Barthes and by Simon Schama's critique of Barthes in "Perishable Commodities: Dutch Still-Life Painting and the 'Empire of Things,'" in *Consumption and the World of Goods*, ed. John Brewer and Roy Porter (London: Routledge, 1993), 478–88. I am also indebted to Luce Irigaray's "Women on the Market," in *This Sex Which Is Not One*, trans. Catherine Porter and Carolyn Burke (Ithaca: Cornell University Press, 1985), 170–91, which applies Marx's analysis of commodities to a reading of women in patriarchy.

7. For trade between England and the Low Countries, see Vanessa Harding, "Cross-Channel Trade and Cultural Contacts: London and the Low Countries in the Later Fourteenth Century," in *England and the Low Countries in the Late Middle Ages*, ed. Caroline Barron and Nigel Saul (New York: St. Martin's Press, 1995), 153–68. For Rouen's importance as a center of devotional book production, see L. M. J. Delaissé, James Marrow, and John de Wit, *Illuminated Manuscripts: The James A. De Rothschild Collection at Waddesdon Manor* (London: Published for the National Trust by Office du Livre, 1977), 130.

8. Delaissé, Marrow, and de Wit, *Illuminated Manuscripts*, 559.

9. L. M. J. Delaissé, "The Importance of Books of Hours for the History of the Medieval Book," in *Gatherings in Honor of Dorothy Miner* (Baltimore: Johns Hopkins University Press, 1974), 2.

10. For service books in wills, see JoAnn Hoeppner Moran, *The Growth of English Schooling, 1340–1548: Learning, Literacy, and Laicization in Pre-Reformation York Diocese* (Princeton: Princeton University Press, 1985), 196. For books of hours printed by early English printers, see *William of Machlinia's Primer*, ed. George Smith (London: Ellis, 1929), 10. Felix Soleil, *Les Heures gothiques et la littérature pieuse aux XVe et XVIe siécles* (Rouen: Auge, 1882), lists sixty-five editions of books of hours printed between 1487 and 1498, and Paul Lacombe's catalog, *Livres d'heures imprimés au XVe et XVIe siècle, conservés dans les Bibliothèques Publiques de Paris: Catalogue* (Paris, 1907; reprint, Nieuwkoop: de Graaf, 1963), describes some five hundred books of hours printed in the fifteenth and sixteenth centuries.

11. See Malcolm B. Parkes, "The Literacy of the Laity," in *The Medieval World*, ed. David Daiches and Anthony Thorlby (London: Aldus, 1973), 564.

12. For another example of liturgical material converted to popular use, see *The Lay Folks' Mass Book*, ed. T. F. Simmons, EETS os 71 (London: Trübner, 1879). A characteristic of late medieval piety is the assimilation of liturgical texts to private use. Richard Kieckhefer views devotional religion as lying between and drawing on liturgical and contemplative religion and so representing a middle ground between the completely public and the purely private; see his "Major Currents in Late Medieval Devotion," in *Christian Spirituality: High Middle Ages and Reformation*, ed. Jill Raitt (New York: Crossroad, 1987), 76.

13. The printed books of hours that reached their height of popularity in the sixteenth century featured changed contents, including the addition of new texts arranged in quasi-liturgical order for use at church services, especially Mass and vespers; see John P. Harthan, *Books of Hours and Their Owners* (London: Thames and Hudson, 1977), 39.

14. See Lacombe, *Livres d'heures*, xlvii.

15. See the discussion of how various owners used their books of hours by Virginia Reinburg, "Prayer and the Book of Hours," in Roger S. Wieck, *Time Sanctified: The Book of Hours in Medieval Art and Life* (New York: Braziller, 1988), 40–42.

16. See Edgar Hoskins, *Horae Beatae Mariae Virginis, or Sarum and York Primers* (London, 1906; reprint, Westmead, Eng.: Gregg International, 1969), xvii. The question of literacy in relation to the owners of books of hours is as vexed as the question of literacy in general in the Middle Ages. Some owners may not have read, or been able to read, either the Latin or the vernacular texts of the hours, but may have used the images to guide their meditations. On the general question of lay literacy, see Parkes, "Literacy of the Laity." For the relation between literacy and image, see Michael Camille, "Seeing and Reading: Some Visual Implications of Medieval Literacy and Illiteracy," *Art History* 8 (1985): 26–49. For a discussion of women as readers of books of hours, see Susan Groag Bell, "Medieval Women Book Owners: Arbiters of Lay Piety and Ambassadors of Culture," in *Women and Power in the Middle Ages*, ed. Mary Erler and Maryanne Kowaleski (Athens: University of Georgia Press, 1988), 149–87.

17. See the discussion in C. A. J. Armstrong, "The Piety of Cicely, Duchess of York: A Study in Late Medieval Culture," in *England, France, and Burgundy in the Fifteenth Century* (London: Hambledon, 1983), 140–42. See also Reinburg, "Prayer," 39–44.

18. For useful discussions of the laicization and privatization of religion in the late Middle Ages, see John Van Engen, "The Christian Middle Ages as an Historiographical Problem," *American Historical Review* 91 (1986): 547–48; Francis Oakley, *The Western Church in the Later Middle Ages* (Ithaca: Cornell University Press, 1979), esp. 118 (for the "Mass factories" that developed to meet the demand for more church services); and Goldthwaite, *Wealth and the Demand for Art*, 122–29.

19. For these examples, see Lacombe, *Livres d'heures*, lxxxiv, and Moran, *Growth of English Schooling*, 44.

20. Although in the fourteenth century nearly all books were priced out of the reach of anyone except the nobility or upper bourgeoisie, in the fifteenth century books of hours became much less costly as something akin to mass production increased their distribution; see Bell, "Medieval Women Book Owners," 152–54. Parkes, "Literacy of the Laity," 564, claims that by the fifteenth century small devotional books could be bought in England for less than one shilling. For a list of bequests of books of hours, see *Horae Eboracenses*, ed. Christopher Wordsworth (London: Quaritch, 1920), xxxviii–xxxix.

21. For a useful discussion of poststructuralist understandings of fetishism, as well as a rehabilitation of a Marxist theory of fetishism defined as a theory of social desire, see William Pietz, "Fetishism and Materialism: The Limits of Theory in Marx," in *Fetishism as Cultural Discourse*, ed. Emily Apter and William Pietz (Ithaca: Cornell University Press, 1993), 119–51.

22. See the discussion of the cultural function of these "devotional toys" by Christiane Klapisch-Zuber, "Holy Dolls: Play and Piety in Florence in the Quattrocento," in *Women, Family, and Ritual in Renaissance Italy*, trans. Lydia Cochrane (Chicago: University of Chicago Press, 1985), 310–29.

23. Delaissé, Marrow, and de Wit, *Illuminated Manuscripts*, 264.

24. See *The Prymer, or Lay Folk's Prayer Book*, ed. Henry Littlehales, EETS os 109 (London: Kegan Paul, Trench, Trübner, 1897), xliv.

25. See Lawrence Poos, "Social History and the Book of Hours," in Wieck, *Time Sancti-*

*fied*, 34. For a discussion of the intersection of private and public devotion in the late Middle Ages, see Jean Leclercq, "Dévotion privée, piété populaire et liturgie au moyen âge," *Études de pastorale liturgique* (Paris: Editions du Cerf, 1944), 149–83.

26. See *A Relation . . . of England*, ed. C. A. Sneyd, Camden Society 37 (London: Nichols, 1847), 23; and *Middle English Sermons*, ed. Woodburn O. Ross, EETS os 209 (London: Oxford University Press, 1940), 154, lines 27–28.

27. See Delaissé, Marrow, and de Wit, *Illuminated Manuscripts*, 264.

28. For the late medieval fascination with spectacle and display, see Sylvia L. Thrupp, *The Merchant Class of Medieval London* (Chicago: University of Chicago Press, 1948), 143–54.

29. Kathleen L. Scott, "A Mid-Fifteenth Century Illuminating Shop and Its Customers," *Journal of the Warburg and Courtauld Institutes* 31 (1968): 176.

30. Delaissé, Marrow, and de Wit, *Illuminated Manuscripts*, argue that some owner-portraits are "too common to . . . have any personal significance" (296) and might often have been "simply a formula often reproduced in this workshop" (508). But even if owner-portraits have become formulaic by the late fifteenth century, that says something important about the extent of the desire to see the "owner," whoever that might be, inscribed within devotional space.

31. This has been suggested by Charles Sterling and Claude Schaeffer, *The Hours of Etienne Chevalier*, trans. Marianne Sinclair (New York: Braziller, 1971), 7–8.

32. The defense of images often used terms that tried to decommodify the image, by making a distinction between the representation and the thing represented. See the advice in *Dives and Pauper* to worship "aforn þe ymage, nought to þe ymage," in *Dives and Pauper*, ed. Priscilla Heath Barnum, vol. 1, EETS os 275 (London: Oxford University Press, 1976), 85. See also the discussion in Eamon Duffy, *The Stripping of the Altars: Traditional Religion in England, 1400–1580* (New Haven: Yale University Press, 1992), 428–30.

33. Critics of modern consumer culture argue that, in Mike Featherstone's words, "the inner logic of consumer culture depends upon the cultivation of an insatiable appetite to consume images"; see his "The Body in Consumer Culture," *Theory, Culture and Society* 1, no. 2 (1982): 22. Owner-portraits in books of hours are, to a lesser degree, caught up in the same dynamics.

34. *The Fifty Earliest Wills in the Court of Probate, London*, ed. Frederick J. Furnivall, EETS os 78 (London: Trübner, 1882), 116. This tombstone is discussed in Gail McMurray Gibson, *The Theater of Devotion: East Anglian Drama and Society in the Late Middle Ages* (Chicago: University of Chicago Press, 1989), 11–12.

35. Jeffrey F. Hamburger, *The Rothschild Canticles: Art and Mysticism in Flanders and the Rhineland circa 1300* (New Haven: Yale University Press, 1990), 4.

36. Another, less common, form of owner portraiture found in books of hours is the portrait head; cf. the Visconti Hours in which Giangaleazzo Visconti's head appears three times alone in a medallion unrelated to the religious scenes. Millard Meiss and Edith W. Kirsch, *The Visconti Hours* (New York: Braziller, 1972), 8–9, suggest that this usage was probably inspired by portraits in frescoes and on ancient coins and medals. The Psalter and Hours of John, Duke of Bedford, ca. 1420 (British Library MS Additional 42131), also contains many small portrait heads of unidentified individuals.

37. For a discussion of the meanings of nakedness in late medieval art, see Ruth Mellinkoff, *Outcasts: Signs of Otherness in Northern European Art of the Late Middle Ages*, 2 vols. (Berkeley: University of California Press, 1993), 1:204–8.

38. For the painting of Andrew, see the Hours of Pope Leo X, France, ca. 1470, Walters Art Gallery, Baltimore, Md., MS W. 285, fol. 90; for Sebastian, see the Egmont Hours, Belgium, ca. 1440, Walters Art Gallery, MS W. 719, fol. 134; for Erasmus, see the Llangattock Hours, Low Countries, ca. 1440, J. Paul Getty Museum, Ludwig IX 7, fol. 18v; for Catherine,

see the Hours of Guillebert de Lannoy, Low Countries, ca. 1430, Rothschild Collection at Waddesdon Manor MS 4, fol. 114; and for Adrian, see the Cumberland Hours, Tours, early sixteenth century, New York, Pierpont Morgan Library, MS H. 8, fol. 181v. The painting of Catherine is the only one I have seen that shows her partially nude; usually she is depicted fully clothed.

39. John Plummer, *The Hours of Catherine of Cleves* (New York: Braziller, 1966), 15–16.

40. The Hours of Adolph of Cleves and La Marck, Belgium, ca. 1480, Walters Art Gallery, Baltimore, Md., MS W. 439, fol. 13v.; reproduced in Wieck, *Time Sanctified*, fig. 5.

41. For a related discussion of the use of domestic and familial space to defend mercantile culture, see Margaret D. Carroll, "'In the Name of God and Profit': Jan van Eyck's Arnolfini Portrait," *Representations* 44 (1993): 96–125, esp. 106–8.

42. For the lady distributing alms, see *The Hours of Catherine of Cleves*, ed. John Plummer (New York: Braziller, 1966), 40; for Margaret of York practicing seven pious acts, see *Miniatures médiévales de la Librairie de bourgogne au Cabinet des manuscrits de la Bibliothèque Royale de Belgique*, ed. L. M. J. Delaissé (Geneva: Editions des Deux-Mondes, 1959), 196–97.

43. The Beaufort/Beauchamp Hours (British Library, MS Royal 2 A.XVIII) consists of two parts: part of a psalter dating from ca. 1410, whose owner is unknown, and a book of hours, 1430–40, probably made for Margaret Beauchamp, wife of the first Duke of Somerset. The Annunciation scene is reproduced in Richard Marks and Nigel Morgan, eds., *The Golden Age of English Manuscript Painting, 1200–1500* (New York: Braziller, 1981), plate 32.

44. Owner-portraits in books of hours agree with the sentiments of *Jacob's Well* that prayer and meditation are the highest form of spiritual practice, better than alms-giving or fasting, since "for almes comyth of þi temperall godys, fastyng comyth of þi body, but þi prayere comyth out of þin herte"; see *Jacob's Well*, ed. Arthur Brandeis, EETS os 115 (London: Kegan Paul, Trench, Trübner, 1900), 190, lines 31–33.

45. For a related discussion of the disciplining practices of bodily enclosure as it applies to female anchorites, see Sarah Beckwith, "Passionate Regulation: Enclosure, Ascesis, and the Feminist Imaginary," *South Atlantic Quarterly* 93 (1994): 803–24.

46. Walters Art Library, MS W. 236, fol. 77; see Lilian M. C. Randall, *Medieval and Renaissance Manuscripts in the Walter Art Gallery*, 2 vols. in 3 (Baltimore: Johns Hopkins University Press, 1989), 2, 2:453; fol. 77 is reproduced in 2, 2: fig. 342.

47. For a description of the household goods found in English aristocratic households, see Christopher Dyer, "Aristocracy as Consumers," in his *Standards of Living in the Later Middle Ages: Social Change in England, c. 1200–1520* (Cambridge: Cambridge University Press, 1989), 49–85; K. M. McFarlane, *The Nobility of Later Medieval England* (Oxford: Clarendon Press, 1973), 96–98; and Thrupp, *Merchant Class*, 140–42.

48. Penelope Eames, "Documentary Evidence Concerning the Character and Use of Domestic Furnishings in England in the Fourteenth and Fifteenth Centuries," *Furniture History* 7 (1971): 47.

49. Belgium, Bruges, 1480s, Washington, D.C., Library of Congress, Rosenwald 9, fol. 87.

50. The Buves Hours, northern France or southern Belgium, 1450s, Walters Art Gallery, Baltimore, Md., MS W. 267, fol. 13v.

51. This depiction of a safe domestic space as a locale for devotion is consistent with late medieval advice on meditation. See, for example, the *ABC of Aristotle*, which counsels the individual to find a "priue place" secluded from "alle manere noyse" and to "sitte þe or knele as is þi mooste ese," MS Bodley 789, fol. 140; quoted in John C. Hirsh, "Prayer and Meditation in Late Medieval England: MS Bodley 789," *Medium Aevum* 48 (1979): 57.

52. This cozy domestic interior seems socially analogous to the rural landscapes depicted in many books of hours, which, as Poos has noted, portray a bucolic terrain that in its detachment from everyday reality could be described as a form of cognitive dissonance rep-

resenting a deliberate escape from the turmoil and rapid changes of the late Middle Ages; see his "Social History," in Wieck, *Time Sanctified*, 37. Even some outdoor scenes are treated as if they were interiors, with grass underneath but with rich tapestries and architectural enclosures serving to shut the individual off from the open exterior space; see, for example, a book of hours from Reims, ca. 1460, Walters Art Library, Baltimore, Md., MS W. 269, in which the owner who is named Collette is shown kneeling on grass outdoors before the Virgin and child surrounded by elaborate tapestries and wall hangings (fol. 76); reproduced in Randall, *Medieval and Renaissance Manuscripts*, 2, 2: fig. 232.

53. The self-absorbed interiority of owner-portraits in books of hours is in striking contrast to fourteenth-through-sixteenth-century European portraiture, in which the classic pose features the subject, pictured from the waist up and filling the frame of the painting, gazing outward; see the reproductions in Lorne Campbell, *Renaissance Portraits: European Portrait-Painting in the Fourteenth, Fifteenth, and Sixteenth Centuries* (New Haven: Yale University Press, 1990). For an English example, see the portrait of Margaret Beaufort (1488), National Portrait Gallery, London; reproduced in O. E. Saunders, *English Art in the Middle Ages* (Oxford: Clarendon Press, 1932), fig. 62.

54. John F. Benton has described this self-absorption, whose origins he locates in the twelfth century, as a "renewed commitment to the examination of the inner life"; see his "Consciousness of Self and Perceptions of Individuality," in *Renaissance and Renewal in the Twelfth Century*, ed. Robert L. Benson and Giles Constable (Cambridge: Harvard University Press, 1982): 263–95, esp. 264.

55. The Vienna Hours, Vienna, Nationalbibliothek, Cod. 1857, fol. 14v; reproduced in Christopher de Hamel, *A History of Illuminated Manuscripts* (Oxford: Phaidon, 1986). See the discussion of this miniature's "real" and "imaginary" spaces in Otto Pächt, *The Master of Mary of Burgundy* (London: Faber and Faber, 1948).

56. The Vienna Hours, fol. 43v; reproduced in Franz Unterkircher, *European Illuminated Manuscripts in the Austrian National Library*, trans. J. Maxwell Brownjohn (London: Thames and Hudson, 1967), plate 58.

57. For a related discussion of visions conjured up during devotions, see Craig Harbison, "Visions and Meditations in Early Flemish Painting," *Simiolus* 15 (1985): 87–118, esp. 94–99.

58. The Boucicaut Hours, fol. 26v, Paris, Musée Jacquemart-André.

59. Benton, "Consciousness of Self," 285, notes that within late medieval devotional culture, looking inward "brought one closer to the uniqueness, not of self, but of God."

60. Owners also appear outside of sacred space, in borders or within initials; see, for example, the illumination of Catherine of Cleves praying to the Virgin in the Hours of Catherine of Cleves, where the owner is located just outside the frame that contains the Virgin holding the Christ child; New York, Guennol Collection, fol. 4. In an example not from a book of hours, the donor is painted into an exterior scene with a holy figure; see Dirk Bouts, *Christ with St. John the Baptist and a Donor*, Munich, Wittelsbacher Ausgleichsfonds, on loan to the Bayerische Staatsgemäldesammlungen, Alte Pinakothek.

61. Guy Debord, *Society of the Spectacle* (Detroit: Black and Red, 1983), thesis 1.

62. See the discussion in Greil Marcus, *Lipstick Traces: A Secret History of the Twentieth Century* (Cambridge, Mass.: Harvard University Press, 1989), 96–112; Marcus illustrates Debord's ideas in a reading of Michael Jackson's *Thriller* album.

63. Debord, *Society of the Spectacle*, thesis 47. Or, as Marcus puts it, "capitalism as spectacle . . . turned upon individual men and women, seized their subjective emotions and experiences, changed those once evanescent phenomena into objective, replicable commodities . . . and sold them back to those who had, once, brought emotions and experiences out of themselves" (101).

64. See Sixten Ringbom, "Devotional Images and Imaginative Devotions," *Gazette*

*des Beaux Arts*, 6th ser., 73 (1969): 159–70, for a discussion of the role of images in late medieval lay piety. Ringbom claims that private devotion, under the influence of mysticism, became more individualistic in nature, as is evidenced in the popularity of books of hours (164).

65. *Zardino de oration;* cited in Michael Baxandall, *Painting and Experience in Fifteenth-Century Italy: A Primer in the Social History of Pictorial Style*, 2d ed. (Oxford: Oxford University Press, 1988), 46.

66. Baxandall, *Painting and Experience*, 46–47.

67. The quotation is from Bishop Reginald Pecock's defense of images in his *Repressor of Over Much Blaming of the Clergy*, published between 1449 and 1455; discussed in W. R. Jones, "Lollards and Images: The Defense of Religious Art in Late Medieval England," *Journal of the History of Ideas* 34 (1973): 41–42. Wyclif argued that although images might be valuable when they were used to induce religious emotions, they were dangerous when the image itself became an object of idolatry or veneration. As K. B. McFarlane, *John Wycliffe and the Beginnings of English Nonconformity* (London: English Universities Press, 1952), 96, notes, Wyclif was conventional in his criticism. Later Lollards often used lavish images (especially statues and paintings in churches) as the basis of class attacks against ecclesiastical privilege; see John A. F. Thomson, *The Later Lollards: 1414–1520* (London: Oxford University Press, 1965), 239–50. For a useful discussion of Lollardism and images, see Margaret Aston, *Lollards and Reformers: Images and Literacy in Late Medieval Religion* (London: Hambledon Press, 1984).

68. See the discussion of medieval visual theory in Margaret R. Miles, *Image as Insight: Visual Understanding in Western Christianity and Secular Culture* (Boston: Beacon, 1985), 7–9.

69. Michel de Certeau, *The Practice of Everyday Life*, trans. Steven F. Randall (Berkeley: University of California Press, 1984).

70. Hans Belting, *The Image and Its Public in the Middle Ages: Form and Function of Early Paintings of the Passion*, trans. Mark Bartusis and Raymond Meyer (New Rochelle, N.Y.: Caratzas, 1990), esp. 56–58.

71. See Richard Trexler, *Public Life in Renaissance Florence* (New York: Academic Press, 1980), 176–80.

72. Belting, *Image and Its Public*, 83.

73. Ibid., 90.

74. See Goldthwaite, *Wealth and the Demand for Art*, 145. Goldthwaite argues that this is more marked for Italy than for other countries, but it seems to be a widespread Anglo-European phenomenon.

75. Jacques Lacan, *The Four Fundamental Concepts of Psycho-Analysis*, ed. Jacques-Alain Miller, trans. Alan Sheridan (New York: Norton, 1977), 67–78.

76. Ibid., 84–85.

77. Belting, *Image and Its Public*, 58.

78. Peter Brown, "The Saint as Exemplar," *Representations* 1 (1983): 1–25.

79. See James D. Breckenridge, "'Et prima videt': The Iconography of the Appearance of Christ to His Mother," *Art Bulletin* 39 (1957): 31–32.

80. Benton, "Consciousness of Self," 266.

81. Erving Goffman, *The Presentation of Self in Everyday Life* (New York: Doubleday, 1959).

82. See Jacques Derrida, "Structure, Sign, and Play in the Discourse of the Human Sciences," in *The Structuralist Controversy*, ed. Richard Macksey and Eugenio Donato (Baltimore: Johns Hopkins University Press, 1972), 247–72.

83. Cf. Baudrillard's similar claim about the controlling nature of images: "It is useless to fantasize about state projection of police control through TV. . . . TV, by virtue of its mere

presence, is a social control in itself"; Baudrillard, "Requiem for the Media," in *For a Critique of the Political Economy of the Sign*, trans. Charles Levin (St. Louis, Mo.: Telos, 1981), 172. Although television is obviously a much different and more penetrating medium than the manuscript illumination, Baudrillard's remarks point to a connection between the social functioning of the two.

84. Norbert Elias, *The History of Manners* (1939), vol. 1 of *The Civilizing Process*, trans. Edmund Jephcott (New York: Pantheon, 1978), 78 and 104–8.

85. Schama, "Perishable Commodities," 478–88, similarly argues that Dutch still-life paintings are preoccupied with issues of perishability and loss, despite their opulent materiality.

86. France, Tours or Bourges, ca. 1510–20, Walters Art Gallery, Baltimore, Md., MS W. 446, fol. 15v.

87. Book of hours, Bruges, ca. 1450, Walters Art Gallery, Baltimore, Md., MS W. 220, fol. 150v.

88. Ervin Panofsky, "Jan van Eyck's Arnolfini Portrait," *Burlington Magazine* 64 (1934): 117–27.

89. University Library, Utrecht, MS 15.C.5, fol. 15v; reproduced in Koert van der Horst, *Illuminated and Decorated Medieval Manuscripts in the University Library, Utrecht: An Illustrated Catalog* (Cambridge: Cambridge University Press, 1989), fig. 357.

90. The quotation is from Mary Ann Caws, *The Eye in the Text: Essays on Perception, Mannerist to Modern* (Princeton: Princeton University Press, 1981), 88.

91. Barthes, "Monde-objet," 22.

92. Ibid., 25.

93. Schama, "Perishable Commodities," esp. 481–83.

94. For an eloquent description of these instances of disturbance of the supposedly placid surface of Dutch paintings, see Paul Claudel, *The Eye Listens*, trans. Elsie Pell (New York: Philosophical Library, 1950), 47–48; discussed in Schama, "Perishable Commodities," 480–81.

95. Schama, "Perishable Commodities," 482.

96. Catherine Presenting a Patroness to Christ; reproduced in Wieck, *Time Sanctified*, fig. 11.

97. For a direct confrontation of an owner and death, see the illumination discussed earlier in this chapter in which Death with a spear attacks a woman, who is possibly the book's owner; Walters Art Library, Baltimore, Md., MS W. 236, fol. 77; reproduced in Randall, *Medieval and Renaissance Manuscripts*, 2, 2: fig. 342.

98. The Butler Family at Mass, in the Butler Hours, England, ca. 1340, Walters Art Gallery, Baltimore, Md., MS W. 105, fol. 15; for a color reproduction, see Wieck, *Time Sanctified*, plate 13.

99. For a discussion of the role of consumption in self-creation, see Grant McCracken, *Culture and Consumption: New Approaches to the Symbolic Character of Consumer Goods and Activities* (Bloomington: Indiana University Press, 1990), esp. 71–92.

100. Rosalind Coward and John Ellis, *Language and Materialism: Developments in Semiology and the Theory of the Subject* (London: Routledge and Kegan Paul, 1977), 76.

101. For a discussion of both the conservative and the innovative role of goods, see McCracken, *Culture and Consumption*, 130–37.

# Chapter 6. Violated Bodies:
## The Spectacle of Suffering in Corpus Christi Pageants

1. See Sarah Beckwith, *Christ's Body: Religious Culture and Late Medieval Piety* (London: Routledge, 1994), and Miri Rubin, *Corpus Christi: The Eucharist in Late Medieval*

*Culture* (Cambridge: Cambridge University Press, 1991), for discussions of the cultural importance of the *corpus Christi* in the late Middle Ages.

2. The appropriateness of the term "Corpus Christi pageants" to describe these performances has been questioned, since, although Corpus Christi Day was a popular occasion for plays, any play could be performed then; see Alexandra F. Johnston, "What If No Texts Survived? External Evidence for Early English Drama," in *Contexts for Early English Drama*, ed. Marianne G. Briscoe and John C. Coldewey (Bloomington: Indiana University Press, 1989), 6. Of the civic cycles, only the York cycle seems to have taken place on Corpus Christi; the Chester cycle was performed at Whitsun, and the performance history of the N-Town and Towneley plays remains unclear. Richard Beadle, "The York Cycle: Texts, Performances, and the Bases for Critical Enquiry," in *Medieval Literature: Texts and Interpretation*, ed. Tim Machan (Binghamton, N.Y.: Medieval and Renaissance Texts and Studies, 1991), 111, notes also that the term "the York cycle" is "no more than a convenient notional term to describe what was, in reality, a literary and dramatic entity capable of marked variation in form from year to year."

3. John Shaw, "The Life of Master John Shaw," in *Yorkshire Diaries and Autobiographies in the Seventeenth and Eighteenth Centuries*, ed. Charles Jackson, Surtees Society 65 (London, 1877), 121–62; the quotation is from 139.

4. For a discussion of violence in the Croxton play, see Richard L. Homan, "Devotional Themes in the Violence and Humor of the *Play of the Sacrament*," *Comparative Drama* 20 (1986–87): 327–40. An analogous scene to that in the *Mystery* appears in the N-Town Assumption of Mary, in which one of the three Jewish knights sent to attack the Virgin's funeral procession touches the coffin and finds his hands stuck fast to it.

5. John Spalding Gatton, "'There must be blood': Mutilation and Martyrdom on the Medieval Stage," in *Violence in Drama*, ed. James Redmond (Cambridge: Cambridge University Press, 1991), 80. For violence in late medieval society, see Marc Bloch, *Feudal Society* (Chicago: University of Chicago Press, 1962), 411, who claims that "violence [was] the distinguishing mark of [the] epoch and [the] social system"; and Rodney Hilton, *A Medieval Society* (London: Weidenfeld and Nicolson, 1967), 55, who describes the West Midlands in the thirteenth and fourteenth centuries as a place "where violence, bribery and corruption were normal means of settling the issues which arose between men."

6. One exception to this general avoidance is Gatton, "'There must be blood,'" 79–91. Gatton argues that violence on the medieval stage sanctioned not just virtuous suffering but also "sensationalism, voyeurism, sadism, and anti-Semitism" (79). Another exception is Anthony Kubiak, *Stages of Terror: Terrorism, Ideology, and Coercion as Theatre History* (Bloomington: Indiana University Press, 1991), who describes much of medieval drama as a "theatre of punishment" wherein the pleasure of the spectator's gaze is directed toward spectacles of suffering (49).

7. V. A. Kolve, *The Play Called Corpus Christi* (Stanford, Calif.: Stanford University Press, 1966), 175–205. In "Mixed Feelings about Violence in the Corpus Christi Plays," in *Violence in Drama*, ed. James Redmond (Cambridge: Cambridge University Press, 1991), 93–100, Richard Homan expresses similar feelings about the York Crucifixion, arguing that "the violence done to Christ in this play would have inspired pity for the ignorance of the doers" (95).

8. See John R. Elliott, *Playing God: Medieval Mysteries on the Modern Stage* (Toronto: University of Toronto Press, 1989), 91, and Robert A. Potter, *The English Morality Play: Origins, History and Influence of a Dramatic Tradition* (Boston: Routledge and Kegan Paul, 1975), 222.

9. This reading has been most fully developed in feminist work on the body of the cyborg; see Donna Haraway, "A Cyborg Manifesto: Science, Technology and Socialist-Feminism in the 1980s," in her *Simians, Cyborgs, and Women* (New York: Routledge, 1989), 149–81. See also Arthur Kroker and Marilouise Kroker, "Theses on the Disappearing

Body in the Hyper-Modern Condition," in *Body Invaders: Panic Sex in America*, ed. Arthur Kroker and Marilouise Kroker (New York: St. Martin's Press, 1987), esp. 21.

10. In an influential essay, Mervyn James drew on the work of Mary Douglas to argue that Corpus Christi processions and plays used the body as a dense symbolic system within which late medieval urban societies could represent and understand themselves. According to James, "the concept of body provided urban societies with a mythology and ritual in terms of which the opposites of social wholeness and social differentiation could be both affirmed, and also brought into a creative tension, one with the other"; see Mervyn James, "Ritual, Drama and Social Body in the Late Medieval English Town," *Past and Present* 98 (1983): 3–29; the quotation is from 4.

11. The ordinance reads: "[N]o man of the Crafte take no prentys but that he be an Engelysch man borne & nother Frensche Skottysche ne Iryyssh And . . . that he haue all his ryght lymes"; C.R.O. access. 34: Weavers 2a, rule no. 13. See the discussion in Peter Travis, "The Social Body of the Dramatic Christ in Medieval England," in *Early Drama to 1600*, ed. Albert H. Tricomi (Binghamton, N.Y.: Center for Medieval and Early Renaissance Studies, 1987), 23.

12. For a discussion of economic issues relating to the Corpus Christi cycles, see John C. Coldewey, "Some Economic Aspects of the Late Medieval Drama," in *Contexts for Early English Drama*, ed. Marianne G. Briscoe and John C. Coldewey (Bloomington: Indiana University Press, 1989), 77–101.

13. See the studies of merchant oligarchies by Jennifer Kermode, "The Merchants of Three Northern Towns," in *Profession, Vocation, and Culture in Later Medieval England*, ed. Cecil H. Clough (Liverpool: Liverpool University Press, 1982), 7–50; Maryanne Kowaleski, "The Commercial Dominance of a Medieval Provincial Oligarchy: Exeter in the Late Fourteenth Century," *Medieval Studies* 46 (1984): 355–84; and David Harris Sacks, *Trade, Society and Politics in Bristol, 1500–1640*, 2 vols. (New York: Garland, 1985), esp. 2:662–72; as well as the classic study of the mercantile class by Sylvia L. Thrupp, *The Merchant Class of Medieval London, 1300–1500* (Chicago: University of Chicago Press, 1948).

14. Heather Swanson, *Medieval Artisans: An Urban Class in Late Medieval England* (Oxford: Blackwell, 1989), esp. 110–13. As Swanson notes, however, this picture has to be complicated by other alliances and divisions, particularly those uniting master craftsmen with the mercantile elite against journeymen and apprentices (115–16).

15. Printed in Bertha H. Putnam, *The Enforcement of the Statutes of Labourers during the First Decade after the Black Death, 1349–1359* (New York: Columbia University Press, 1908; reprint, New York: AMS, 1970), appendix 8–12. Putnam descibes the statute as "the first thorough-going attempt to impress uniform economic standards on the country at large" (217) and views the statute as "on the whole equitable" (223).

16. Swanson, *Medieval Artisans*, 113–15.

17. See Travis, "Social Body," esp. 23–25.

18. The argument that the plays were an explicit force in supporting and maintaining an urban economy that favored the mercantile elite has been made with regard to York by Sarah Beckwith, "Making the World in York and the York Cycle," in *Framing Medieval Bodies*, ed. Sarah Kay and Miri Rubin (Manchester: Manchester University Press, 1994), 254–76.

19. Beckwith, "Making the World," 266. Beckwith's essay importantly opens up the York cycle plays to ideological critique, linking them with the economic policies of a mercantile elite but pointing out how an artisanal emphasis on "making" in the plays, particularly in the Crucifixion play, undercuts the mercantile position.

20. Although there were important differences among the various Corpus Christi plays and, as Nigel Goose argues in "English Pre-Industrial Urban Economies," *Urban History Yearbook* 1 (1982): 24–30, among English towns, ample evidence of common and widely

shared attitudes toward labor exists. Peter Travis's reading of the homologies between Christ's broken body and the breakdown of the late medieval city is also relevant here; see Travis, "Social Body," esp. 29–32.

21. For the texts of the liturgical plays on the Slaughter of the Innocents theme, see Karl Young, *The Drama of the Medieval Church*, 2 vols. (Oxford: Clarendon Press, 1933), vol. 2, chap. 20. The biblical source for the Slaughter of the Innocents is Matthew 2; the incident does not appear in the other Gospels.

22. *The Records of Early English Drama: Chester*, ed. Lawrence M. Clopper (Toronto: University of Toronto Press, 1979), 36 (hereafter *REED: Chester*).

23. See Gatton, "'There must be blood,'" 86–88, for a discussion of these special effects. T. W. Craik, however, believes that the Slaughter scenes might have been treated in a sedate way, as is suggested by the text of Towneley; see T. W. Craik, "Violence in the English Miracle Plays," in *Medieval Drama*, ed. Neville Denny (London: Arnold, 1973), 181–82.

24. *The Towneley Plays*, ed. Martin Stevens and A. C. Cawley, 2 vols., EETS ss 13 (Oxford: Oxford University Press, 1994), 16/697. Other editions cited in this chapter include *The Chester Mystery Cycle*, ed. R. M. Lumiansky and David Mills, 2 vols., EETS ss 3 (London: Oxford University Press, 1974); *The Late Medieval Religious Plays of Bodleian MSS. Digby 133 and e Museo 160*, ed. Donald C. Baker, John L. Murphy, and Louis B. Hall Jr., EETS os 283 (Oxford: Oxford University Press, 1982); *The N-Town Play: Cotton MS Vespasian D.8*, ed. Stephen Spector, 2 vols., EETS ss 11 (Oxford: Oxford University Press, 1991); and *The York Plays*, ed. Richard Beadle (London: Arnold, 1982). Subsequent citations appear in the text by play and line number.

25. See Gustave Cohen, *Le Livre de Conduite du Régisseur . . . pour le Mystère de la Passion joué à Mons en 1501* (Paris: Honoré Champion, 1925), 103 and 104 n. 13.

26. E. K. Chambers, *The Mediaeval Stage*, 2 vols. (Oxford: Clarendon Press, 1903), 2:345. The Valenciennes *Passion* of 1547 also apparently featured blood pouring from the slaughtered children's bodies; see Louis Petit de Julleville, *Les Mystères*, 2 vols. (Paris: Librairie Hachette, 1880), 2:155.

27. For this argument, see Robert Weimann, *Shakespeare and the Popular Tradition in the Theater*, ed. Robert Schwartz (Baltimore: Johns Hopkins University Press, 1978), 66–68, and Rosemary Woolf, *English Mystery Plays* (Berkeley: University of California Press, 1972), 205, both of whom follow the description of Herod as a feudal tyrant advanced by G. R. Owst, *Literature and Pulpit in Medieval England* (Cambridge: Cambridge University Press, 1933), 331–34 and 493–95.

28. Theresa Coletti, "'Ther Be But Women': Gender Conflict and Gender Identity in the Middle English Innocents Plays," *Mediaevalia* 18 (1995): 245–61; the quotations are from 248 and 252, respectively. For a discussion of gender and the Towneley plays, see Ruth Evans, "Feminist Re-Enactments: Gender and the Towneley Vxor Noe," in *A Wyf Ther Was: Essays in Honour of Paule Mertens-Fonck*, ed. Juliette Dor (Liege: University of Liege Press, 1992), 141–54.

29. It is worth noting that not all late medieval depictions of violence against children focus on masculine power. *La Vengeance de Notre-Seigneur* (The vengeance of our Lord), for example, a collection of fifteenth-century French plays that features the destruction of Jerusalem by Titus in A.D. 70, shows mothers violating the bodies of their own offspring: during the siege of the city mothers are forced by famine to eat their children; see Stephen K. Wright, *The Vengeance of Our Lord: Medieval Dramatizations of the Destruction of Jerusalem* (Toronto: Pontifical Institute of Medieval Studies, 1989).

30. The Towneley manuscript dates from ca. 1500 and contains thirty-two pageants arranged continuously with no blank spaces; it was probably a "regenall," i.e., an original or authorial text, and does not for the most part identify guilds associated with the pageants or include marginalia. Stevens and Cawley, eds., *Towneley Plays*, xix–xxi, see little doubt

about the manuscript's association with Wakefield, although there are only a few external references from the 1550s to a Corpus Christi cycle at Wakefield.

31. Clopper, ed., *REED: Chester*, liv, believes that the early Chester Corpus Christi play was a Passion play, not a complete cycle. Antiquarians of Chester promoted the notion of Whitsun plays dating to the early fourteenth century, but records refute their claim (liii–liv).

32. J. W. Robinson, *Studies in Fifteenth-Century Stagecraft* (Kalamazoo, Mich.: Medieval Institute, 1991), 164–65, notes that the Towneley version of the Slaughter develops the York pageant's linking of knights and violence into a full-fledged satire of the first estate, with Herod being portrayed as a fifteenth-century magnate and his knights resembling the small private armies of the times and so representing well-known evils of unchecked and corrupt power.

33. Coletti, "'Ther Be But Women,'" 250–51.

34. See Barbara A. Hanawalt, *Crime and Conflict in English Communities, 1300–1348* (Cambridge: Harvard University Press, 1979), 61.

35. See the succinct summary of these processes in John Brenkman, "Mass Media: From Collective Experience to the Culture of Privatization," *Social Text* 3 (1984): 94–109, esp. 94–95.

36. See James B. Given, *Society and Homicide in Thirteenth-Century England* (Stanford, Calif.: Stanford Universty Press, 1977), 177, and P. J. P. Goldberg, *Women, Work, and Life Cycle in a Medieval Economy: Women in York and Yorkshire, c. 1300–1520* (Oxford: Clarendon Press, 1992), 158–202. Urban poll tax evidence shows that 20 to 30 percent of the population over the age of fourteen were servants, compared with only 10 percent in rural areas; see Maryanne Kowaleski, "The History of Urban Families in Medieval England," *Journal of Medieval History* 14 (1988): 53–54.

37. For an instance of this equating of children with potential profit, see the labor statute of 1405–6 (7 Henry IV) for the assertion that laborers and servants are apprenticing their children in order to be able to afford fashionable clothing and pay for what the statute sees as other items of indulgence.

38. Cf. the early-fifteenth-century misericord from Saint Mary's Church, Whalley, Lincolnshire, in which a kneeling warrior, his weapons put aside, is beaten by a woman with a frying pan; described in Robinson, *Stagecraft*, 168. The N-Town, Chester, and Digby versions of the Slaughter of the Innocents all use the symbolism of the rebellious housewife to stage the mothers' resistance to the murder of their sons.

39. The words are Craik's, "Violence in the English Miracle Plays," 195.

40. The Shearmen and Taylors play from Coventry, printed in *Two Coventry Corpus Christi Plays*, ed. Hardin Craig, EETS es 87, 2d ed. (London: Oxford University Press, 1957), 867, explicitly identifies the women's weapons as "womanly gere." Gail McMurray Gibson, *The Theater of Devotion: East Anglian Drama and Society in the Late Middle Ages* (Chicago: University of Chicago Press, 1989), 42–43, argues that the scene functions not as comic intrusion, but rather as juxtaposition of the biblical event in Bethlehem with the celebration of Saint Distaff's Day on January 7, when women returned to their spinning after the holidays. Saint Distaff's Day was traditionally celebrated with games and jokes, especially mock battles between the sexes. In East Anglia, Gibson notes, which was a center of the cloth industry, the distaff would have also had larger communal and economic implications. Coletti, "'Ther Be But Women,'" 251, also discusses the invocation of female versus male labor through the weapons they fight with and points out that through their epithets ("hoore" and "bawd") the men attempt to reduce the women to sexualized bodies.

41. Coletti, "'Ther Be But Women,'" esp. 251. For the role of women in urban economies, see Kowaleski, "History of Urban Families," 49–50.

42. Relevant to this dynamic is Klaus Theweleit's work on the *Freikorps*. Theweleit suggests that male soldiers desire to destroy the female and reduce her to a bloody mass,

thereby ratifying their own masculine identities. Theweleit goes on to develop an analogy between the working class and women in this position, thus describing how militaristic violence against women has class valences. See his *Male Fantasies*, trans. Stephan Conway in collaboration with Erica Carter and Chris Turner, 2 vols. (Minneapolis: University of Minnesota Press, 1987–89), esp. 1:218ff.

43. John Mirk, *Festial*, ed. T. Erbe, EETS es 96 (London: Trübner, 1905), 29.

44. See the discussion of this shift in Kolve, *Play Called Corpus Christi*, 175–76; the quotation is from 176.

45. *REED: Chester*, 37.

46. Travis, "Social Body," 25–26, says of these pageants that "Christ, stripped of his clothing and required to remain naked throughout his Passion, calls attention to his body and to the vulnerabilities of his flesh." This dramatic representation of Christ evokes the devotional iconography of the late Middle Ages, where Christ similarly appears with all the effects of physical torture visible on his body, vividly revealed in sometimes exaggerated ways; see Grace Frank, "Popular Iconography of the Passion," *PMLA* 46 (1931): 333–40, and Gertrud Schiller, *Iconography in Christian Art*, trans. Janet Seligman (Greenwich, Conn.: New York Graphic Society, 1972), 2:190–97.

47. For these added stories, see James H. Marrow, *Passion Iconography in Northern European Art of the Late Middle Ages and Early Renaissance* (Kortrijk, Belgium: Van Ghemmert, 1979), 95–170.

48. See Meg Twycross and Sarah Carpenter, "Masks in Medieval English Theatre: The Mystery Plays 2," *Medieval English Theatre* 3 (1981): 101.

49. For a discussion of violence against Jewish bodies in the *Canterbury Tales* and in the Croxton *Play of the Sacrament*, see Steven F. Kruger, "The Bodies of Jews in the Late Middle Ages," in *The Idea of Medieval Literature: New Essays on Chaucer and Medieval Culture in Honor of Donald R. Howard*, ed. James M. Dean and Christian K. Zacher (Newark: University of Delaware Press, 1992), 301–23.

50. The spitting in Jesus' face during the buffeting is mentioned by Margery Kempe, chaps. 79 and 80, where she gives her version of the Passion; see *The Book of Margery Kempe*, ed. Sanford Meech and Hope Emily Allen, EETS os 212 (London: Oxford University Press, 1940). Marrow, *Passion Iconography*, 132, claims that of all the incidents of the mocking at Caiaphas's house mentioned in the Gospels, the spitting seemed to capture the interest of medieval writers. This interest in spitting also seems to represent a preoccupation with issues of violation of bodily integrity, in which the ultimate degradation features an invasion of bodily fluids.

51. Martin Stevens, "Processus Torontoniensis: A Performance of the Wakefield Cycle," *Research Opportunities in Renaissance Drama* 28 (1985): 189–90. The performance being described is the 1985 Toronto Towneley cycle.

52. Peter Travis, "The Dramatic Strategies of Chester's Passion Pagina," in *The Chester Mystery Cycle: A Casebook*, ed. Kevin J. Harty (New York: Garland, 1993), 147, sees the Chester Passion scenes as much different from the other cycles, aiming at demonstrating the "salvific power of Christian belief" by emphasizing ritual and making the evil characters a collective, impersonal force.

53. Ibid., 150.

54. For a discussion of women and the body, see Elizabeth Spelman, "Women as Body: Ancient and Contemporary Views," *Feminist Studies* 8 (1982): 109–31. For women's bodies in late medieval spirituality, see Caroline Walker Bynum, "The Female Body and Religious Practice in the Later Middle Ages," in *Zone: Fragments for a History of the Human Body*, ed. Michel Feher, with Ramona Nadaff and Nadia Tazi, 3 vols. (New York: Urzone, 1989), 1: 166–67.

55. See Mary Douglas, *Purity and Danger: An Analysis of Concepts of Pollution and Taboo* (Harmondsworth: Penguin, 1970), esp. 144–45.

56. Kolve, *Play Called Corpus Christi*, 175–205. In Middle English, "game" has a range of meanings, including trick, scheme, or plot, as well as sport, amusement, or contest; see John C. Coldewey, "Plays and 'Play' in Early English Drama," *Research Opportunities in Renaissance Drama* 28 (1985): 181–88.

57. See Owst, *Literature and Pulpit*, 510–11.

58. See Kolve, *Play Called Corpus Christi*, esp. 199. By foregrounding the element of play, the pageants also raise questions about the problem of play itself, as Glending Olson, "Plays as Play: A Medieval Ethical Theory of Performance and the Intellectual Context of the *Miraclis Pleyinge*," *Viator* 26 (1995): 215–16, notes, linking the "play" that is the performance with illicit forms of play such as dicing.

59. Kolve, *Play Called Corpus Christi*, 138.

60. *The Tretise of Miraclis Pleyinge*, ed. Clifford Davidson (Kalamazoo, Mich.: Medieval Institute, 1993), 39. Davidson argues that identification with the suffering Christ, often manifested in the form of weeping spectators at Corpus Christi Passion plays, was a characteristic of northern spirituality; see his "Northern Spirituality and the Late Medieval Drama of York," in *The Spirituality of Western Christendom*, ed. E. Rozanne Elder (Kalamazoo, Mich.: Cistercian Publications, 1976), 125–51.

61. *Book of Margery Kempe*, ed. Meech and Allen, 192, lines 1–8.

62. This is how Maureen Flynn reads public rituals of flagellation in medieval Spain, seeing such rituals as the "theatrical production of private practices in a narrative format that reiterated the moral message of compensatory suffering" (164); see her "The Spectacle of Suffering in Spanish Streets," in *City and Spectacle in Medieval Europe*, ed. Barbara A. Hanawalt and Kathryn L. Reyerson (Minneapolis: University of Minnesota Press, 1994), 153–68. Elaine Scarry's discussion of torture as a public projection of private pain is also useful here; see her *The Body in Pain: The Making and Unmaking of the World* (Oxford: Oxford University Press, 1985), 27–59. See Jody Enders, "Rhetoric, Coercion, and the Memory of Violence," in *Criticism and Dissent in the Middle Ages*, ed. Rita Copeland (Cambridge: Cambridge University Press, 1996), 24–55, for a general discussion of rhetoric and violence in medieval Europe.

63. See Bynum, "Female Body," 160–219.

64. Mikhail Bakhtin, *Rabelais and His World*, trans. Helene Iswolsky (Bloomington: Indiana University Press, 1984), 334–35.

65. See Marie-Christine Pouchelle, *The Body and Surgery in the Middle Ages*, trans. Rosemary Morris (Cambridge: Polity Press, 1990), 115–23, for a discussion of these ideas of cleansing through purging.

66. See Geoffrey Galt Harpham, *The Ascetic Impulse in Culture and Criticism* (Chicago: University of Chicago Press, 1987).

67. See, for example, Kolve, *Play Called Corpus Christi*, 186.

68. For a discussion of representations of Christ's sexuality in the early modern period that is relevant to the eroticizing of his body in the Corpus Christ crucifixion scenes, see Leo Steinberg, *The Sexuality of Christ in Renaissance Art and in Modern Oblivion* (New York: Pantheon, 1983).

69. For a discussion of the "shame" of female bleeding and for how such shame can become attached to male as well as female subjects, see Gail Kern Paster, *The Body Embarrassed: Drama and the Disciplines of Shame in Early Modern England* (Ithaca: Cornell University Press, 1993), 65–112.

70. For a discussion of Christ's feminized body, see Caroline Walker Bynum, *Jesus as Mother: Studies in the Spirituality of the High Middle Ages* (Berkeley: University of California Press, 1982). For a striking depiction of the wound-vagina, see the Psalter and Hours of Bonne of Luxembourg, Metropolitan Museum of Art, the Cloisters, MS 69, fol. 331; reproduced in Lucy Freeman Sandler, "Jean Pucelle and the Lost Miniatures of the Belleville Breviary," *Art Bulletin* 66 (1984), fig. 17.

71. For a discussion of blood as an ambiguously figured sign in medieval culture, see Kathleen Biddick, "Genders, Bodies, Borders: Technologies of the Visible," *Speculum* 68 (1993), esp. 401–9; Biddick reads blood as marking "a crisis of exteriority and interiority in the construct of Christendom" (401).

72. Scarry, *Body in Pain*, 27.

73. See, for instance, the labor statutes of 1388 (12 Richard II) and 1405–6 (7 Henry IV), which limit access of the poor to crafts.

74. See Jacques Le Goff, *Time, Work, and Culture in the Middle Ages*, trans. Arthur Goldhammer (Chicago: University of Chicago Press, 1980), 115.

75. Charles Phythian-Adams, *The Desolation of a City: Coventry and the Urban Crisis of the Late Middle Ages* (Cambridge: Cambridge University Press, 1979), 117.

76. One result of the labor shortages that came in the wake of the Black Death was a decline in almsgiving and the rise of a work culture. Secular and religious authorities alike showed increased interest in preventing begging and encouraging labor; see Michel Mollat, *The Poor in the Middle Ages: An Essay in Social History*, trans. Arthur Goldhammer (New Haven: Yale University Press, 1986); and Miri Rubin, *Charity and Community in Medieval Cambridge* (Cambridge: Cambridge University Press, 1987), esp. 291–93.

77. For the corporate solidarity modeled by the plays, see James, "Ritual, Drama, and Social Body"; for the divisions they created, see Beckwith, "Making the World," 263–64, and Swanson, *Medieval Artisans*, esp. 120.

78. *The Records of Early English Drama: York*, ed. Alexandra F. Johnston and Margaret Rogerson (Toronto: University of Toronto Press, 1979), 1:11 (hereafter *REED: York*).

79. This point has been suggested by James, "Ritual, Drama and Social Body," 27.

80. Seeing the image of the dying Christ could also lead to pardons; see *REED: York*, 2:855 and 859.

81. Beckwith, "Making the World," 265; the quotations are from 266 and 257, respectively.

82. Medieval urban elites understood the need to subdue the body. As Phythian-Adams, *Desolation of a City*, 139, notes, these elites "jealously guarded the dignity or 'worship' of the group" by regulating the behavior of the individual's body, especially the body's sexual behavior.

83. Michel Foucault, *Discipline and Punish*, trans. Alan Sheridan (New York: Vintage Books, 1979), 26.

84. Ibid., 55.

85. Philippa Maddern's finding that violence in East Anglia in the fifteenth century was used in the service of authority and order endorses Foucault's view; see her *Violence and Social Order: East Anglia, 1422–1442* (Oxford: Clarendon Press, 1992), esp. 227–29.

86. René Girard, *Violence and the Sacred*, trans. Patrick Gregory (Baltimore: Johns Hopkins University Press, 1977); the quotation is from 14.

87. Given, *Society and Homicide*, 90.

88. See Bynum, "Female Body," esp. 1:162.

89. Late medieval attitudes toward play and theatrical performance have been recently explored by Olson, "Plays as Play."

90. *The Records of Early English Drama: Coventry*, ed. R. W. Ingram (Toronto: University of Toronto Press, 1981), 107. On the potential for confusion between real violence and stage violence, see Jody Enders, *Rhetoric and the Origins of Medieval Drama* (Ithaca: Cornell University Press, 1992), 102–5 (hereafter *REED: Coventry*).

91. C. Clifford Flanigan, "Liminality, Carnival, and Social Structure: The Case of Late Medieval Biblical Drama," in *Victor Turner and the Construction of Cultural Criticism: Between Literature and Anthropology*, ed. Kathleen M. Ashley (Bloomington: Indiana University Press, 1990), 54.

92. *REED: York*, 2:728; Latin original on 1:43.

93. A number of other kinds of performances are also known to have sparked riots, including a Lent carnival at Norwich in 1443; the staging of a play of Thomas the Apostle at York in the 1550s, which was followed by a papist disturbance; and the Kett revolt set off by a Robin Hood play at Wymondham. For a discussion of all three, see James, "Ritual, Drama and Social Body," 29.

94. See Rupert H. Morris, *Chester in the Plantagenet and Tudor Reigns* (Chester, 1893), 405–8; *REED: York*, 2:717–18; and *REED: Coventry*, 83, respectively, for these instances of violence.

95. See Foucault, *Discipline and Punish*, 135–38.

96. See *REED: Chester*, 28, 184, 197, and 292–93, respectively.

97. Natalie Zemon Davis, "The Rites of Violence: Religious Riot in Sixteenth Century France," *Past and Present* 59 (1973): 51–91, is also useful in understanding the links between religious events and violence.

98. See *York Memorandum Book*, ed. Maud Sellars, 2 vols., Surtees Society 120, 125 (London, 1912 and 1915), 2:124.

99. Quoted in the Latin original and in translation in Siegfried Wenzel, "*Somer Game* and Sermon References to a Corpus Christi Play," *Modern Philology* 86 (1989): 278–79.

100. In a sermon on the Slaughter of the Innocents, John Mirk assumes that such a pattern of identification is possible, likening his audience to the Innocents; see his *Festial*, 35.

101. R. B. Pugh, *Imprisonment in Medieval England* (Cambridge: Cambridge University Press, 1968), 25.

102. For the trade in relics, see Patrick J. Geary, "Sacred Commodities," in *The Social Life of Things: Commodities in Cultural Perspective*, ed. Arjun Appadurai (Cambridge: Cambridge University Press, 1986), as well as his *Furta Sacra: Thefts of Relics in the Central Middle Ages* (Princeton: Princeton University Press, 1978), esp. 152–54.

103. For dismemberment, see Elizabeth A. R. Brown, "Death and the Human Body in the Later Middle Ages: The Legislation of Boniface VIII on the Division of the Corpse," *Viator* 12 (1981): 221–70.

104. See Schiller, *Iconography in Christian Art*, 2:190–91.

105. For a fascinating discussion of one medieval artist's self-record of his own bodily disintegration, see Michael Camille, "The Image and the Self: Unwriting Late Medieval Bodies," in *Framing Medieval Bodies*, ed. Kay and Rubin, 62–99.

106. In a similar reading, Travis, "Social Body," 29, sees the naked, vulnerable, wounded Christ acting as a homology for the late medieval "city close to the verge of economic collapse."

107. Phythian-Adams, *Desolation of a City*, 276.

108. Foucault, *Discipline and Punish*, 59–60.

109. Ibid., 10.

## Afterword. Domination, Resistance, and the Consumer

1. See, for example, Ien Ang, *Watching Dallas* (London: Methuen, 1985); Tony Bennett and Janet Woollacott, *Bond and Beyond: The Political Career of a Popular Hero* (New York: Methuen, 1987); David Morley, *The "Nationwide" Audience* (London: British Film Institute, 1980); and Patricia Palmer, *The Lively Audience: A Study of Children around the TV Set* (Sydney: Allen and Unwin, 1986).

2. John Fiske, "British Cultural Studies and Television," in *Channels of Discourse*, ed. Robert C. Allen (Chapel Hill: University of North Carolina Press, 1985), 254–90; Dick Hebdige, *Subculture: The Meaning of Style* (New York: Methuen, 1982); Tania Modleski,

*Loving with a Vengeance: Mass-Produced Fantasies for Women* (New York: Routledge, 1984); and Janice Radway, *Reading the Romance: Feminism and the Representation of Women in Popular Culture* (Chapel Hill: University of North Carolina Press, 1984).

3. Barbara Klinger, "Digressions at the Cinema: Commodification and Reception in Mass Culture," in *Modernity and Mass Culture*, ed. James Naremore and Patrick Brantlinger (Bloomington: Indiana University Press, 1991), 17–34; the quotation is from 18.

# Index

✛

Wallace, David, 169 n. 42
Warwick, Isabella, 113
Whitford, Richard, *The Boke of Pacience*, 81
Wiles, David, 173 n. 14
Willis, Paul, 68–69
Wimbledon, Thomas, 7, 17–18
work, 153–60; improper, 34–35, 87; proper,

86–87; and violence, 143–46; women's, 145–46
Wright, Stephen K., 197 n. 29

youth: suspicion of, 90–91

*Zardino de oration*, 121–22

# MEDIEVAL CULTURES

**VOLUME 2**
Edited by Andrew MacLeish
*The Medieval Monastery*

**VOLUME 1**
Edited by Kathryn Reyerson and Faye Powe
*The Medieval Castle*

**Claire Sponsler** is currently assistant professor of English at the University of Iowa and has taught at George Washington University and the Bread Loaf School of English. She has published articles in *CLIO, Theatre Journal, Assays, Semiotica,* and *Contemporary Literature,* among others.